TYPE

TELLS

TALES

STEVEN HELLER & GAIL ANDERSON

TYPE TELLS TALES

Yale University Press

CONTENTS

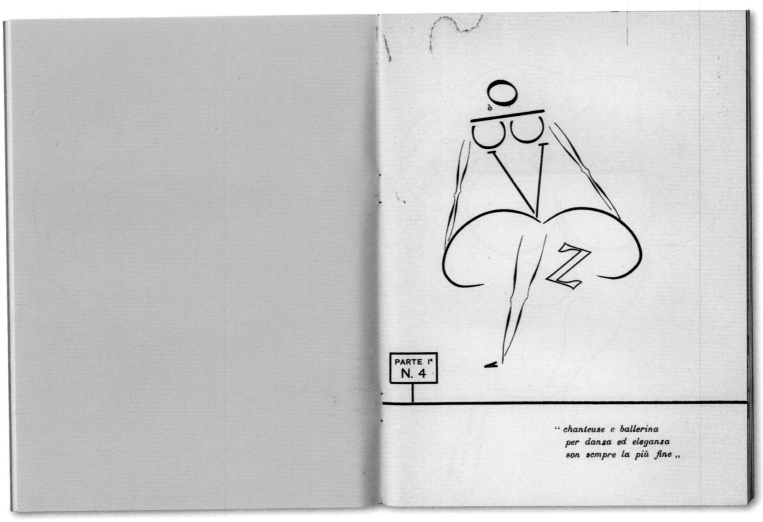

PARTE I^a
N. 4

" chanteuse e ballerina
per danza ed eleganza
son sempre la più fine „

PARTE I^a
N. 5

dal pubblico
una voce trasecolata
sacramento !

nella canzonetta d'attualità:
« Il maggiore in guerra va
hip - hip Urrà ! »

INTRODUCTION

Type is like a ventriloquist's dummy. It cannot speak or think on its own. However, with a skilled author writing the words and a keen designer pulling the strings, there is no limit to how typography can emote, express, engage and, of course, guide the reader from one thought to the next.

Typefaces have individual characteristics and family traits that make most better suited to one particular subject rather than any other, yet type's primary role is as the compliant actor, and not the star, in a text or message. The majority of book and magazine designs demand functional performance from type – so should a designer ever seek to upstage the well-written word?

History says yes.

Central-axis type composition was long considered the ideal format for presenting text; it was (and continues to be) viable. However, it represents the old order. Since the days of Gutenberg, printers and compositors have been constrained to some extent by the rectangular boundaries of the press. Yet pushing those boundaries became inevitable. Changes in printing technology ushered in shifts in language, which in turn had an impact on typography. If the vanguard of change is art, then graphic design is the messenger. In this equation typography speaks volumes about the intention and consequence of printed work. Although elegantly pristine typesetting, with perfect leading and exact margins, is the quintessence of fine printing, traditional practices that refuse to question the status quo are not necessarily the most virtuous. Even the Bible has been redesigned countless times over the past two millennia.

The word is THE WORD, yet different words, sentences and paragraphs can have a wide range of intentions. Not all words are created equal, nor should they be typeset with equal weight. While great writers are skilled enough in the construction and rhythm of their words that typographic manipulation becomes unnecessary, sometimes an unconventional marriage of design and content gives a stronger, more dramatic emphasis. Helping the reader engage fully with a text is the goal of such an effect.

The communication of a message or narrative through the amplification of what will be called the 'typographic voice' was a late nineteenth- and early twentieth-century phenomenon, born of social, technological and even political upheavals in Europe and the United States. It was also a natural outcome of a certain restlessness. The world was moving at a faster pace and print communications had accelerated to meet the demands of increasingly literate populations. As distribution of printed material became more commercial and globalized (think of the web today), visionaries sought to recast the standards governing typography.

LETTERFORMS AS CHARACTERS Francesco Cangiullo's *Cangiullo Futurista, Caffè-concerto: Alfabeto a sorpresa* (Alphabet Surprise), published by Agenzia Editrice Canzonettistica Marinetti, Milan, 1919. This is a programme for a Futurist musical performance, illustrated with animated letterforms that suggest they are characters in the show.

7

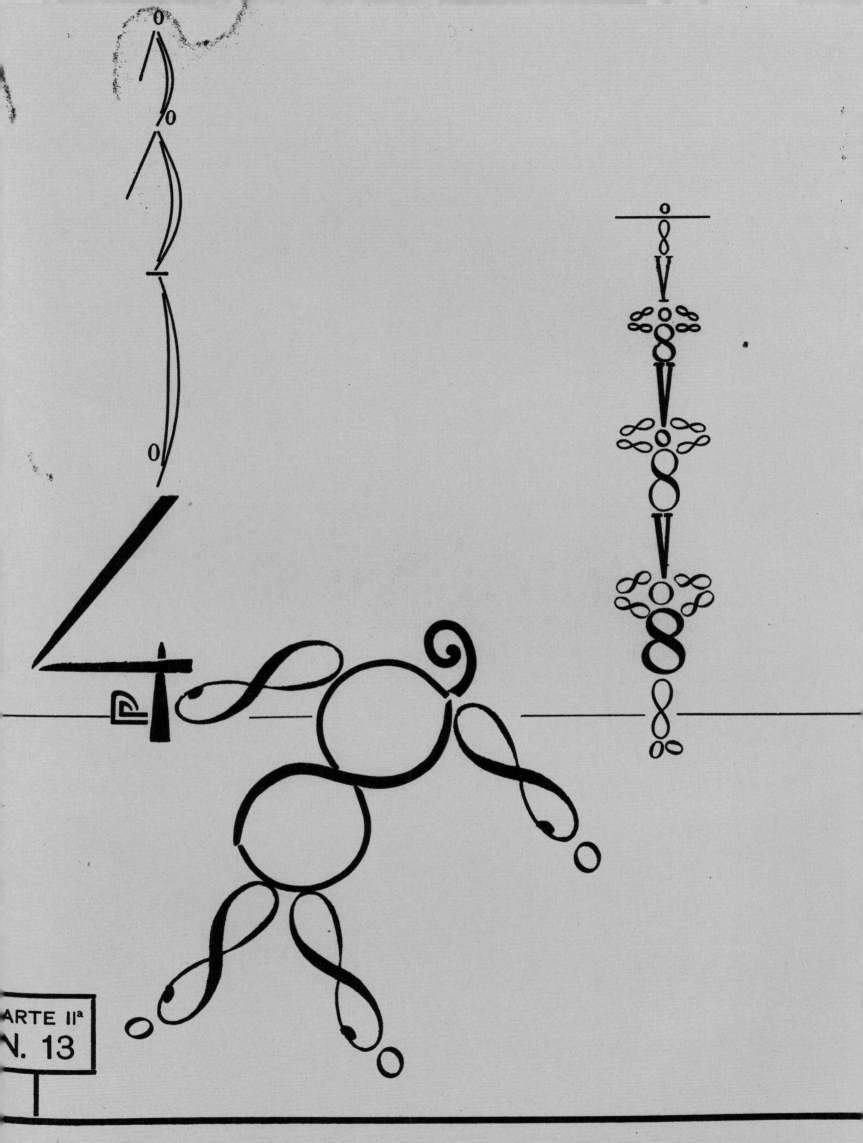

Oplà !

ORCHESTRA Sospensione perplessa

At first, incremental shifts in weight and colour occurred as a way to modulate a surge in printed noise. With rising competition for attention, the louder or larger the type, the better.

The consequent cacophony of typographic forms trending at the turn of the century was as crucial, in a way, to the state of communication as the invention of radio, film and television. Devising new typefaces and type products was a necessity in the print-centric world, but it was also a field ripe for experimentation. Discovering fresh ways to telegraph contemporary messages through what was ostensibly a fifteenth-century medium was not just a challenge for commercial type foundries; it was one of the principal objectives for progressive artists, poets and designers.

That the written word could be transformed and used to illustrate the ideas in a text was one of the defining aspects of Guillaume Apollinaire's poetry, notably his *Calligrammes*, which introduced typography parlant (type that speaks), that was in turn a variant of F.T. Marinetti's *parole in libertà* (words in freedom) in which type and lettering were loudspeakers for the word.

The Czech artist, writer and graphic designer Karel Teige was another of a growing number of avant-gardists who embraced the printed letter, both for function and as a tool for expression in its own right. Discussing new approaches to advertising in his essay 'Modern Type', he said that typography is not merely a mediator between content and the reader but 'a self-contained construction' that optically realizes 'on its basis an optical composition'.

The idea behind 'a self-contained construction', or typography that is designed to actually be its own content, is modern but not born of modernity. Arguably, ornate illuminated initials from medieval manuscripts through to the nineteenth century represent the beginning of typographic interventions with text. Even in the early twentieth century the Futurists, Dadaists and Surrealists – with their disruptive typography – tipped their collective hat to largely anonymous pioneers. Even today, much of the typography parlant is accomplished with vintage or pastiche forms.

Robert Massin is a French designer best known for '*faire du neuf avec de l'ancien*' – making something new with the old – notes Richard Hollis, in *Eye* (vol. 4, no. 16, 1995). Massin's shedding of light and colour on passé typefaces is not meant to evoke nostalgia for bygone ages, but rather to show that in new narrative contexts even old letterforms have relevance. In Jean Cocteau's *Les mariés de la Tour Eiffel* (The Wedding on the Eiffel Tower) Massin composes the author's words in such a way that each phrase is expressed through a clash of old and new letters that subtly illuminates the absurdist story of a new couple's wedding breakfast on Bastille Day at the Eiffel Tower.

Cocteau's writing did not need Massin's typographic interpretation, but giving those words a more demonstrative presence shows how the skilled designer can either give the vernacular a boost or create an entirely new dialect, accent or language. This book shows how a range of voices have contributed to the richness of typographic language.

TYPE SAMPLE This is a type specimen sample from the Morgan Press type catalogue (*c.*1965). It represents a long tradition of using often meaningless yet curiously poetic fragments to illustrate how specific letters of typefaces work in tandem.

No. 56D (1)—Antique Pointed (No A)   36 pt.

TYPES 5
to be very

No. 56E—Antique Pointed No. 2   36 pt.

PRETTY ?
or will one!

No. 57A—Broadgauge (no fig. 2 ; caps only)   6 pt.

MOST IMPRESSIVE AND $34

No. 57B—Broadgauge (caps only)   8 pt.

ATTRACTIVE WE SAY 1

No. 57C—Broadgauge (caps only)   10 pt.

BUT NATURALLY 2

No. 57—Broadguage (caps only)   12 pt.

WE DO NOT TRY

No. 57D—Broadgauge (caps only)   18 pt.

CHIEFLY 3

No. 58—Broadguage (caps only)   24 pt.

TO SAY ?

No. 58A—Broadgauge Shaded (caps only)   6 pt.

WITH RESPECTS AIMED &6

No. 58B—Broadgauge Shaded (caps only)   8 pt.

TOWARD ALL THOSE 7

No. 58C—Broadgauge Shaded (caps only)   10 pt.

SENTIMENTALS 8

No. 58D—Broadgauge Shaded (caps only)   36 pt.

NOW -

As a prelude to writing this introduction we read Keith Houston's *The Book: A Cover-To-Cover Exploration of the Most Powerful Object of Our Time* (Norton, 2016). It is difficult to ignore such an evocative subtitle or such a surprisingly well-illustrated and smartly designed little brick of a volume, splendidly conjoining classic and contemporary aesthetic traits and technical methods. Before starting to read, however, we spent some silent time savouring the physical object itself, which was designed by Abbate Design. Delving into the text was an intense pleasure for the eye and mind – what a meditative state should be like; a state that today's media cannot duplicate (although virtual reality may get us there one day).

Nonetheless, Houston's book is nothing like what you will find or experience throughout this book – which is not to say that the kineticism of our content is intended to be any less consequential or pleasurable. Houston's book was a brief respite from the radical, experimental, occasionally unprecedented eccentric typography and graphic design that we had been exploring for the past two years. 'This book is about the history and the making and the *bookness* of all those books,' writes Houston in his introduction; 'the weighty, complicated, inviting artifacts that humanity has been writing, printing and binding for more than fifteen hundred years.'

Our book, on the other hand, is about taboo-challenging alternatives to the book's ancient history, and both the legacy and continued practice of expanding type's status as the venerable crystal goblet, or unobtrusive vessel, of words and meaning. It ignores the glorious '*bookness*' that Houston so eloquently (and wittily) addresses, but his role is one of keeper of the classical flame – those 'weighty, complicated, inviting artifacts' – while our book is about well-meaning heretics who challenged and continue to bust standards.

Type Tells Tales is also not exclusively about books. It is about how content that uses type as the primary medium – including books, as well as periodicals, websites, walls, textiles, clothing and other potential *tabulae rasae* – is used by designers and writers to tell stories, proclaim ideologies and express and shout their ideas. It is not concerned with pristine composition, perfect spacing and generous margins – although perfection is quite debatable.

Selected are those examples where type and typography, but also hand-lettering and calligraphy, transmit or illuminate the content in ways that might contain references to old manuscripts and fine-press bookmaking, but were devised from the outset of early twentieth-century modernism: alternately clean, raw, primitive and professional. This was during a time of removal of artistic barriers, when typography was integrally related to architecture, which influenced furniture, and had an effect on industrial products and machines, and so on. Many of the designers represented are multifaceted (or trans-disciplinary in today's terms), but all use type and lettering as the core of each work. Letterforms are sometimes metamorphosed into players as though on a theatre stage; some are exaggerated in size and shape to approximate the timbre of the voice or voices, and some are printed in overlapping ways to resemble sound or movement. There are layouts where

STYLES ADD EXPRESSION Advertisement (*c.*1909) for the Inland Type Foundry, 'This is Not Pi'. It shows in an expressive way how different type styles, sizes and colours can add expression to everyday typography.

12

THIS IS NOT PI

Nor is it an *attempt* at being **odd** or funny. It is simply a specimen *of* **STANDARD LINE** TYPE. Notice that **all** faces **line at the bottom.** Of course you **would not** use your type in *this* **manner,** but you can readily **see** *the* **advantage** of having it all **line.** All different *faces* on **one body** if STANDARD LINE **will** line with each other and **with leaders,** *and* they **will** line with **all** other **sizes or** **6**-to-pica brass *rule* by **means** of regular leads and slugs. **These** are but a few of *the* **advantages** which enable the printer **to make and save money** by using our type....... If **you** wish **to keep** abreast of the **times send** for a copy of the **PRINTERS' QUARTERLY**...................

INLAND TYPE FOUNDRY

217-219 OLIVE ST.  ST. LOUIS

ÉGYPTIENNES DENTELÉES

Corps 14.

Ouverture SAMEDI 12 Juin

Corps 24.

Le feu et l'eau sont

LIEU MALSAIN

Corps 36.

Le Moderne

ROCHELLE

Corps 48.

Courses

MORAL

typefaces, words and sentences have interpersonal relationships that run over contiguous spreads and entire page signatures. Others appear seemingly random and ad hoc.

A common theme is that type and letters are not passive, but are active participants in an entire composition. Without the intelligence imbued within and emanating from the type or letters, there is no story. Avoided are those works where type is made to do gymnastics on a page for no particular reason – that's not a good enough rationale for inclusion. Personality of the characters is important. There is an evolutionary path with this kind of typographic experimentation and implementation, and technology certainly plays a role. It was harder to achieve the typographic hijinks when Marinetti used metal and wood on letterpress than when Massin transferred type on to rubber, and stretched and photographed it. But today's digital options make printing on fabric just as easy as laser-cutting words and sentences into virtually any material.

We're glad we read Houston's book, and particularly his first introductory sentence set with a classic red initial cap and a larger first-line point size than the body text, which reads 'This is a BOOK about books.' We loved that simplicity, but don't exactly practise it here. This is a book about TYPE filtered through the typographer's skill and talent, whose knowledge and instinct has helped evolve the book and other analogue and digital platforms into something that does not just provide a shy text but offers active words, resulting in a cognitive experience that makes us think more about what we read, hold and feel. This book shows that a range of voices have contributed richness to the typographic language.

FRAGMENTS DEMONSTRATE TYPE This type specimen page, like the one preceding it, is from the Paris Fonderie Warnery (1903) and adheres to the common practice of fragmented wordplay to show type specimens.

ONE

POETICS

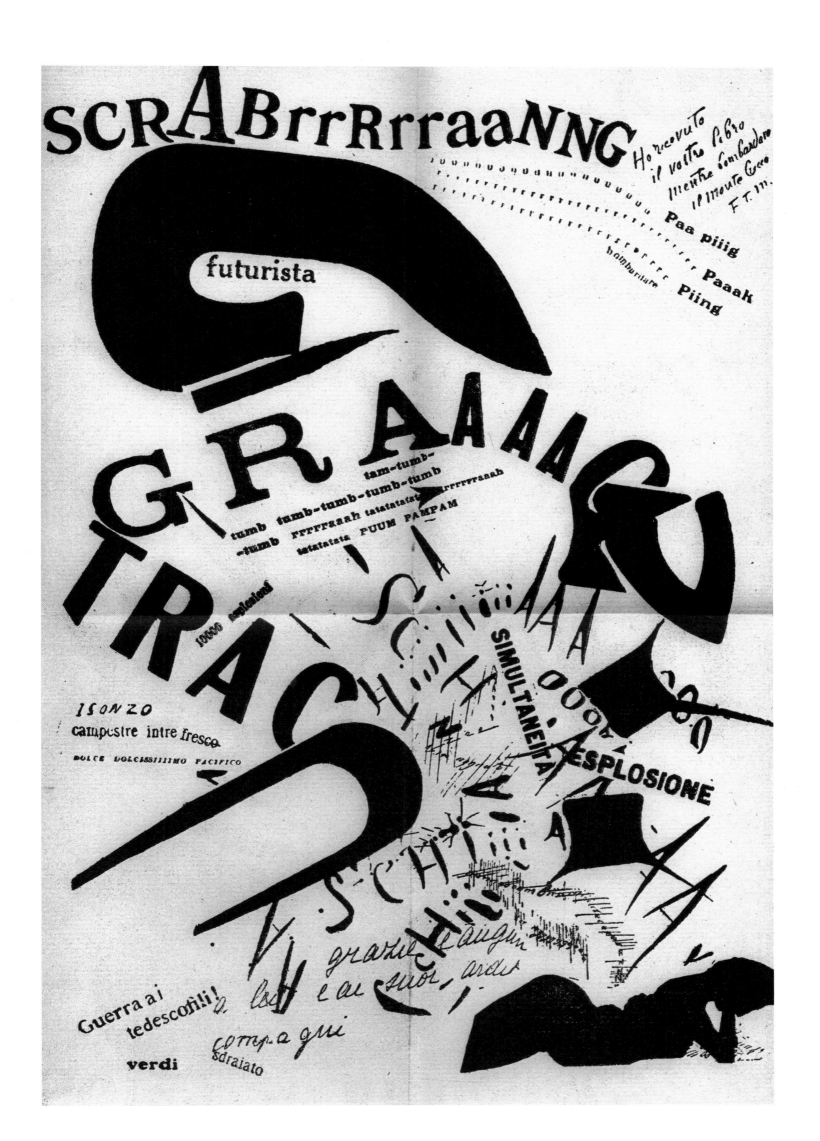

FILIPPO TOMMASO MARINETTI

Les mots en liberté futuristes (Futurist Words in Freedom)

Marinetti's *Les mots en liberté futuristes* draws on a long tradition of modern concrete poetry or calligrams, a form of artistic wordplay in which the typeface composition echoes or illustrates the words on the page. The precursor to this genre was Lewis Carroll's 'The Mouse's Tale', a passage in *Alice's Adventures in Wonderland* where the words of the mouse's story are typeset in a way that reflects the shape of its tail. The genre was later taken up by Guillaume Apollinaire in his *Calligrammes: Poèmes de la paix et de la guerre 1913–1916* (1918), in which the typeface composition echoed the words on the page by giving them representational form. This represents a typographic legacy that has injected a physical and sonic dimension to texts of all kinds.

Apollinaire was ahead of a howling pack of avant-gardists whose art was influenced by the First World War, yet it was the writing and typographic experiments of Italian poet and theorist Filippo Tommaso Marinetti (1876–1944) that brought the concept of *parole in libertà* (words in freedom) well into the modernist orbit. As the founder of Italian Futurism, Marinetti trailblazed the idea that the so-called 'crystal goblet' of typography (the aim for type to be unobtrusive) was a fallacy. Type of any style or

quality could indeed be as expressive as words, and when used freely could make sounds that both accompanied and led those words into vocal and visual realms.

Les mots en liberté futuristes, written and designed by Marinetti and printed as an insert on a single sheet of newsprint, is arguably the iconic Futurist typographic experiment – cutting, smashing and violating type and the words it represented.

What's more, these were fighting words: as Marinetti proclaimed in the 1909 *Futurist Manifesto* (published in *Le Figaro*): 'United, we must attack! We must create with absolute faith in the imperishable richness of the earth! There can be no nostalgia! No pessimism! There's no turning back! Boldly, let us advance! Forward! Faster! Farther! Higher! Let us lyrically renew our joy in being alive!'

Marinetti espoused a permanent artistic and political revolution. He rejected traditionalism in favour of 'the new religion of speed', mythologizing the machine as a totem of the modern spirit. Technology, though somewhat primitive in Italy, was the saviour of mankind, and Futurism was the avant-garde movement of the masses.

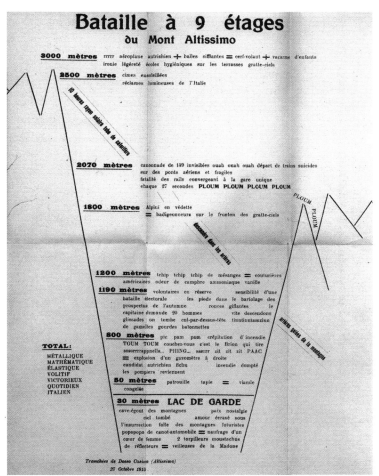

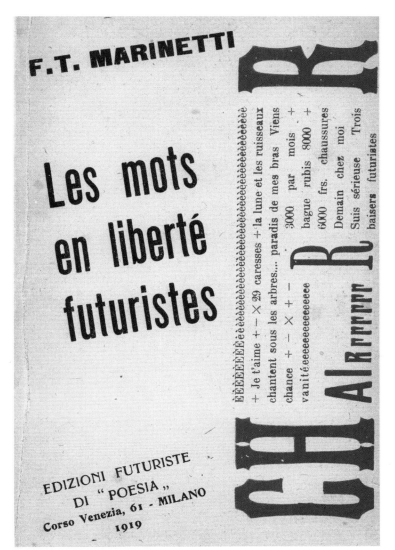

TITLE: *Les mots en liberté futuristes*
(Futurist Words in Freedom)
DESIGNER/AUTHOR: F.T. Marinetti
YEAR: 1919

HENDRIK NICOLAAS WERKMAN
The Next Call

Being a typographer and printer is not usually a dangerous profession. However, it turned out to be a deadly one for the neophyte Dutch designer and artist Hendrik Nicolaas Werkman (1882–1945). On 10 April 1945 – two days before his home town of Groningen in the Netherlands was liberated by Allied forces from the occupying German army, and less than five months before the end of the Second World War – Werkman and ten others were executed by the SS in the town of Bakkeveen.

Werkman, who prior to the war had been a printer with a particular interest in typographic experimentation, had published a small, clandestine publication produced by a tedious stencil method. *De Blauwe Schuit* (The Blue Barge) was a combustible mixture of avant-garde aesthetics, anti-Nazi politics and a few texts by the Jewish writer Martin Buber, and was distributed to a very few friends. To this day it is unclear how Werkman was targeted, but the SS response was characteristically brutal.

Werkman is best known in the history of graphic design, however, less for his clandestine contraband publishing than his earlier work as a 'typographic maverick'. Neither modernist nor classicist, he was in a class of his own – one might say a world of his own making – born of a true passion for ink, type and paper.

A failed journalist, he became a prosperous printer with a successful Groningen business, working on commercial jobs. Yet he was drawn to the more abstract and expressive aspects of art, which he believed could be replicated on the printing press. In 1920 he joined the local progressive artists in the De

Ploeg (Plough) movement, and found inspiration in work by De Stijl designers of the moment. His inevitable indifference to his printing business ensured it would fail, yet gave him a sense of freedom; he used his printing expertise to make odd ephemeral items that underscored his compulsive love of art and design.

One such item announced the forthcoming release of a nine-issue experiment titled *The Next Call*, which Werkman historian Alston Purvis says would appear at irregular intervals from 1923 until 1926. 'Except for two numbers printed on single foldout sheets, each issue consisted of eight pages, including front and back covers, and was printed on inexpensive paper in editions never exceeding forty copies.'

It was given away for free to friends, and they never knew what to expect. The contents varied, as did the compositional quality of the type and printing – while one issue would be anarchic, another would be serene. He further gave a name to his typographic creations: '*druksels*' – poems or prose (nonsense or some sense) composed with cuts of wood or metal type. About his technique Werkman once wrote (as quoted by Purvis): 'I use an old hand press for my prints ... Sometimes you have to press hard, sometimes very lightly ...' – but in all of his work he pushed the basic letterpress capabilities into uncharted artistic realms. He was 'entranced' with the printing process itself, and 'often thought of the materials as animate beings', Purvis wrote, regarding the non-functional quality of the work. But unfortunately it seems that what his art symbolized, and the content of his publications, proved fatal for Werkman in the end.

TITLE: *The Next Call*
DESIGNER/AUTHOR: H.N. Werkman
YEARS: 1923–1926

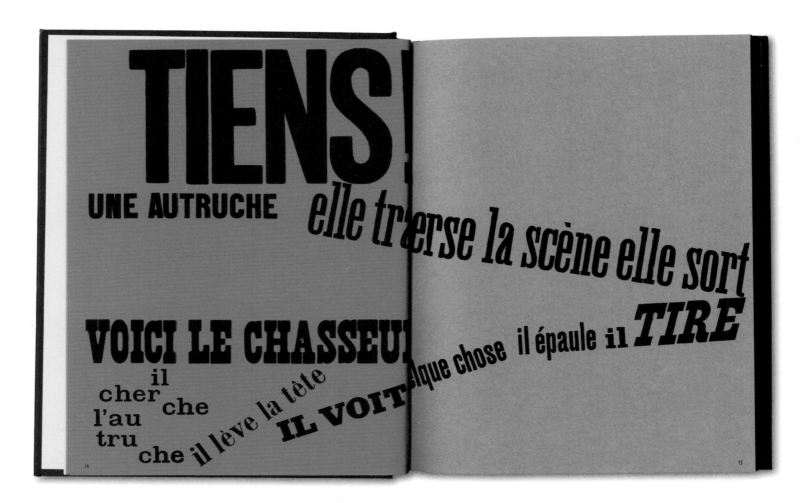

ROBERT MASSIN
Les mariés de la Tour Eiffel

Les mariés de la Tour Eiffel (The Wedding on the Eiffel Tower), is Jean Cocteau's satiric ballet, choreographed by Jean Börlin in 1921 for the Ballets suédois (see *La Danse*, page 62), the avant-garde Swedish troupe directed by Rolf de Maré in Paris. It satirizes the French bourgeoisie through a series of serendipitous mishaps during a wedding tea set on the first-storey platform of the Eiffel Tower in 1900.

Cocteau wryly comments on social conventions and more: 'Making fun of mothers-in-law and old generals is too easy,' wrote Anna Kisselgoff in *The New York Times* in 1988. 'In 1921, Cocteau had a more difficult task: to convince an audience that art can be refreshed by looking in the most ordinary of places. Cocteau used *Les mariés* to officially proclaim his creed (in a preface published in 1922) of the 'rehabilitation of the commonplace'.

This text was the inspiration for Massin's typographic designs recalling nineteenth-century book title pages, musical score covers and voluminous type specimen catalogues. Although he began the project when phototype and press-down type were de rigueur, he continued his work when the computer typesetting revolution began. '[In] September 1988 Massin set himself a challenge,' design historian Richard Hollis quoted in 'Language Unleashed', a 1995 article in *Eye*. 'From tomorrow, I'm going to start layout on screen.' This reversed Massin's earlier dictum, adds Hollis, '"to do something new with the old", and

using the Macintosh has done something old with the new', which allowed him the freedom to finish *Les mariés*, originally his twenty-page homage to Cocteau, who had died three years earlier. In a harsh critique of the project, Hollis wrote: 'These initial pages, created by pasting up lines of type letter by letter, were scanned into the Macintosh. The final book typography was printed in black on sixteen-page sections of coloured paper. *Les mariés* is an indulgence belonging to the period of Massin's earlier interest in letterforms. What began as a labour of love, a technical tour de force, has become a nostalgic series of exercises in style.'

Yet it may also be Massin's overt satire of his own work. Just as Cocteau was criticized for 'insulting' France's most famous engineering marvel, so Massin was toying with his own process. Cocteau was not anti-modern; he was extolling what one of his characters implied was the spirit of the new. 'It wasn't Notre Dame but the Eiffel Tower that was now queen of Paris, said the character in the text Cocteau wrote as narration for the ballet,' notes Kisselgoff, with reference to 'Cocteau's view of reality in the post-Cubist Parisian world of his time'.

Massin was typographically reinterpreting Cocteau's sensibility in a manner that revealed Massin's own intimate involvement with the inner 'organism' of books, and it has made him acutely aware of how writing functions in the world.

TITLE: *Les mariés de la Tour Eiffel*
AUTHOR: Jean Cocteau
TYPOGRAPHY: Robert Massin
PUBLISHER: Éditions Hoébeke
YEAR: 1994

ENCORE, SI JE SAVAIS D'AVANCE LES SURPRISE QUE ME RÉSERVE MON APPAREIL DÉTRAQUÉ, POURRAIS ORGANISER SPECTACLE. HÉLAS! JE TREMBLE CHAQUE FOIS QUE JE PRONONCE LES MAUDITES PAROLES. SAIT-ON JAMAIS CE PEUT SORTIR? PUISQUE CES MYSTÈRES ME DÉPASSENT, FEIGNONS D'EN ÊTRE L'ORGANISATEUR.

Il salue.

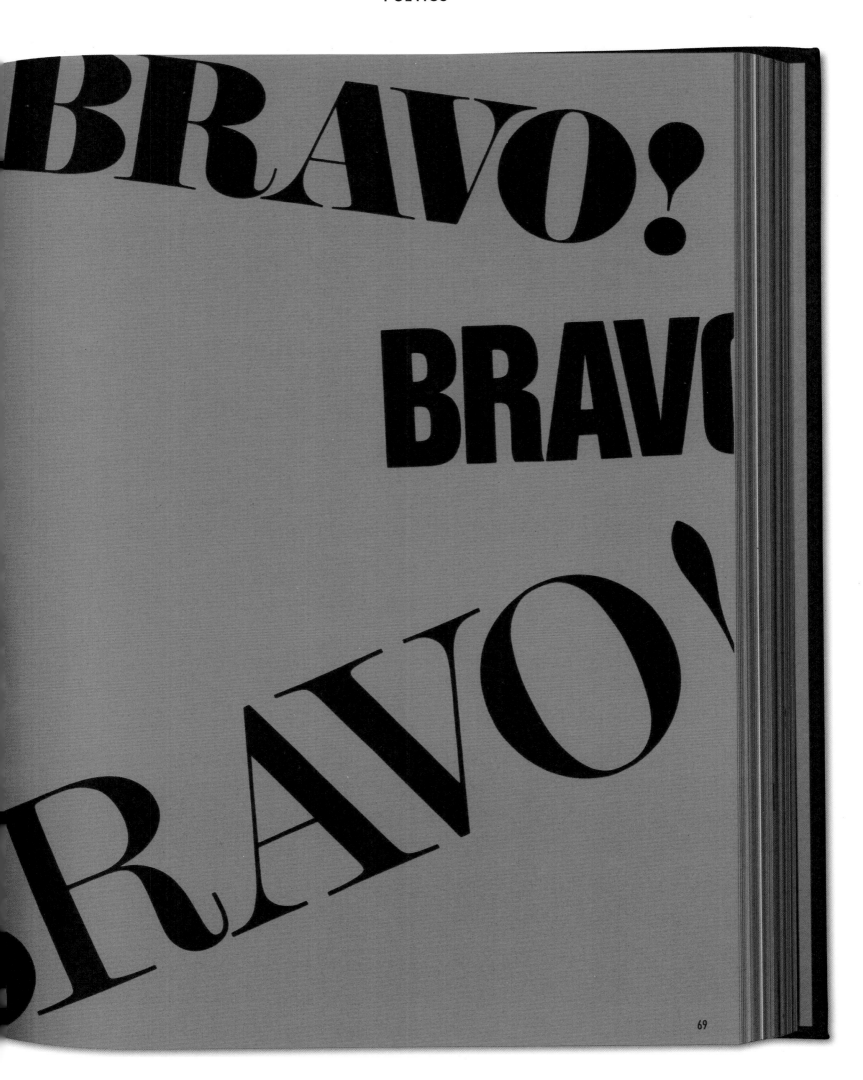

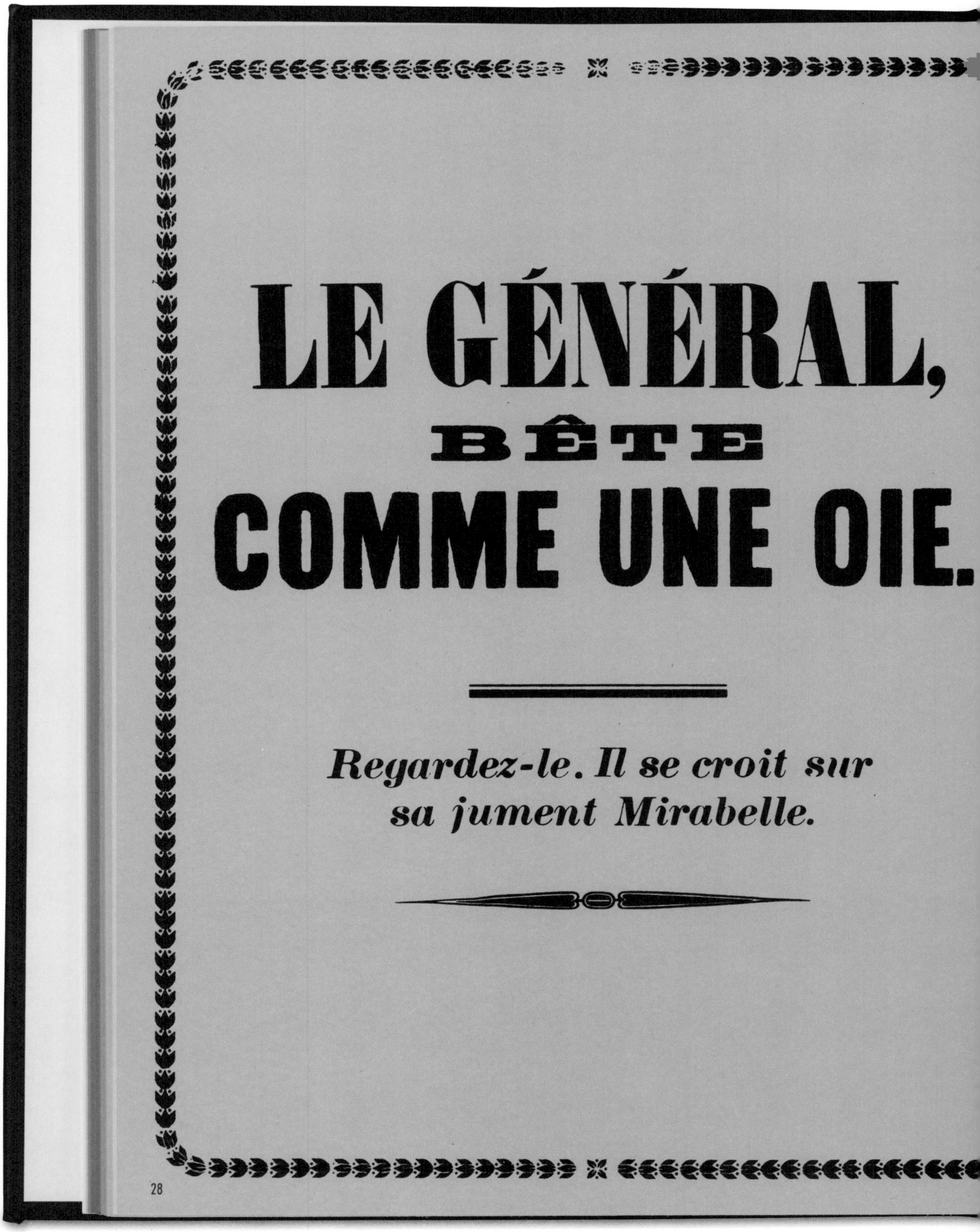

LE GÉNÉRAL,
BÊTE
COMME UNE OIE.

———

Regardez-le. Il se croit sur
sa jument Mirabelle.

28

Les
GARÇONS
D'HONNEUR
FORTS
comme des
TURCS

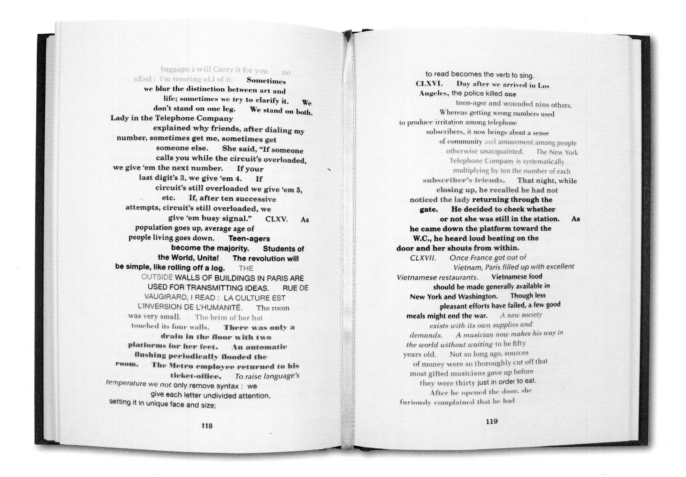

JOHN CAGE
Diary: How to Improve the World
(You Will Only Make Matters Worse)

Marching neatly in the footsteps of the Futurists and the Dadaists, John Cage's *Diary: How to Improve the World (You Will Only Make Matters Worse)* began as a recording over a year before his death in 1992. Compiled over the course of sixteen years, the content includes musings, observations and quotes from Buckminster Fuller, Henry David Thoreau and a host of insightful others of his generational ilk, as well as philosophical sensibility.

The diaries, originally typed on an IBM Selectric (the classic one with the removable type balls) did appear in print in the early 1970s, which is when Cage started changing font and text size in a somewhat random manner in a rhythmic central column width that suggested a vase or candlestick holder. But it was the quirkily hypnotic audio version, accomplished by changing the position of the microphone and the recording volume, that gives the entire enterprise its alluring cadences.

'The *Diary* is repository', notes the Siglio Press in its promotion for the publication of the splendid 2015 edition, 'of anecdotes, proclivities, obsessions, jokes and koan-like stories … *Diary* registers Cage's assessment of the times in which he lived as well as his often uncanny portents about the world we live in now.'

Cage was randomly precise when it came to the application of typefaces, the number of letters per line and the patterns of indentation, to ensure the tonal and rhythmic quality of the text. His musical mind and mathematical acuity did the trick.

Again from Siglio's text: 'While Cage used chance operations to expand the possibilities of creating and shaping his work beyond the limitations of individual taste and perspective, *Diary* nonetheless accumulates into a complex reflection of Cage's own particular sensibilities as a thinker and citizen of the world, illuminating his social and political awareness, as well as his idealism and sense of humour: it becomes an oblique but indelible portrait of one the most influential figures of the 20th century American avant garde.'

This slim new edition also involves 'chance operations' to compose the text in various fluctuating forms of flush left and rag right, and central-axis and wide and tight margin patterns, highlighted by dark and light reds, purples and blues.

The editor's note elucidates 'the procedure of chance operations and demonstrate[s] its application, giving readers a rare opportunity to see how the text is transformed' – and how Cage thought and conjured for sixteen of his eighty-two years.

TITLE: *Diary: How to Improve the World*
(You Will Only Make Matters Worse)
AUTHOR: John Cage
EDITORS: Joe Biel and Richard Craft
PUBLISHER: Siglio Press
YEAR: 2015

that nowadays there's no equation),
saying, "How can you speak of money and
virtue in the same breath?"   XII.   Where
there doesn't seem to be any space,
know we no longer know what space is.
        Have faith space is there, giving one
        the chance to renovate his way of
recognizing it, no matter the means,
psychic, somatic, or means
involving extensions of either.
        People still ask for definitions, but
        it's quite clear now that nothing
                can be defined.   Let alone art, its
                purpose etc.   We're not even sure of
                carrots (whether they're what we think
they are, how poisonous they are, who
        grew them and under what circumstances).
                She was indignant when I suggested
        the use of an aphrodisiac.   Why?
        Naturally she considers TV a waste of
        time.   **XIII.   The purpose of one**
        activity is no longer separate from the
        purpose of any other activity.   All
        activities fuse in one purpose which
is (cf. Huang-Po Doctrine of Universal
        Mind) no purpose.   Imitate the
        Ganges' sands, becoming indifferent to
perfume, indifferent to **filth.**
        Influence.   Where does it come from?
        Responsibility?   Sick ones now are
        heartsick.   Narcissi, they became
entranced with emotions, purposes,
                mystified by living in the twentieth
                century.   We've invented something else,
not the wheel.   We extended nervous

16

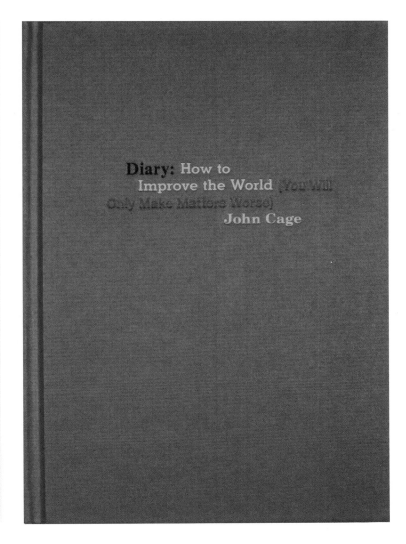

TITLE: *Hot & Sour Soup*
DESIGNER: Walasse Ting
PUBLISHER: Sam Francis Foundation
YEAR: 1969

WALASSE TING
Hot & Sour Soup

Chinese-American abstract painter Walasse Ting (1929–2010) was among a handful of twentieth-century Chinese artists who moved to France and then to America. He was born in Shanghai, but was famously a nomad, 'having lived variously in Jiangsu, Shanghai, Hong Kong, Paris, New York and Holland', as noted on the Sotheby's website; he was based in New York from 1961. Ting wrote poetry and prose; he also sang and danced, drawing from life as much as he could. Apart from painting female figures, cats, horses and birds are all familiar images in his paintings, and Ting often injected them with whimsy. He also had an inexhaustible love of colour, about which he wrote:

I put on a floral-print shirt today and I've turned into a butterfly ... From the garden I gather flowers, making honey from them. Paintings are my honey; colours are my flowers; velocity is what's required of a thief – he must paint as speedily as he draws a gun. My nickname 'flower thief' has nothing to do with martial arts novels. I create oil paintings, utilising vibrant colours to fashion a magnificent garden. The flower thief is merely a honey butterfly.

Hot & Sour Soup takes the form of a box folio, with seventeen loose folded sheets, as issued, illustrated with twenty-two colour lithographs throughout that either include text in type or hand scrawl. It is a mix of free-form abstraction and playful sexual joy, as this poem – typeset large – expresses.

> *I masturbate in dark room*
> *Put sperm in blue envelope*
> *Add Stamp*
> *Open telephone book*
> *Find girl's name*
> *Three years pass*
> *Everyday*
> *Waiting*
> *My son come*

The collection contains fifty of Ting's provocative poems, illustrated by the lithographs. 'His work,' states an online book dealer, 'is characterized by bold colours featuring such subjects as sensuous women, cats, birds, fish, giant penises, etc.' Ting called himself a 'butterfly' or 'flower thief', 'his art inspired by beauty and goodness, emotions and desires'. He was never tied to any one medium, including the typographic book.

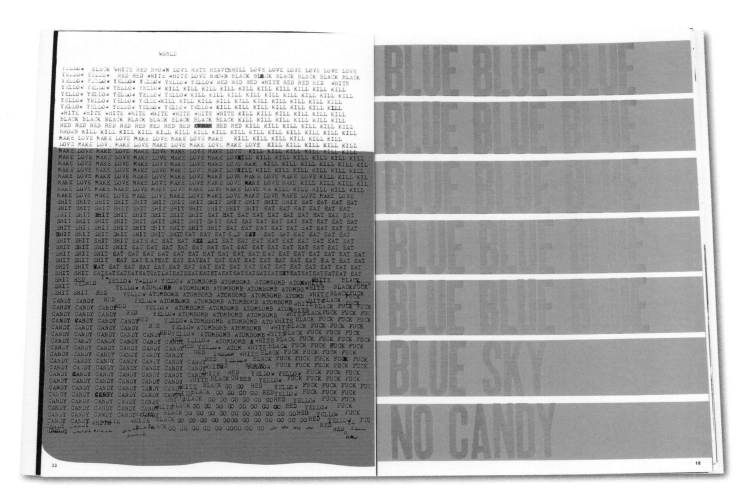

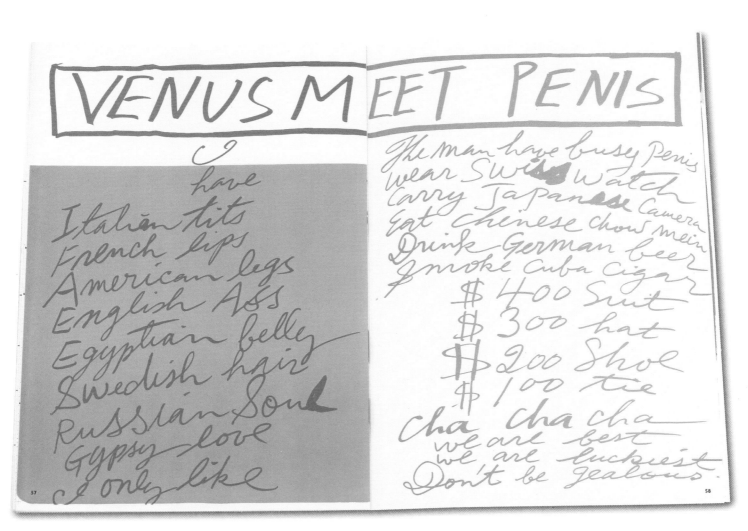

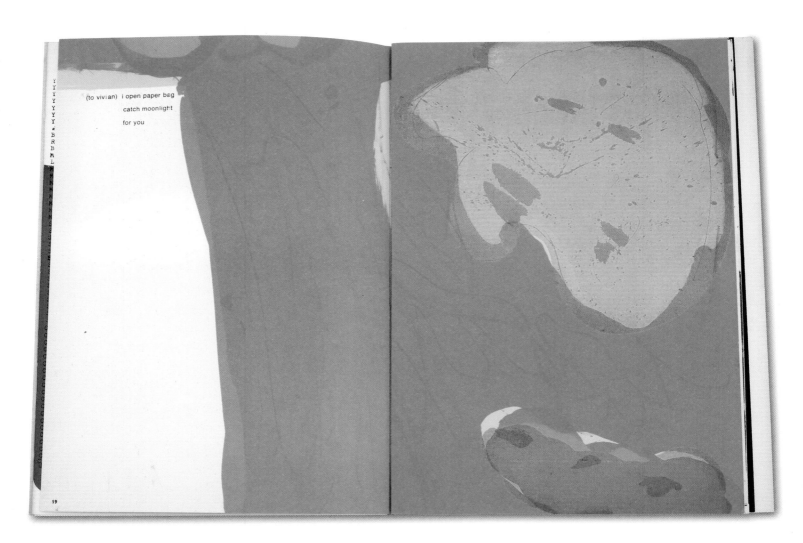

(to vivian) i open paper bag

catch moonlight

for you

19

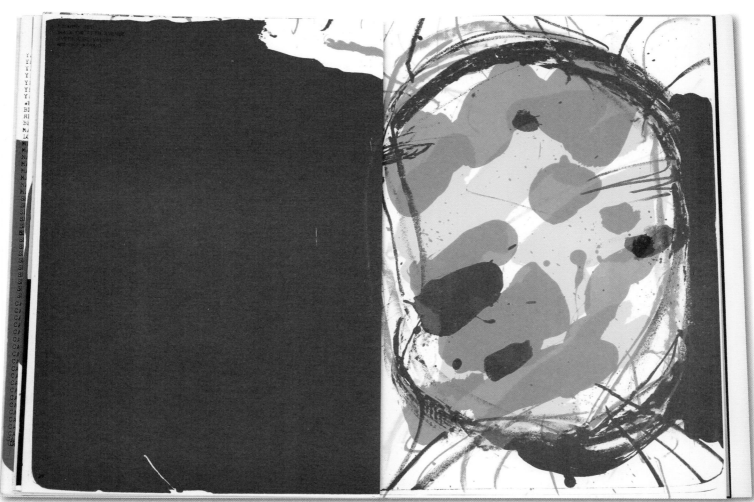

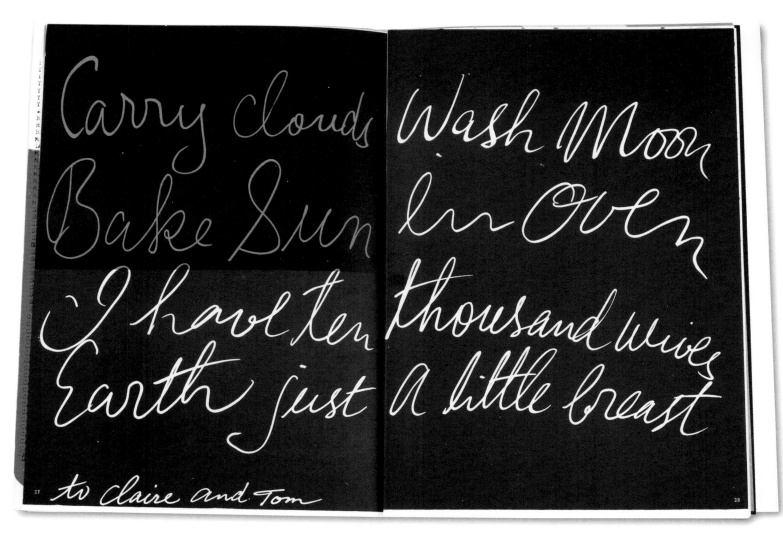

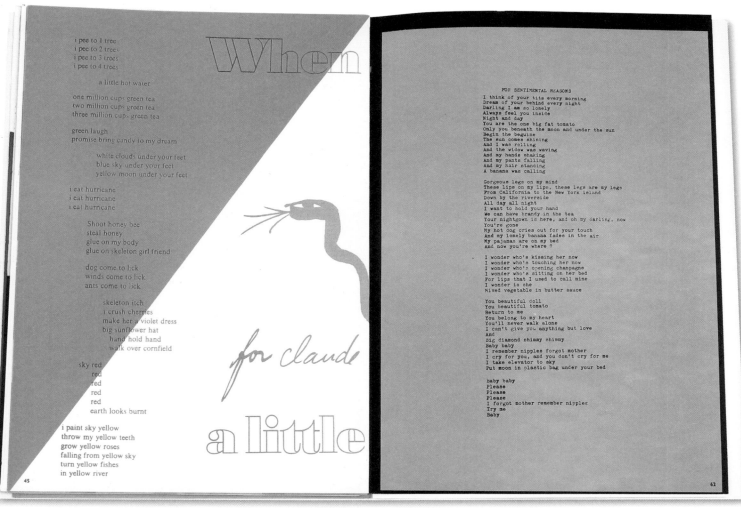

TITLE: *The typographic Dante*
ART DIRECTOR/DESIGNER: Barrie Tullett
YEAR: 1989 onwards

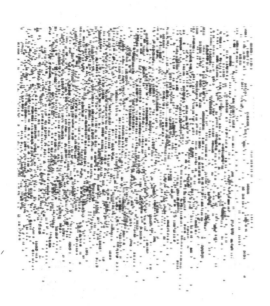 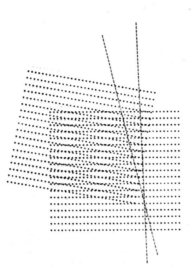  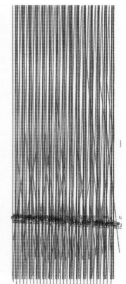

BARRIE TULLETT
Selections from *The typographic Dante*

The typographic Dante started when Barrie Tullett was a student at the Chelsea School of Art has continued for over twenty-five years, and is still going strong. Tullett quotes the artist Gordon Brennan as saying that 'making art might not make you happy, but not making it makes you sad'. So there is something very positive in physically making, disseminating, teaching and enabling other people to make artwork and develop their own creative voice – at least, that's what Barrie Tullett believes.

'The joy of the Caseroom Press [which he co-directs, enabling his creative freedom] allows me to tell as many stories as I like.' As it's self-published – usually books are made by hand, or go to press with small digital print runs – there are no commercial pressures at all. 'I have the opportunity to work on so many different things, either individually, or as part of the collaborative process,' Tullett says.

Various themes run through Tullett's books: word art, concrete poetry, typewriter art, letterpress, fairy tales. 'I'm a firm believer in John Furnival's philosophy that rather than think

about an idea, you should make the idea happen. So I think that's a good place to start and then you can worry about the "why" later.'

Tullett has a huge range of references and visual languages that inspire him. 'Working between digital and analogue processes throws up interesting juxtapositions,' he notes, 'and the fact the analogue processes often lead the work, either through restrictions or mistakes ... it always keeps things interesting. Even the print production methods involve compromise or creative thinking, depending whether or not you're asking more of the kit than it's designed for.

'I'm sure there will be unique voices in the book – I'm not sure I'm one of them. The combination of the idea, one's own sense of design and composition, combined with the production methods one chooses, will all create a unique piece of work – after all, it wouldn't exist otherwise, and no one would make it in the same way you do.'

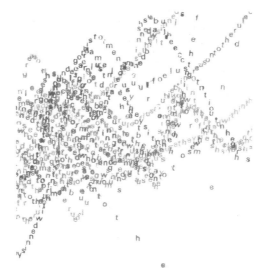

three throats 'barking

d o g l i k e

CERBERUS

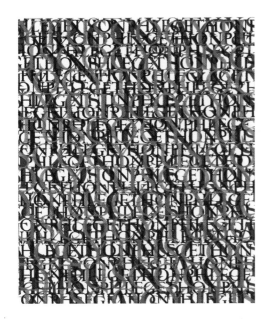

and he had made a **trumpet** of his *ass*

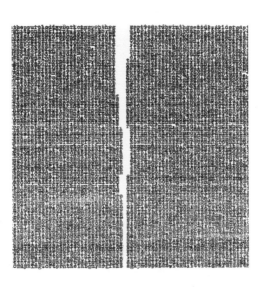

TITLE: *Your Song*
DESIGNER: Antonius Bui
YEAR: 2013

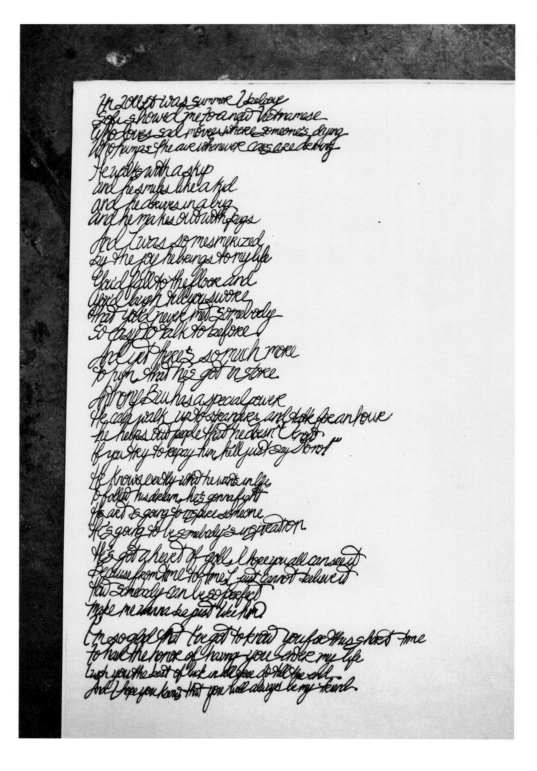

ANTONIUS BUI
Your Song

Your Song is a visual translation of a song once written and performed for Antonius Bui by his dear friend. 'He was the true storyteller,' Bui says, about one who has gone from his life. 'Now I am holding on to the remnants of a memory.'

Bui adds that 'Hand-cutting the lyrics was a meditative process that allowed me to confront a fading relationship. The project was a means of immortalizing the present feeling before it became the past.'

As a fine artist without graphic design experience, Bui hand-wrote and hand-cut this piece because that's what he knew how to do: 'My direct and honest relationship with the work makes it one of a kind.' Bui's choice of material, paper, is significant in its paradoxical qualities, which he says 'are embodied in every human; immense resistance and strength contrasted with fragile sensitivity. The tactility of the piece is not only fragile but impractical, just like my insistence on remembering the past. When lifted off the page, shadows of the text remind me that life is meant to be ephemeral.'

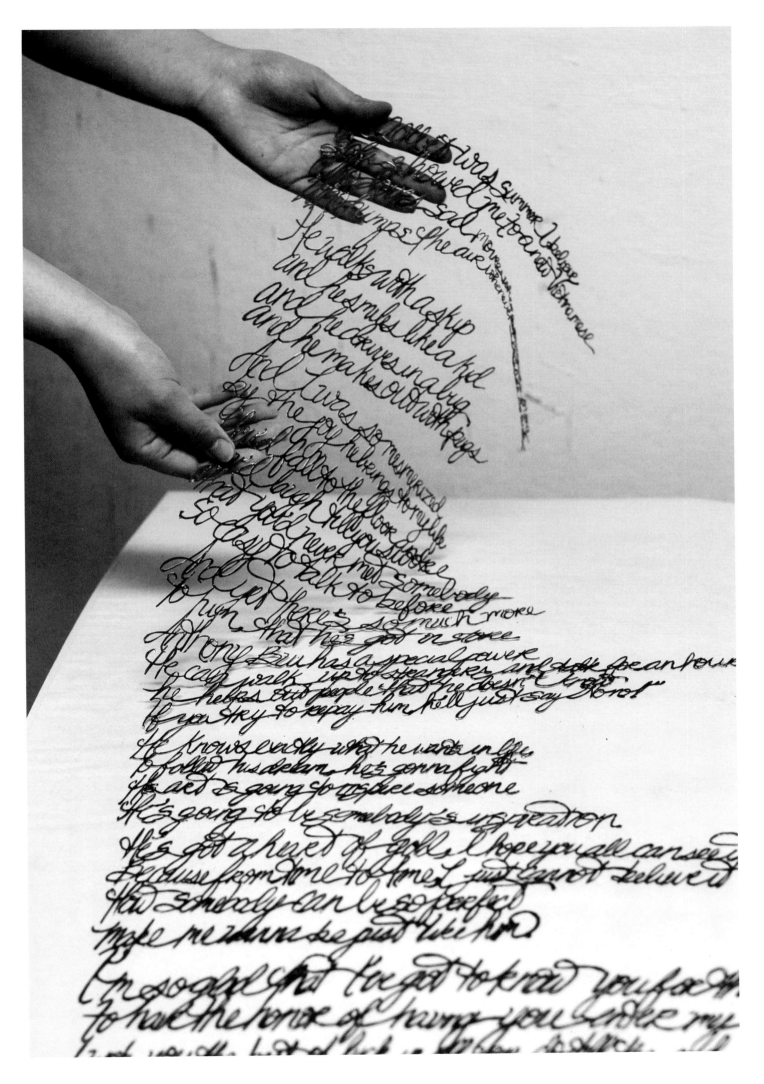

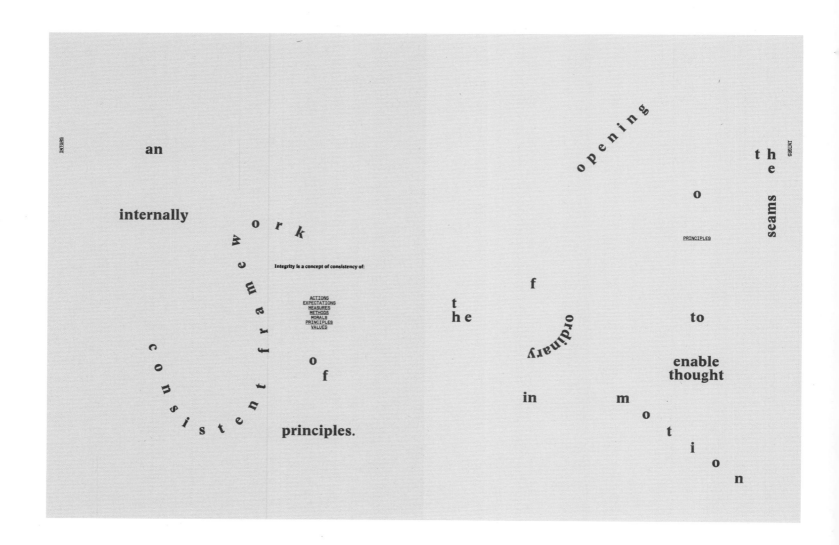

DYLAN McDONOUGH
INTGRS

Dylan McDonough's *INTGRS*, commissioned by fashion designer and writer Cluny McCullagh, tells the story of fashion as a social mechanism. It uses 'integrity as a lens to examine fashion', producing three core concepts: structural integrity, social integrity and moral integrity. The three are documented historically, abstractly and empirically throughout the text, often crossing over between categories. This is a deliberate decision, says McDonough, about the typographic and layout hierarchy: 'The removal of page numbers, the unbound pages, the lack of headings and so on all put the onus on the reader' to make sense of it all.

'*INTGRS* is intended as an alternative presentation of fashion at the place where it intersects with integrity.' All design choices revolved around the notion of functionality as it related to the concept and content. It is designed in a very minimalist way, says McDonough, in order to engage the reader in a physical/wearable 'reading' of the work. 'Central to the production of *INTGRS* was not just to document a project on fashion integrity but that it actually be a functioning work of fashion integrity itself.'

The typography is meant to incite the reader/user/wearer to act. *INTGRS* is meant as a 'toolkit, so the lettering had to reflect this in a two-dimensional sense'. The shapes chosen also mimic (to an extent) the shapes in clothing – armholes, collars, etc.; referencing the content, which is ultimately fashion in its many iterations. Wherever lettering was not directly referencing fashion it was creating movement – for the eye, hand and body (often challenging movement) – to encourage a deeper cognition of the material.

The book uses the language, objects and images of fashion and can be experienced as a traditional 'book', but is also the opposite in a limitless way, determined by the individual.

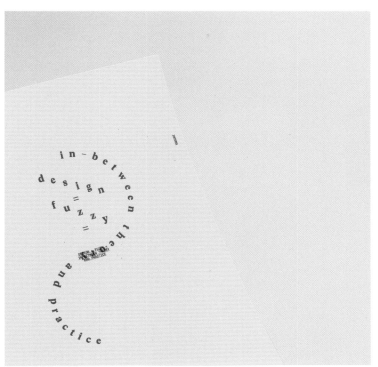

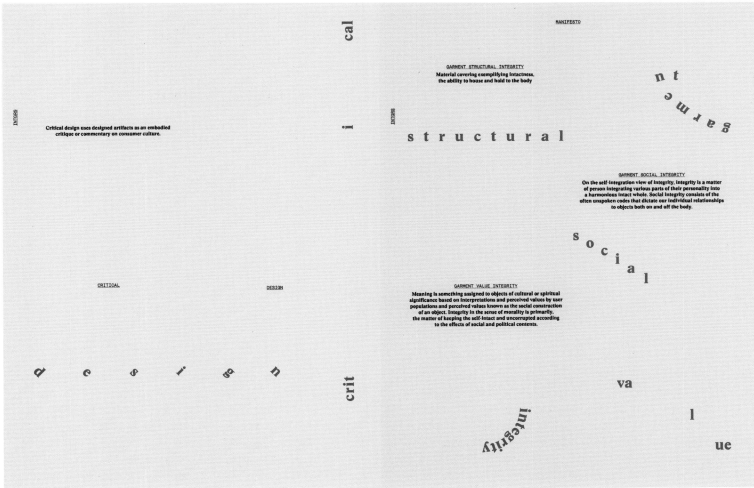

TITLE: *INTGRS*
DESIGN FIRM/AGENCY: Dylan McDonough
DESIGNER: Dylan McDonough
CLIENT: Cluny McCullagh
YEAR: 2014

BELOW, LEFT

TITLE: *Pissn n d deep blu sea n d spring tym, d dstnt lyts of d CT*
ART DIRECTOR/DESIGNER/ PHOTOGRAPHER/ILLUSTRATOR: Dirk Hagner
YEAR: 2012

BELOW, RIGHT

TITLE: *Distracted w d flowas amazd @ d m%n – d)i(!*
ART DIRECTOR/DESIGNER/ PHOTOGRAPHER/ILLUSTRATOR: Dirk Hagner
YEAR: 2012

OPPOSITE

TITLE: *A swallo flw outa d noz of d gr8 bddha*
ART DIRECTOR/DESIGNER/ PHOTOGRAPHER/ILLUSTRATOR: Dirk Hagner
YEAR: 2012

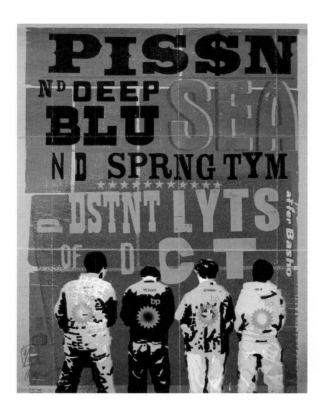

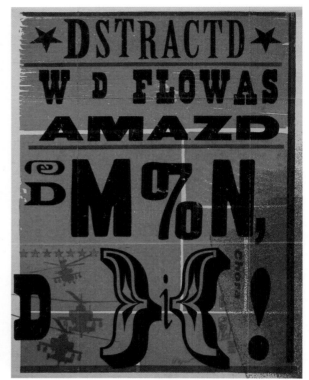

DIRK HAGNER
Texted Haiku Broadsides

With these typographic 'Haiku broadsides', which were started in 2010, Dirk Hagner audaciously bridged Western and Eastern cultural traditions. He used a traditional broadsheet paper size, letterpress printing, European 'bite of the print' visual commentary and American typographic traditions, combined with the contemplative nature of Japanese haiku measured verse. 'My students helped me with the texting,' he admits.

'The goal is to bring the important confluence of seeing and understanding the goings-on in the world across to the viewer,' he goes on to say, about the mashing of different cultures, old and new processes, references to history and contemporary issues, calm and unease, the beauty of the printing process and the written word. 'My hope is that the result is unexpected with a hint of familiarity – then it becomes interesting. I like people to feel something when they look at the work, so they get curious and start thinking about what this might be all about and look closer.'

Using texting words, he notes, 'was like jpeg-ing a picture'. Texts used less space, so larger type could fit in the lines. 'The result was a loss/compression, introducing some interesting artefacts. However, just like in a jpeg, the words resurrected to their full meaning when read. Here the typography is the story,

the content.' Most of the visual elements are woodcuts he made, and most of the large type is letterpress wood type. He used his own type and a full-sheet-size Showcard Signmaster press, dating (probably) from the 1960s. All pieces are hand-printed in up to eight colours in an edition of fifteen each, measuring 22 × 17 inches. Words, and by extension poetry, are frequently part of Hagner's art. He uses them not only for their meaning but because of the marks that letters and writing make. 'I used traditional haikus, mostly from the famous poets,' he explains. 'Nowadays there is a perceived sweetness to haikus which I wanted to acidify by introducing some elements of unease.'

These are indeed acidified. There are visual clues that hint at drones, smoke rising from some explosives, frogs with six legs, police shootings, a watchtower of a concentration camp, CCTV, consumerism, and so on. 'While working on it, the BP oil spill in the Gulf and later the tsunami/earthquake at Japan's Fukushima happened – of course those incidents became pieces in the series.' He includes some QR codes embedded in the images that, when scanned with a smartphone, give instant access to websites about the printing process with letterpress, background on the poets and, thankfully, an explanation of what a haiku is.

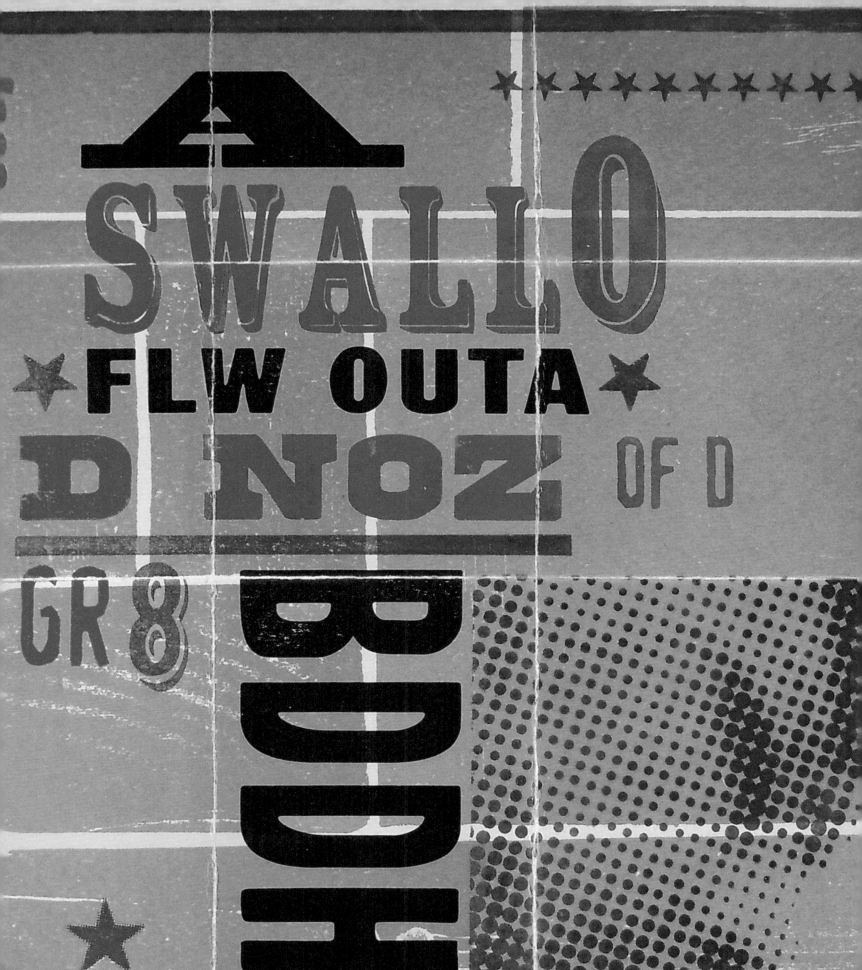

TITLE: *The Five Books* by Hrytsko Chubay
DESIGN FIRM/AGENCY: Agrafka Studio
ART DIRECTORS: Romana Romanyshyn and Andriy Lesiv
PHOTOGRAPHERS/ILLUSTRATORS: Romana Romanyshyn
and Andriy Lesiv
CLIENT: Old Lion Publishing House
YEAR: 2013

AGRAFKA STUDIO
The Five Books by Hrytsko Chubay

The Five Books is a collection of poetry by celebrated Ukrainian underground dissident Hrytsko Chubay (1949–1982). The designers Romana Romanyshyn and Andriy Lesiv note that the format and typewriter font are based on 'an original self-published prototype of [a] book, which existed in two pieces and [was] made by the author himself'. The photos, from a family archive, were never published. The collage aesthetic was chosen after the designers visited the author's own room, which was decorated with collages of texts pasted on the walls and made by Chubay.

This poetry is filled with questions about faith, the place of humans in this world, and about the pressures of political regimes. 'Words were always his shelter, so he cut paper strings from his original book [which] are like [the] carcass for [the] new book,' says Lesiv. 'Sometimes these paper strings are entangled like [a] nest, and sometimes they are frames for photos or put together in shapes [to] create numbers, letters and signs.'

'It was an interesting experience to use small elements of typography for building big symbols of letters for every chapter of [the] book,' Romanyshyn says. 'Like small letters are the building blocks that build the poetry.'

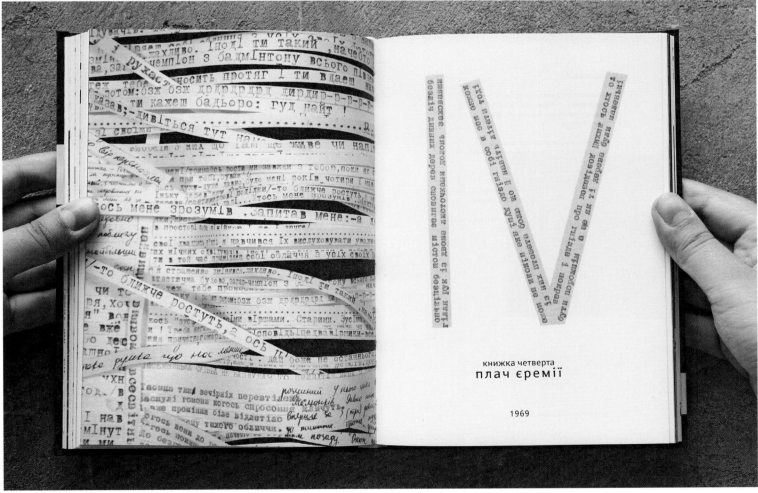

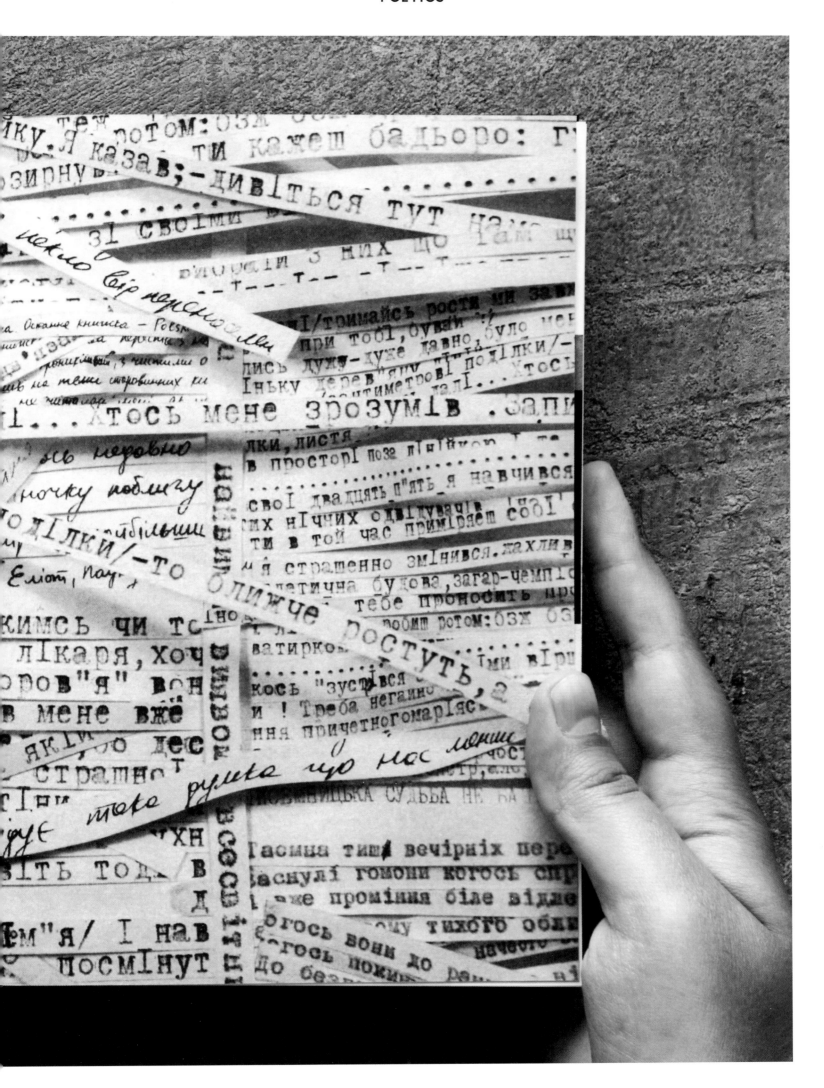

TITLE: *Whitman Illuminated: Song of Myself*
DESIGN FIRM/AGENCY: Plankton Art Co.
ART DIRECTOR: Diane Chonette, Tin House Books
DESIGNER/ILLUSTRATOR: Allen Crawford
CLIENT: Tin House Books
YEAR: 2014

ALLEN CRAWFORD
Whitman Illuminated: Song of Myself

'If you've read the 1855 edition of "Song of Myself",' says Allen Crawford, 'you'll notice that the self, the "I" of the poem, starts out very particular and specific, but the self of the poem gradually broadens to include a multitude of selves – hunters, firemen, slaves, you name it – until eventually, the self of the poem dissipates, becoming everything, including the reader. The poem quite literally begins with "I" and ends with "you".' Walt Whitman not only espoused democratic values in the poem, but he also forged a democratic literary aesthetic – what Ralph Waldo Emerson called the 'clear eyeball'.

Crawford's 'job as the illustrator and designer' of this book was to chart his own path through the poem or, as he describes it, 'to draw from life as Whitman had when he wrote his poem, based on notes he took as he walked through the city, rode on ferries, and eavesdropped on omnibuses'. Whitman wanted 'Song of Myself' to be a different poem for each person who read it, and Crawford has made 'Song of Myself' his own by drawing all the type in the volume by hand.

He was influenced not only by the various drawn type elements used in the covers and frontispieces throughout the seven editions of Whitman's *Leaves of Grass* (1855), but also nineteenth-century scrimshaw, which is something Crawford has been interested in for decades. 'I like the irregularity of the handmade letterforms, their artful artlessness,' he notes. 'But ultimately, I decided to just get out of my way and draw as plainly as I could. The coarse way I naturally draw lent itself well to Whitman's plainspoken aesthetic.'

Making the spreads monochromatic was a practical decision, because making full-colour spreads would have taken many years 'and would not have improved the final result'. The limited palette also lent itself to the unburnished aesthetic that he wanted – nautical colours that repeat throughout the book: red, green, blue. But most important, the limited colour palette gives the book visual continuity, even when the images and type fluctuate stylistically. The book itself is the sketchbook, in that every day Crawford started from scratch: 'It was entirely improvised.' Crawford says a limited palette was necessary to give the book a strong presence as an object. 'Throwing a ton of colours into it would have weakened the cohesion and impact.'

48

do i contradict myself?

very well then.... i contradict myself. I AM LARGE..... i contain MULTI-TUDES.

A CHILD SAID, WHAT IS THE GRASS? FETCHING IT TO ME WITH FULL HANDS; how could I answer the child.... I do NOT KNOW WHAT IT IS ANY MORE THAN HE. I GUESS IT MUST BE THE FLAG OF MY OWN DISPOSITION, OUT OF HOPEFUL GREEN STUFF WOVEN. OR I GUESS IT IS THE HANDKERCHIEF OF THE LORD, A SCENTED GIFT AND REMEMBRANCER DESIGNEDLY DROPPED, BEARING THE OWNER'S NAME SOMEWAY IN THE CORNERS, THAT WE MAY SEE AND REMARK, AND SAY WHOSE? OR I GUESS THE GRASS ITSELF IS A CHILD, THE PRODUCED BABE OF THE VEGETATION.

49

BIANCA BUNSAS
Anatomia Poetica

Anatomia Poetica is a literal translation of anatomical terms to discover their original and underlying meaning, which is typographically visualized by connecting them to poems, dramatic extracts and other literary works. The book shows that technical anatomical terms are, in fact, funny and figurative. Bianca Bunsas, who formerly studied human medicine, designed the book as a bachelor degree project at the University of Applied Sciences in Augsburg, Germany. 'I wanted to find a way to connect art and design and science in one project.'

The typography, while expressively randomized, is 'absolutely driven' by its content – 'It is form follows function,' Bunsas insists. The narrative continued throughout the book owing to some constant elements, such as colour and font. 'The level of variation should be similar,' she says about her design logic, 'because if all spreads are completely different, being different is something all spreads have in common.'

TITLE: *Anatomia Poetica*
ART DIRECTOR: Bianca Bunsas
YEAR: 2014

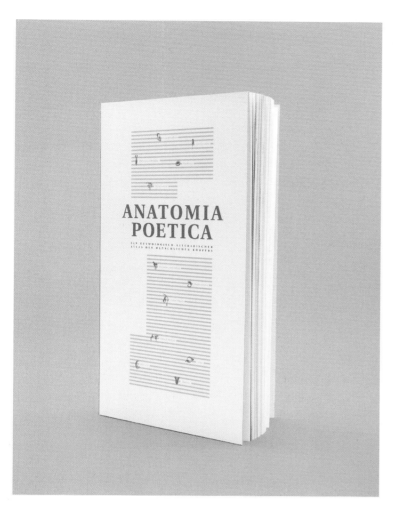

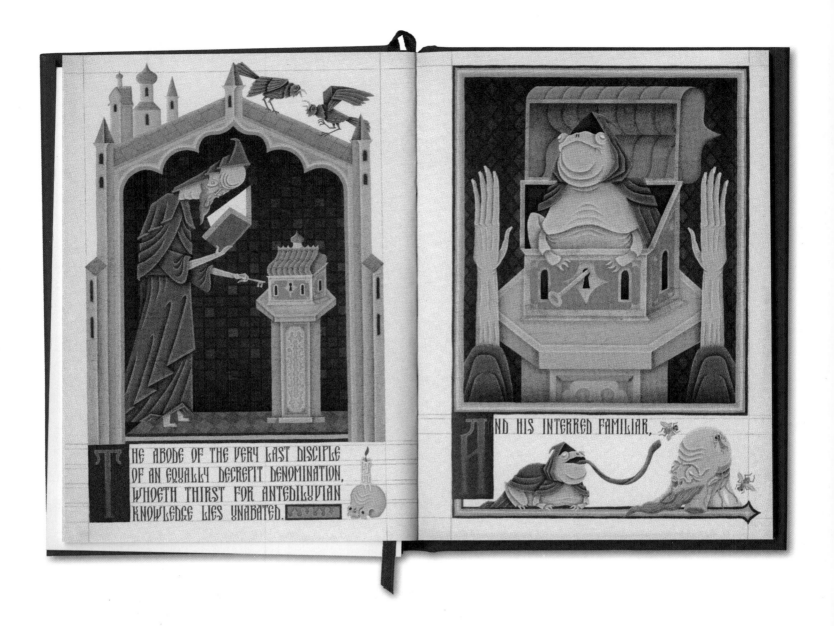

HERMAN INCLUSUS
Dismal Incantation

Herman Inclusus's *Dismal Incantation* is unique among graphic novels: it has the essential beauty of incunabula, with lettering that recalls early typography and is imbued with the spirit of a modern illuminator. It is the tale of a lonely, bedraggled monk; the last follower of a long dead and forgotten faith. He attempts, one last time, to re-establish and revive his bygone religion by conducting a diabolical ritual, with no margin for error.

Dismal Incantation was heavily inspired by Inclusus's personal interest in medieval manuscripts and Byzantine icons, and to a lesser extent, Islamic miniatures and Indian court paintings. 'I needed the typography to have a particular medieval and religious aesthetic,' he says, 'but I didn't want to use an illegible Gothic script font. I rendered my own typeface based on traditional Cyrillic letterforms, in keeping with the

Eastern Orthodox-style artwork of the book, but stripped of any ornamental flair to try and keep it as readable as possible.'

He admits that he had no way to convert letterforms into an actual digital font file. 'So I had to painstakingly arrange each letter by hand in Photoshop; which in a way, is not too dissimilar from the act of the patient print-worker of yesteryear, who would have to compose and lock movable type into the bed of a press – kind of apt considering the influence of early book design on my artwork.'

His primary challenge and the happy outcome was to create a horror comic that does not rely on vintage pre-Comics Code 1950s horror or action comic-book aesthetics, which he does well. But his secondary goal was, he says, to 'disgust and horrify the reader' – over which the jury is still undecided.

TITLE: *Dismal Incantation* (comic book)
DESIGNER: Herman Inclusus
YEAR: 2014

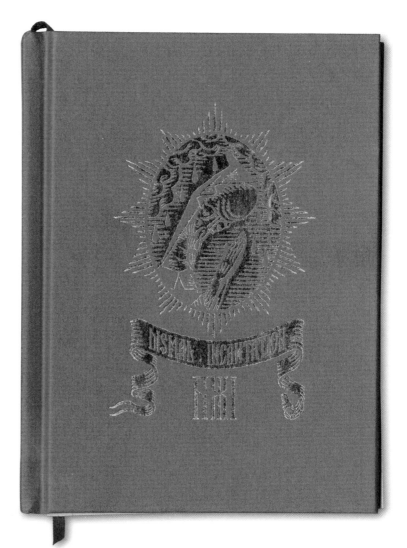

BELOW
TITLE: Livro 1
ART DIRECTOR/DESIGNER: Pedro Antônio
Gabriel Anhorn
YEAR: 2013

OPPOSITE
TITLE: Livro 2
ART DIRECTOR/DESIGNER: Pedro Antônio
Gabriel Anhorn
YEAR: 2014

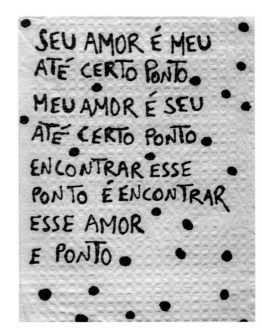

PEDRO ANTÔNIO GABRIEL ANHORN
Eu Me Chamo Antônio
Segundo – Eu Me Chamo Antônio

Pedro Antônio Gabriel Anhorn discloses his inner world: 'shyness, giving voice to the silence, giving courage to the fear of exposing myself … Antônio is me with a little more courage, a character in a novel that has yet to be written.'

For now, Anhorn's two published books are a sort of pre-novel, in which the marriage of the word with the drawing helps in telling the story. *Eu Me Chamo Antônio* (His Name is Antônio) was born spontaneously on a bar counter; in truth it was what he calls 'my first public creative space'.

'I started using the napkins as a form of expression by chance. One day, upon returning home after work', he explains, 'I stopped at a bar but noticed I had forgotten my notebook. The only material I had to externalize my thoughts at that moment was the stack of napkins. I ended up with the love of drawing and writing on this fragile piece of paper. When I realized I had a drawer full of creations, I opened a fan page to have a record of all these arts. Today, I have more than 2,000 napkins.'

The first book, *Eu Me Chamo Antônio*, published in 2013, has the light humour characteristic of bohemian chats. The goal was to enable two ways of reading – either to open the book at any page randomly and read it like a poem of the day, or to read the napkins sequentially, finding out how Antônio externalizes his disappointments, encounters and passions. The second book, *Segundo – Eu Me Chamo Antônio*, published in 2014, is created in the world of dreams – as if the character of Antônio left the bar and walked through the space, the dreamland. On each page, the reader goes a little deeper into the character's notebook of ideas and discovers the richness of his poetic world.

'I believe that drawing our own letters is the most unique way to externalize our inner world,' Gabriel says about writing his first poem when he was twelve years old, a tribute to the Cabo Verde (Cape Verde) islands, the African archipelago where he spent most of his childhood. 'Everyone should have the habit of writing! In an increasingly digitalized world, handwriting is a revolutionary act.'

54

WARREN LEHRER
Stretch Marks

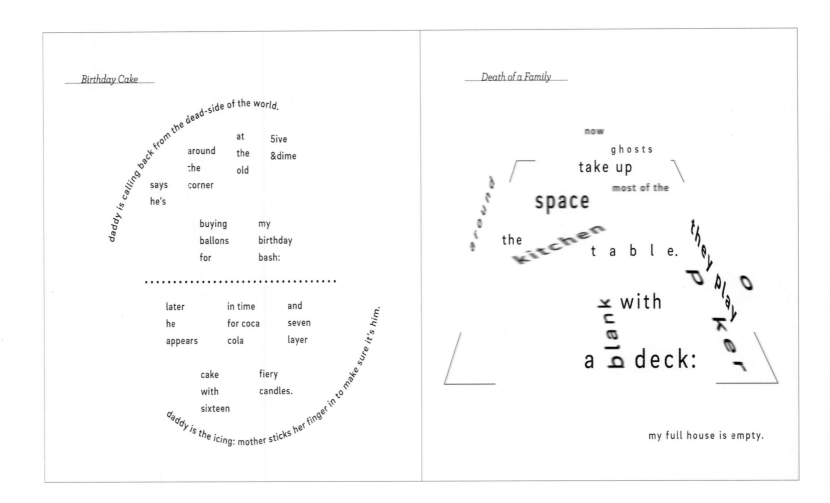

Birthday Cake

daddy is calling back from the dead-side of the world.

	at	5ive
around	the	&dime
the	old	
says	corner	
he's		
	buying	my
	ballons	birthday
	for	bash:

. . . .

later	in time	and
he	for coca	seven
appears	cola	layer
	cake	fiery
	with	candles.
	sixteen	

daddy is the icing: mother sticks her finger in to make sure it's him.

Death of a Family

now

ghosts

take up

space   most of the

the   kitchen   t a b l e.   they play

around

blank   with   poker

a b deck:

my full house is empty.

Stretch Marks is a collaborative book of short poems written by Dennis Bernstein and visualized by Warren Lehrer. In addition to writing *French Fries* (1984, page 72) together, the long-time collaborators wrote a play called *Social Security: The Basic Training of Eugene Solomon* (1980), and other works; many of Bernstein's poems, of all lengths, have been published in leading literary magazines and journals. *Stretch Marks* forms a collection of 250 short poems he has written over thirty years, as selected, visualized and composed for the page by Lehrer.

Lehrer begins working on each of Bernstein's poems with no specific plan. 'I let the poem lead me into a visual setting,' he explains. 'The words, and *emotions* behind the words, lead me, as a reader and writer and interpreter.' Like an actor with

a script, Lehrer's typography performs 'a new kind of life for the text. Behind the words – the experience of a person with Alzheimer's disease, a parent losing their child to a bullet, the love for a mother, surviving open-heart surgery, sensing the ghosts of loved ones, a swarm of insects inspecting a discarded piece of candy, having to flee your home and homeland, being kissed for the very first time – lead me to typographic compositions.'

The aim of each visual setting is not to illustrate the words, he says, but to create an *experience* for the reader, 'an experience of discovery, wonder, empathy. Through the process of interpretation and play, I often find unexpected connections, visual metaphors, double and sometimes triple meanings.'

Getting Tough

frankie you fuckin'
two-bit twerp today i
kick your ass three o'
clock at the flagpole
be there you four-eyed
cock-lickin' half-breed

or i'll come and drag
you by your faggot hair
rub your face in shit
use you as a rag to
check my oil and open
your lip with my fist

Pain Relief

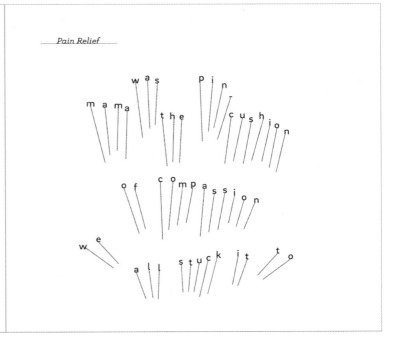

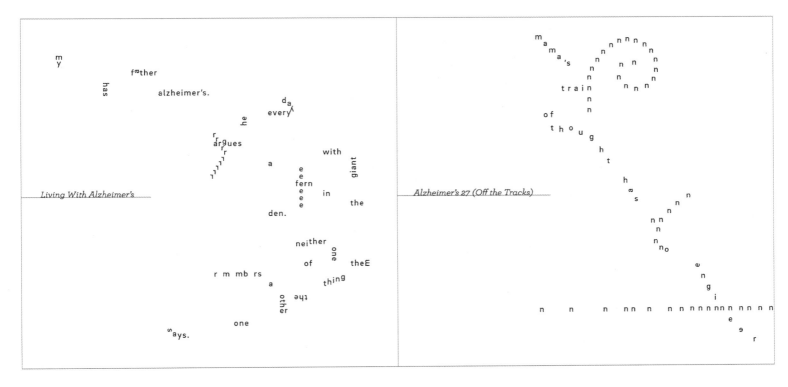

Living With Alzheimer's

Alzheimer's 27 (Off the Tracks)

TITLE: *Stretch Marks*
DESIGNER: Warren Lehrer
POEMS: Dennis Bernstein
VISUALIZATIONS: Warren Lehrer
PUBLISHER: EarSay
YEAR: 2016

The Smaller Picture

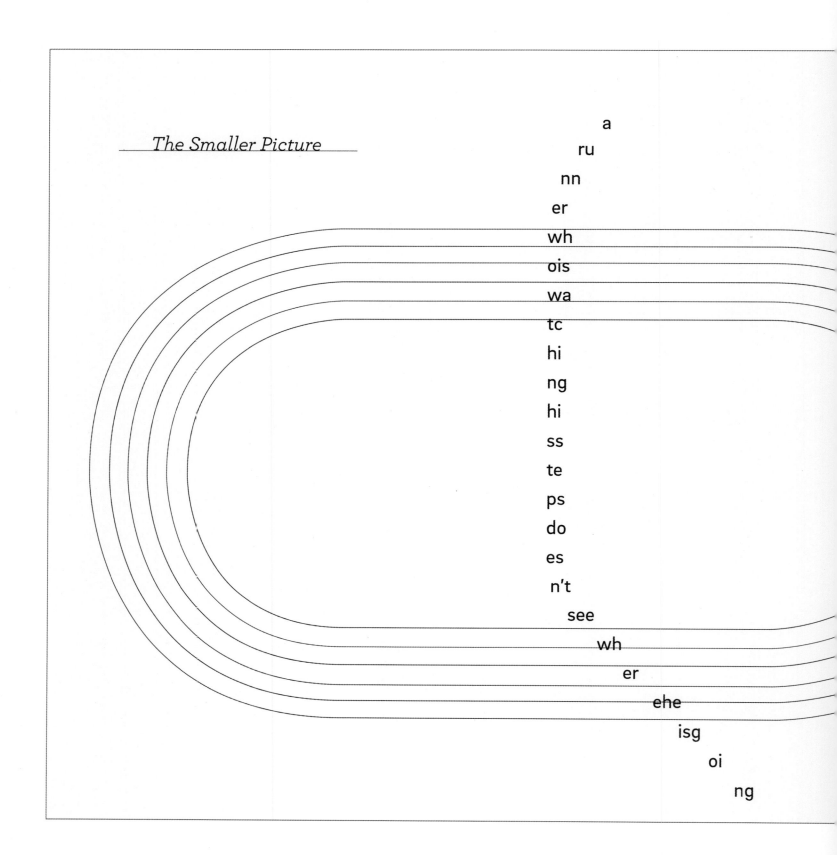

a
ru
nn
er
wh
ois
wa
tc
hi
ng
hi
ss
te
ps
do
es
n't
see
wh
er
ehe
isg
oi
ng

Recovery Room

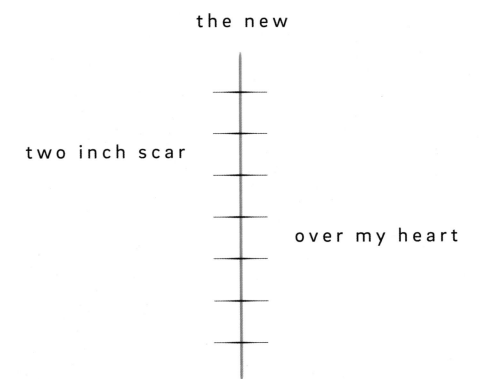

the new

two inch scar

over my heart

is down on its knees,
                praying.

DRAMATICS

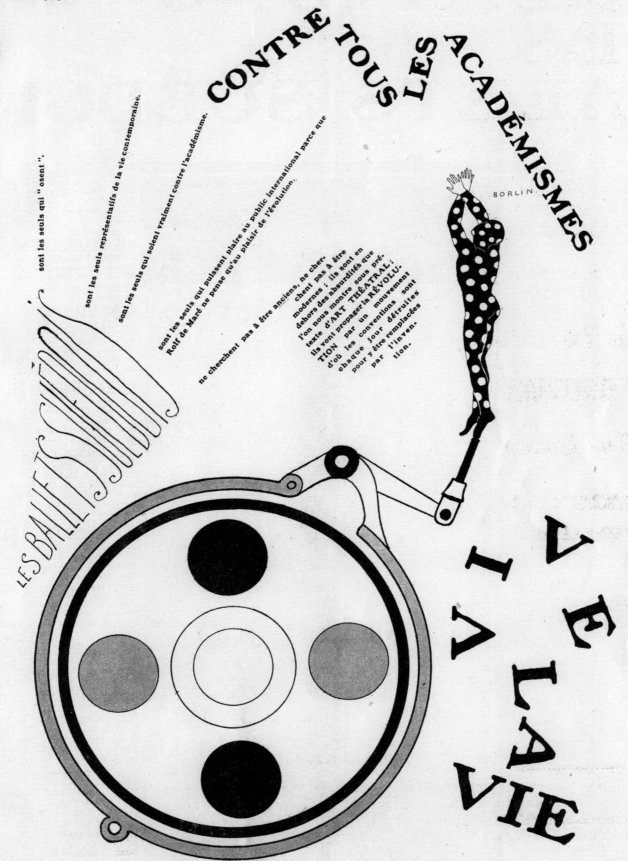

CONTRE TOUS LES ACADÉMISMES

LES BALLETS SUÉDOIS

sont les seuls qui "osent".

sont les seuls représentatifs de la vie contemporaine.

sont les seuls qui soient vraiment contre l'académisme.

sont les seuls qui puissent plaire au public international parce que Rolf de Maré ne pense qu'au plaisir de l'évolution.

ne cherchent pas à être anciens, ne cherchent pas à être modernes ; ils sont en dehors des absurdités que l'on nous montre sous prétexte d'ART THÉATRAL : ils vont propager la RÉVOLUTION par un mouvement d'où les conventions sont chaque jour détruites pour y être remplacées par l'invention.

BORLIN.

VE LA VIE

TITLE: *La Danse*
DESIGNER/AUTHOR: Francis Picabia
YEAR: 1924

FRANCIS PICABIA
La Danse

The Ballets suédois (Swedish Ballet) was one of the leading avant-garde dance troupes in the world, earning its reputation through a distinctive marriage of modern design and a progressive style of movement. Despite the name, it was headquartered at the Théâtre des Champs-Elysées in Paris from 1920 to 1924, and frequently toured throughout Europe and the United States. Its founder was Rolf de Maré, the scion of a wealthy Swedish family, who grew up surrounded by the arts, and although he was not himself an artist, he was a brilliant impresario. He did not specialize in dance alone but modern art in general, with a Cubist collection that included Picasso, Braque and Léger. The latter produced posters and scenery for many of the Ballets suédois performances.

This special issue of *La Danse* (November/December 1924) was devoted to the Ballets suédois, along with its principal choreographer, Jean Börlin, and the many artists, musicians and writers whose talents de Maré had tapped. On the cover, a poster by Maria Vassilieff, the Russian-émigré painter and member of the Montparnasse art scene, is a deceptively naive light-handed drawing and lettering composition, suggesting little evidence of the wild and adventurous typographic contortions taking place on most of the interior pages, which were presumably composed under the direction of the avant-garde gadfly Francis Picabia.

Picabia's page designs echoed – yet didn't slavishly copy – the typographic language of Futurist and Dadaist publications of the era. Each short article by a member of Ballets suédois's brain trust about another member was designed in some way to reflect the subject. Layouts included contoured text blocks that wrapped around portraits and caricatures of leading contributors to the repertoire. *La Danse* was used as the programme for the 1924 season, with listings of dates and venues. However, the expressive typographical hijinks announced that this was more a monumental document than an ephemeral publication.

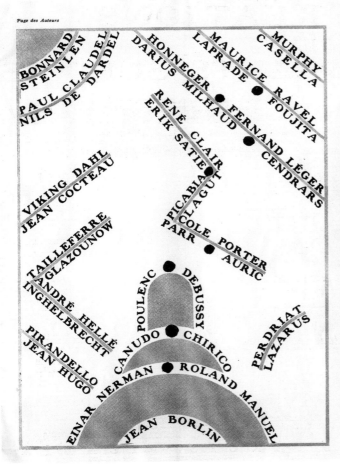

LEO LIONNI
How to Read Fortune *in Bed*

Not many lay-people understand (or care) that typefaces have different names, come in certain point sizes or, most important, project unique symbolic characters and personalities. But when the advertising designer turned children's book author Leo Lionni was art director of *Fortune* in 1952, he conceived and produced the oddly titled *How to Read* Fortune *in Bed*. Typefaces of various shapes and sizes were the protagonists of this off-kilter promotional booklet, presumably aimed at potential advertisers.

It was just one of many content-driven typographic promotions from the self-appointed master of Century type. Each typeface represents the mood of the sentence or phrase in which it is set. The entire booklet humorously tells how the wealthy readers of *Fortune* consume the magazine, using type as a plot-advancing device. And the plot is that the very rich (today

known as the one per cent) could afford a magazine that cost a whopping $1 per copy, even during the Great Depression.

One excerpt from the introductory portion of the booklet goes like this:

> *But how do they read Fortune in bed?*
> [24 pt Horizontal]
> *They don't, They read it while they're wide awake.*
> [24 pt Alert]
> *And then they sleep soundly.*
> [24 pt Double Snored]

That says it all, typographically speaking.

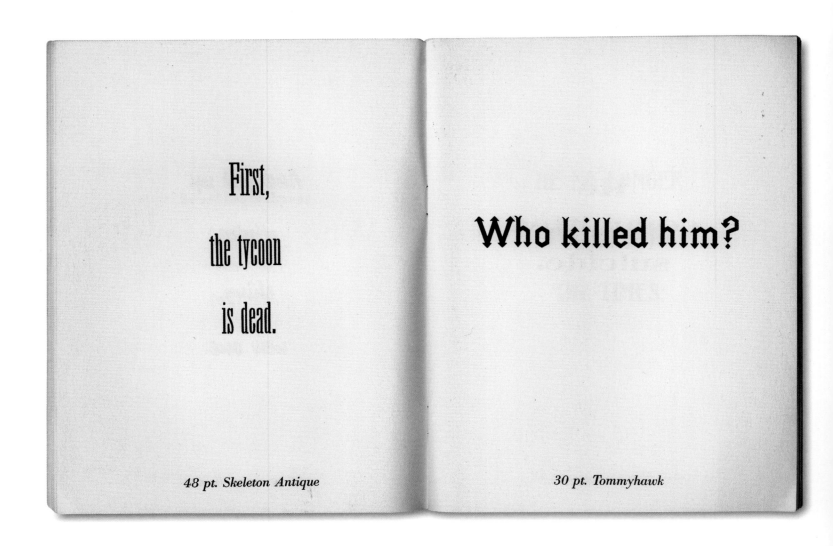

48 pt. *Skeleton Antique*

30 pt. *Tommyhawk*

TITLE: *How to Read* Fortune *in Bed*
DESIGNER: Leo Lionni
PUBLISHER: *Fortune*, Time Inc.
YEAR: 1952

How to read *Fortune* in bed

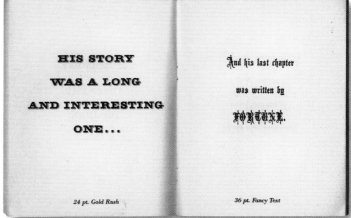

HIS STORY
WAS A LONG
AND INTERESTING
ONE...

24 pt. Gold Rush

And his last chapter

was written by

FORTUNE.

36 pt. Fancy Text

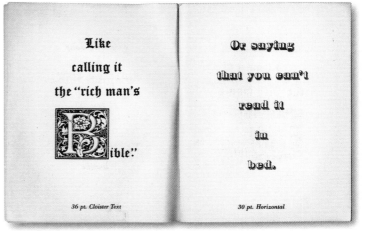

Like
calling it
the "rich man's
Bible."

36 pt. Cloister Text

Or saying
that you can't
read it
in
bed.

30 pt. Horizontal

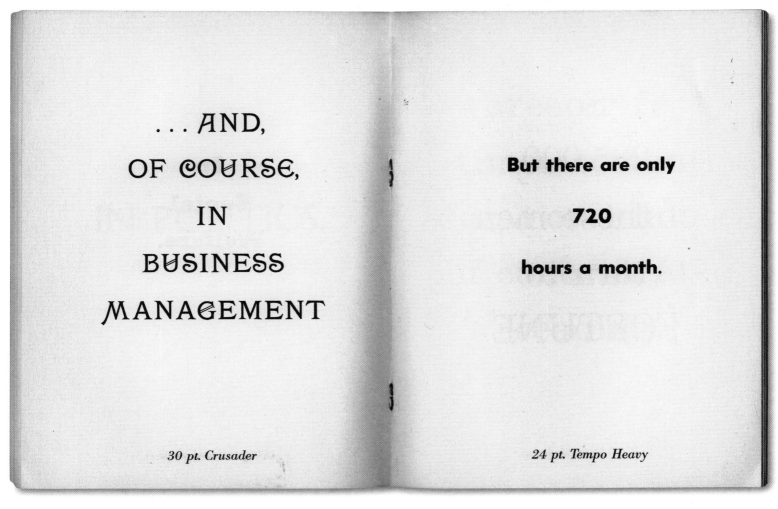

... AND,

OF COURSE,

IN

BUSINESS

MANAGEMENT

30 pt. Crusader

But there are only

720

hours a month.

24 pt. Tempo Heavy

ROBERT MASSIN
The Bald Soprano

If Robert Massin had not done anything else during his career as typographer, art director and editor, the kinetic book he designed in 1964 for Eugène Ionesco's absurd 'anti-play', *La Cantatrice Chauve* – known in its American edition as *The Bald Soprano* (1965) and in the English edition as *The Bald Prima Donna* (1966) – places him in the pantheon of talking typography. Massin invented a raucously narrative form of typo-photo composition that today would be as easy as pressing a button. Back in 1964 Massin only had the digits on his two hands to work with. *The Bald Soprano* was Massin's attempt to capture what Laetitia Wolff, curator of a retrospective exhibition at the Cooper Union, New York (winter 2002), called 'the dynamism of the theatre within the static confines of the book'.

Massin translated the play's theatrical dynamics to the printed page through the nuances, inflections and tics of the actors. Massin transformed Ionesco's players into veritable logos simply by assigning their character to a specific typeface that represented a personalized voice. The typefaces were in parts assigned to high-contrast photographs of the actors, and the readers immediately saw and identified with each player.

The layouts were large storyboards with the dialogue-typefaces integrated from scene to scene. Stage directions were replaced with physical gestures and movements of the actor-images, and type flowed from their respective personages across the pages in varying configurations. Their duelling dialogues became increasingly chaotic as more actors appeared.

Every element was not only arduously composed and pasted up (during the days of glue and photo-mechanicals), but Massin distorted the type to distinguish between quiet and loud conversations by stretching the text that was transferred on to soft rubber – using three dozen condoms, to be exact.

Massin inspired book artists working in pictorial narrative. Most notable was the work of American typographer and performance artist, Warren Lehrer – author of the typographic Babel titled *French Fries* (see page 72), a stage play of intersecting dialogues – who introduced colour, textures and more chaotic typographic interplay to the original Massin model. During the 1990s, with the advent of digital design, neo-Expressionist and Deconstructivist typographers furthered the 'type-as-voice' idea. Yet Massin's work remains the highest peak of these typographic contortions.

TITLE: *The Bald Soprano*
AUTHOR: Eugène Ionesco
ART DIRECTOR: Robert Massin
PHOTOGRAPHER: Henry Cohen
YEAR: 1965

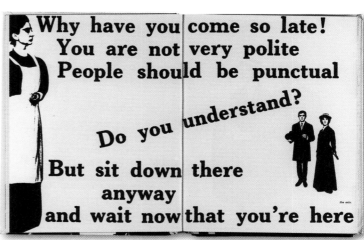

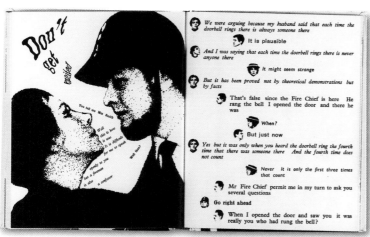

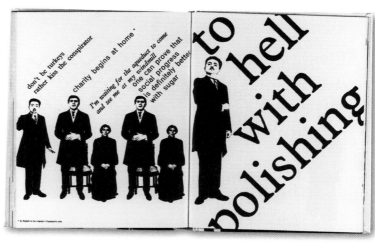

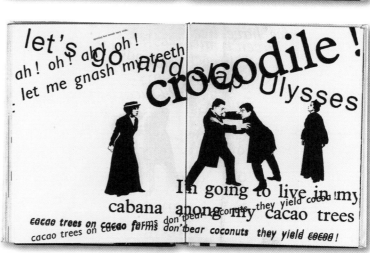

TITLE: *i mean you know*
DESIGNER: Warren Lehrer, EarSay
PHOTOGRAPHER/ILLUSTRATOR: Warren Lehrer
LETTERING: Jan Baker
PUBLISHER: Visual Studies Workshop
YEAR: 1983

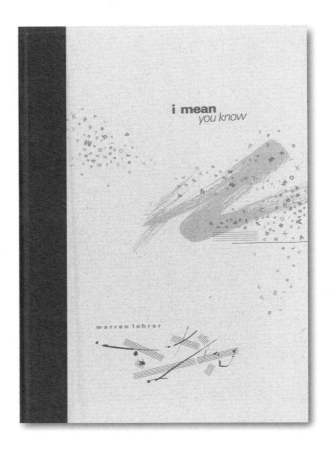

WARREN LEHRER
i mean you know

Warren Lehrer's first offset-printed-book-performance-score, entitled *versations: a setting for eight conversations* (1980), explored the poetics and music of conversation. In his second book, *i mean you know*, he continued his attempt to translate the spoken word on to the printed page – 'but I also set out to capture the shape of thought,' he says.

From the introduction:
'*i mean you know* is a play of voices. it is the music of thought. a day at work. a few hours of one day within the minds of seven people. the characters all inhabit one building, but the architecture is of the mind and not at all concrete.'

'The stories that are told within this "group portrait" are', he explains, 'for the most part, hard fought.' They are not chiselled in typographic slabs or gracefully flowing out of the mouths of their characters, who are all works in progress, searching and fumbling through life as best they can.

Their voices are 'marked by stammers, stutters and revisions; *i mean you know* explores the cracks and synaptic gaps between thoughts and utterances and the iterative nature of memory and story. Looking back on it now, *i mean you know* was a metaphor for the human search for meaning (*i mean*), and the desire to connect with others (*you know*).

'The seven seemingly disparate characters, who happen to inhabit the same building, all have a project going inside their heads, an obsession they're churning about, whether it's an obsession with their family, their work, or something they're trying to improve upon in themselves. In that sense, *i mean you know* is about work.'

i mean you know furthered Lehrer's approach to using typography and lettering as a means of creating graphic representations of character, and translating the shape and rhythms of thought and speech on to the printed page. The result is a kind of real-time notation, instead of using traditional punctuation, which helps expedite time into a compact space. 'I use space to signify time. Lines are broken significantly as in verse so that a line break or a blank space represents a pause. Spaces between words, and silences, are as significant as what is spoken. Since all thoughts are not manifest as sentences or even linear strings, my approach to the composition included fields and clusters of thought as well as trains, bursts, spirals, waves and fragments.'

The musical/theatrical structure of *i mean you know* juxtaposes the seven voices into various arrangements. In order to orchestrate as many as seven simultaneous voices on one page but still maintain readability, Lehrer used a four-column grid superimposed on a three-column grid. 'I also used black and grey inks, which helped differentiate volume and acoustic distance. Each character was typecast into a distinct typographic or calligraphic configuration. Different typefaces and lettering styles tried out for different roles made the "casting" gruelling.'

i mean you know works as both a book – to be read silently alone – and as a score for performance. Its approach to typography leads the reader to actively participate, choose where and who to read next, 'and hopefully make connections to the musicality, humour, pathos, order and chaos in their own daily lives'.

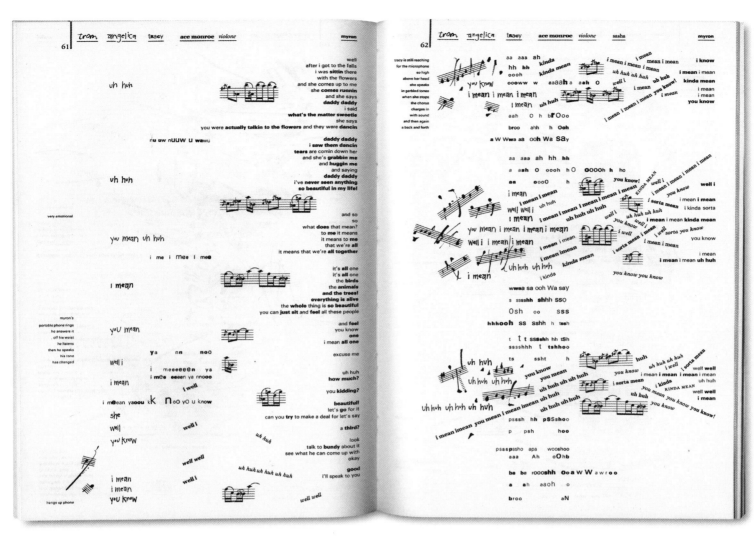

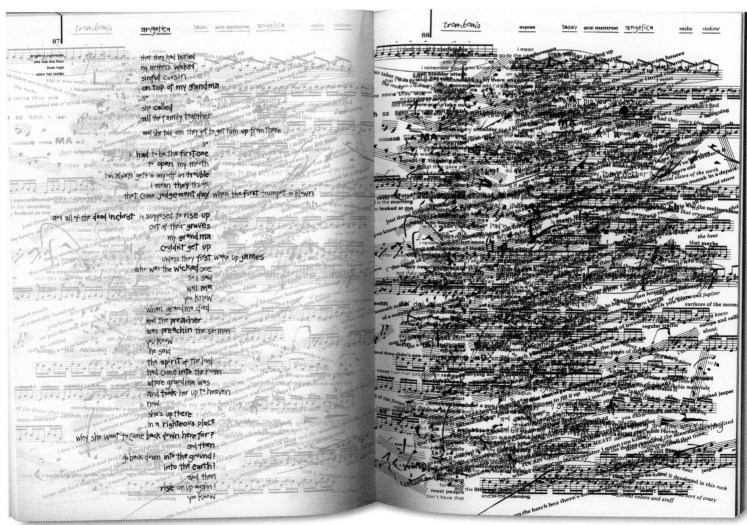

tRAcy myron ace monroe *trombonio*

there is darkness
a smokey
dusty light emerges
from a candle here
a lantern there
everyone is seen
alone
some are crawling
others working
re-arranging
still their dreaming

just those little tiny things
you know all of a sudden you can find a oneness in something

even some smell can do that
the smell of *pizza*
or the smooth touch
of a *metallic* handrail
you know
or just the way the sun
or *buttered popcorn*   may be setting
on a set of keys

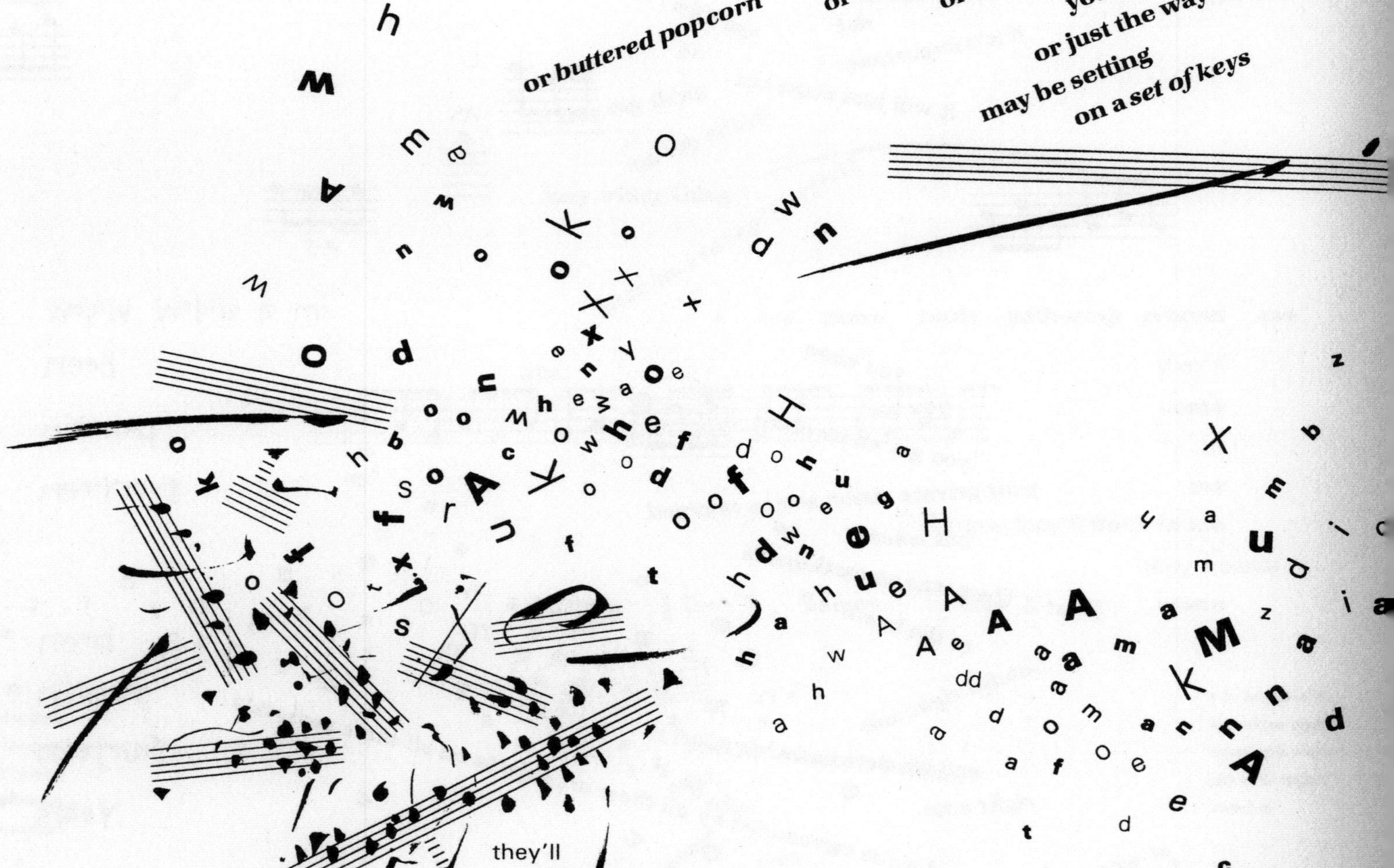

they'll
come
to
me
i see **these birds**
they're   **gatherin   around**
not   this   car
my
other
one
they'll be
the   way   i   **feel   now**
they'll   come   **they'll**   come

they feel
they feel **warm**

warmth

i   **see   these   birds**

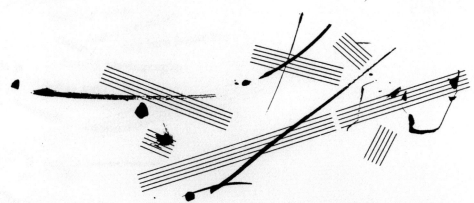

let me tell you something let me put one thing straight to you

no one can make me

do anything that i don't want to do

if i don't want to go anywhere

or take

rhonda or carrie

i don't have to

cause i

i do it cause i want to

no one makes me

i do it

they don't make me do nothin

i do it

cause i want to do it

but when you look closer

there's really nothing there

it just breaks up   it all breaks up

very fleeting

these things   they disappear

i mean as soon as you look any further

they're gone

very momentary   very momentary

TITLE: *French Fries*
DESIGNER: Warren Lehrer, EarSay
AUTHORS: Dennis Bernstein and Warren Lehrer
PHOTOGRAPHER/ILLUSTRATOR: Warren Lehrer
PUBLISHER: Visual Studies Workshop
YEAR: 1984

WARREN LEHRER
French Fries

Performance artist and typographer Warren Lehrer's work is about bringing written and spoken language together. *French Fries* is a play-in-a-book set in an American fast-food restaurant. It is what Lehrer calls a 'slice-of-life play' that reflects on American culture and characters.

French Fries was conceived when Lehrer and journalist Dennis Bernstein were lunching at McDonald's in Greenwich Village. 'At a certain point in the meal, we both realized that the place was living theatre,' says Lehrer, recalling his future cast of characters: a homeless man taking leftover food on the tables; mothers with their kids; college students trying to study; a couple having a fight, while another was smooching. There was the din of cashiers placing and ringing up orders mixed with the sizzle of fryolators and the pulsing in counter time to a customer's bassy boombox. 'On the spot, we decided to write a play called *French Fries*, and I knew the cover of the book should look like a box of French Fries,' says Lehrer.

The play occurs over the course of a few hours of one day in the life of the Dream Queen restaurant (a fictional restaurant that grew to become the third-largest burger chain in the Western Hemisphere). Before the first act begins, Gertie Greenbaum (a steady customer) is found dead in a pool of blood and ketchup. Four customers and three employees give very different testimonies as to how Gertie died – an accident, murder, natural causes. Interspersed throughout the investigatory proceedings characters discuss their own destinies, resulting in a circus of culinary discourse, personal history, dream, memory, loss and twisted aspiration set in an unnamed American city, at the height of the Cold War.

Lehrer dispensed with traditional punctuation and notions of sentence structure in favour of real-time notation techniques – equating time with space on the page; breaking lines significantly; using typography to evoke voice, personality and the nature of interactions; setting physical descriptions and actions as sidebars. Each character was cast in their own typographic arrangement as well as their own colour. The text is illuminated with icons and images that evoke the colourful (if greasy) familiarity of the Dream Queen tableau, and the internal projections of the characters. A multitude of burgers, fries, potatoes and food trays, cascade through the pages. Wayfinding and other chain-restaurant signage/typography also helps to set the stage of the page.

French Fries is a precursor of the digital revolution in design and typography as well as for its technical achievements, as an offset printed book that was composed pre-Macintosh computer using photo-typesetting, mechanicals with numerous overlays and a mix of three (not four) colours.

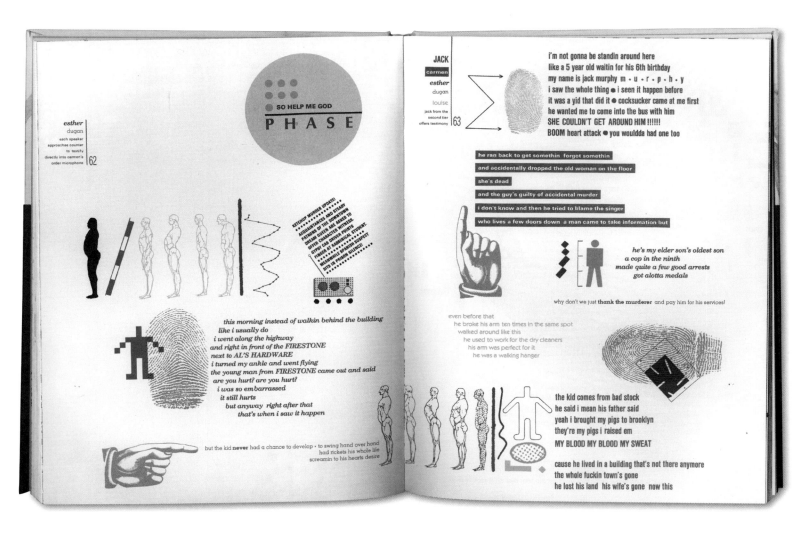

SO HELP ME GOD

PHASE

esther
dugan
each speaker
approaches counter
to testify
directly into carmen's
order microphone | 62

KETCHUP MURDER UPDATE!
ACCOUNTANCES AND STEADY
PATRONS OF THE DOWNTOWN
DREAM QUEEN ARE ASKED TO
OFFER CHARACTER WITNESS
GYPSY CAB DRIVER POINTS
FINGER AT ECONOMICAL STUDENT
MEANWHILE SPANISH SUSPECT
SITS IN PRISON SILENCE!!!

this morning instead of walkin behind the building
like i usually do
i went along the highway
and right in front of the FIRESTONE
next to AL'S HARDWARE
i turned my ankle and went flying
the young man from FIRESTONE came out and said
are you hurt? are you hurt?
i was so embarrassed
it still hurts
but anyway right after that
that's when i saw it happen

but the kid **never** had a chance to develop • to swing hand over hand
had rickets his whole life
screamin to his hearts desire

JACK
carmen
esther
dugan
louise
jack from the
second tier
offers testimony | 63

i'm not gonna be standin around here
like a 5 year old waitin for his 6th birthday
my name is jack murphy m·u·r·p·h·y
i saw the whole thing ● i seen it happen before
it was a yid that did it ● cocksucker came at me first
he wanted me to come into the bus with him
SHE COULDN'T GET AROUND HIM !!!!!!
BOOM heart attack ● you wouldda had one too

he ran back to get somethin forgot somethin
and accidentally dropped the old woman on the floor
she's dead
and the guy's guilty of accidental murder
i don't know and then he tried to blame the singer
who lives a few doors down a man came to take information but

he's my elder son's oldest son
a cop in the ninth
made quite a few good arrests
got alotta medals

why don't we just **thank the murderer** and pay him for his services!

even before that
he broke his arm ten times in the same spot
walked around like this
he used to work for the dry cleaners
his arm was perfect for it
he was a walking hanger

the kid comes from bad stock
he said i mean his father said
yeah i brought my pigs to brooklyn
they're my pigs i raised em
MY BLOOD MY BLOOD MY SWEAT

cause he lived in a building that's not there anymore
the whole fuckin town's gone
he lost his land his wife's gone now this

TITLE: *Max Makes a Million*
DESIGN FIRM/AGENCY: M+Co
ART DIRECTOR: Tibor Kalman, M+Co
DESIGNER/ILLUSTRATOR: Maira Kalman
CLIENT: Maira Kalman
YEAR: 1990

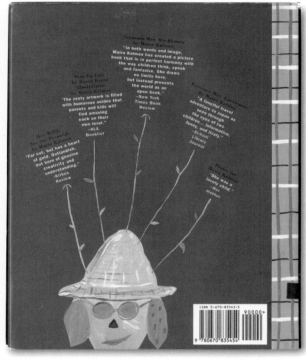

MAIRA KALMAN
Max Makes a Million

Given her flair for personalized lettering, it is not surprising that illustrator and author Maira Kalman says 'My first inkling of art was to be a writer. I had visions of sitting in a quiet country room looking out into a garden, writing. Something happened. I could not stand my writing. It was too serious. Too laden with heavy idiocy.'

So, she next turned to drawing, mistakenly presuming it 'would be a refreshing pastime, not a serious endeavour. And maybe that lack of seriousness allowed me to experiment and to find out something about drawing.' Today she thinks of herself as 'Maybe illustrator. Maybe an author as well. Maybe dilettante.'

Kalman saw her canvas as inclusive. She wanted to write and paint but initially was uncertain as to how, or in which media, she could best accomplish things. Then something in her life became clear – her love of books.

'*Alice in Wonderland* is the greatest children's book ever written. And it stunned me,' she notes. 'Ludwig Bemelmans wrote for adults and children. And then Kay Thompson wrote without any punctuation whatsoever, and maybe her audience was not just children. And then [The] *Wind in the Willows* blew into my life. And *Pippi Longstocking*. I thought the best children's books were good for all audiences. And then I could be smart and stupid. Long and short. Sad and merry. There were no limits of approach.'

That newly found freedom also included licence with type and lettering.

All at once ideas for books started to take form. She saw books as totalities. Some were designed with type at differing sizes and weights, others were hand-lettered using a distinctive, quirky calligraphic writing style. With Kalman's early, critically acclaimed Max (the dog) series she developed ways to seamlessly integrate text and pictures. In *Max Makes a Million*, bold sans-serif type bobs and weaves throughout the images in a choreographed syncopation. Eventually, she mimimized the type in favour of more expressive lettering.

Kalman's stories derive from what she calls a force that allows the brain to observe, assemble and interpret 'in some misty way'. She makes her ideas concrete through the co-mixture of words and pictures, type and lettering, which nonetheless are still not locked in stone.

'It is amazing how often you have no idea why something came to you, or why a particular vision of a perplexed woman wearing a green hat evokes such a strong response. I don't question the sources, I just accept the fact. And then there is longing: for I don't know what. Peace of mind, perhaps? With some spritz of interest.'

I live with Ida and Morris Stravinsky in the spacious Stravinsky apartment. Morris has a ladies' shoe store. Stravinsky Shoes. Every day he goes down to his store and shows women different shoes. Pumps. Sandals. Slippers. Mules. Morris and his assistant Laura are designing shoes for the Queen of Sheba, who must be a very fussy woman, because every time a customer makes Morris crazy he says, "Who do you think you are, the Queen of Sheba?"

Meanwhile, across town, Ida is taking tango lessons with Maurice Chagall.

He has a big black shiny pompadour on his head and tiny shiny pointy shoes on his feet.

Paris.
The city of dreams.
The city of lights.
The city of love.

But do you think it is easy for a dog to pack a small brown suitcase, put on a beret, and hop on a plane? Ha! Plane tickets cost money. Mazuma, shekels, semolians. I have none. Because no one wants to buy my book. I'm flat broke.

Bone dry.

But someday, fat families and skinny families around the world will be reading my poems. And laughing, and crying. I feel it in my bones.

I want to say, before anything, that dreams are very important.

It was on a *sunny summer* day that I met

Mrs. Hoo gen schmidt wearing a fish on her head.

Mr. Hoogenschmidt was walkin

He meant to B**LOW**

the

S A X **O** P H O N E

but man,

he blew his

n
o
s
e

instead

and his glasses

flew off his head

onto the bed

TITLE: *The Stinky Cheese Man & Other Fairly Stupid Tales*
ART DIRECTOR/DESIGNER: Molly Leach
AUTHOR: Jon Scieszka
ILLUSTRATOR: Lane Smith
YEAR: 1992

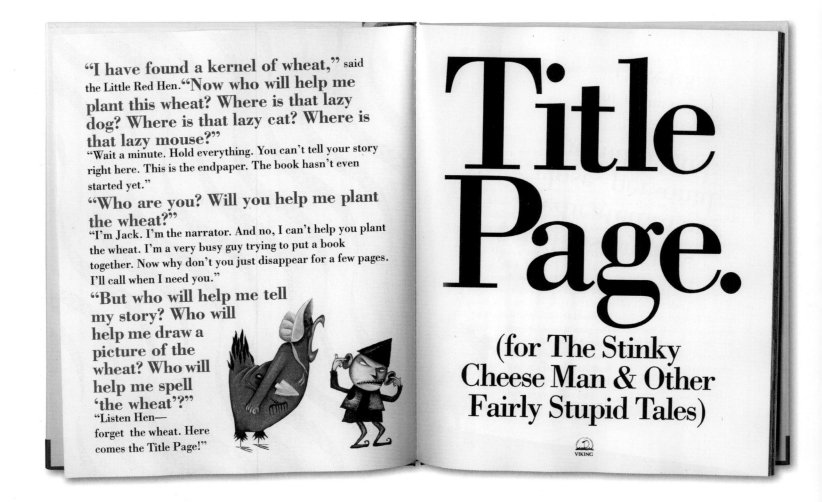

MOLLY LEACH

The Stinky Cheese Man & Other Fairly Stupid Tales

When asked to design the quirkily hilarious *The Stinky Cheese Man* by Jon Scieszka and Lane Smith, Molly Leach hoped that by exaggerating the typography, 'I could make it even more hilarious.' With her background in designing magazines, Leach says she had no preconceived notions about how children's books should look. 'All I knew was it shouldn't be calm and quiet.' She was not only correct in this assumption, but her design revived the art of playful typography for this genre.

Nonetheless, it was not radical typography. 'I'd like to think that I use typography and manipulate it appropriately for the subject matter,' Leach says. 'Typography sets the tone for everything that is to come.'

In fact she selected Bodoni, among the most classic of fonts, 'and used it in unusual ways to emphasize the fact that these were classic fairy tales told in an unconventional way'. The type is put through multiple distortions. It melts, gets stepped on, falls off the page and has other funny mishaps. 'The idea was to fill each page with type and art, no matter how many words, and go straight to the edge for a hyper-kinetic feel.' But apparently, the publisher's production department 'flipped out, and reprints of the book now have margins'.

'These days,' she adds, 'too many children's books use "wacky" type indiscriminately.' It made sense for the irreverent *Stinky Cheese Man*, but she has never repeated that look since.

This book is
dedicated to our
close, personal,
special friend:

(your name here)

—J.S. & L.S.

I know. I know.
The page is upside down.
I meant to do that.
Who ever looks at that
dedication stuff anyhow?
If you really want to read
it—you can always stand
on your head.

A long time ago, people used to tell magical stories of wonder and enchantment. Those stories were called Fairy Tales.
Those stories are not in this book. The stories in this book are almost Fairy Tales. But not quite.
The stories in this book are Fairly Stupid Tales.
I mean, what else would you call a story like "Goldilocks and the Three Elephants"? This girl walking through the woods smells Peanut Porridge cooking. She decides to break into the Elephants' house, eat the porridge, sit in the chairs, and sleep in the beds. But when she gets in the house she can't climb up on Baby Elephant's chair because it's too big. She can't climb up on Mama Elephant's chair because it's much too big. And she can't climb up on Papa Elephant's chair because it's much much too big. So she goes home. The End.
And if you don't think that's fairly stupid, you should read "Little Red Running Shorts" or maybe "The Stinky Cheese Man."
In fact, you should definitely go read the stories now, because the rest of this introduction just kind of goes on and on and doesn't really say anything. I stuck it on to the end here so it would fill up the page and make it look like I really knew what I was talking about. So stop now. I mean it. Quit reading. Turn the page. If you read this last sentence, it won't tell you anything.

JACK
Up the Hill
Fairy Tale Forest
1992

SURGEON GENERAL'S WARNING: It has been determined that these tales are fairly stupid and probably dangerous to your health.

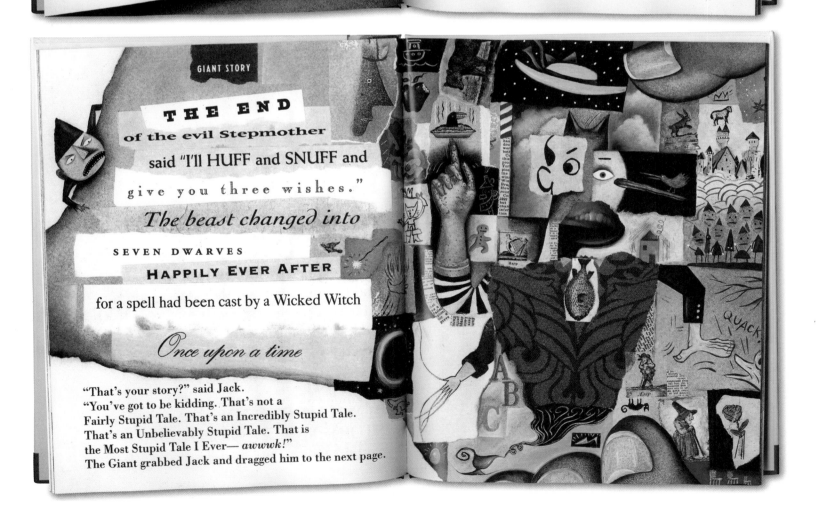

GIANT STORY

THE END

of the evil Stepmother

said "I'll HUFF and SNUFF and

give you three wishes."

The beast changed into

SEVEN DWARVES

HAPPILY EVER AFTER

for a spell had been cast by a Wicked Witch

Once upon a time

"That's your story?" said Jack.
"You've got to be kidding. That's not a Fairly Stupid Tale. That's an Incredibly Stupid Tale. That's an Unbelievably Stupid Tale. That is the Most Stupid Tale I Ever— awwwk!"
The Giant grabbed Jack and dragged him to the next page.

JACK'S BEAN PROBLEM

"Forget that Hen. Now it's time for the best story in the whole book—my story. Because Once Upon a Time I traded our last cow for three magic beans and… hey, Giant. What are you doing down here? You're wrecking my whole story."

"I DON'T LIKE THAT STORY," said the Giant. "YOU ALWAYS TRICK ME."

"That's the best part," said Jack.

"FEE FI FUM FORY. I HAVE MADE MY OWN STORY."

"Great rhyme, Giant. And I'm sure your story is just as good. But there's no room for it. So why don't you climb back up the beanstalk. I'll be up in a few minutes to steal your gold and your singing harp."

"I'LL GRIND YOUR BONES TO MAKE MY BREAD."

"I knew you'd understand. And there's another little thing that's been bugging me. Could you please stop talking in uppercase letters? It really messes up the page."

"I WILL READ MY STORY NOW," said the Giant. And he did.

JACK'S STORY

Once upon a time there was a Giant. The Giant squeezed Jack and said, "TELL ME A BETTER STORY OR I WILL GRIND YOUR BONES TO MAKE MY BREAD. AND WHEN YOUR STORY IS FINISHED, I WILL GRIND YOUR BONES TO MAKE MY BREAD ANYWAY! HO, HO, HO." The Giant laughed an ugly laugh. Jack thought, "He'll kill me if I do. He'll kill me if I don't. There's only one way to get out of this." Jack cleared his throat, and then began his story.

Once upon a time there was a Giant. The Giant squeezed Jack and said, "TELL ME A BETTER STORY OR I WILL GRIND YOUR BONES TO MAKE MY BREAD. AND WHEN YOUR STORY IS FINISHED, I WILL GRIND YOUR BONES TO MAKE MY BREAD ANYWAY! HO, HO, HO." The Giant laughed an ugly laugh. Jack thought, "He'll kill me if I do. He'll kill me if I don't. There's only one way to get out of this." Jack cleared his throat, and then began his story. Once upon a time there was a Giant. The Giant squeezed Jack and said, "TELL ME A BETTER STORY OR I WILL GRIND YOUR BONES TO MAKE MY BREAD. AND WHEN YOUR STORY IS FINISHED, I WILL GRIND YOUR BONES TO MAKE MY BREAD ANYWAY! HO, HO, HO." The Giant laughed an ugly laugh. Jack thought, "He'll kill me if I do. He'll kill me if I don't. There's only one way to get out of this." Jack cleared his throat, and then began his story.

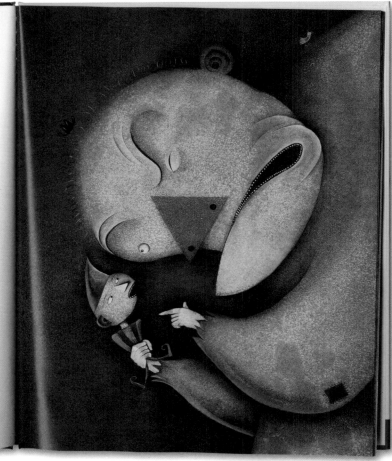

Well, as it turned out, he was just a really ugly duckling. And he grew up to be just a really ugly duck. The End.

The End.

STUART SHARPE
Mouse and Kat and the Evil One

This epic adventure in miniature explores 'the universal theme of good versus evil in classic scenes of hostile confrontation, violent capture, torture and triumphant escape', says Stuart Sharpe.

Sharpe says that he designed one of the characters in *Mouse and Kat and the Evil One* 'just to see if he could, then it needed a friend, and then of course, they needed an evil nemesis'. These three characters begged for some interaction, which occurred in the first image – and this prompted another drawing to continue the story, and so on, until there were ten drawings. 'After showing them to several people, and verbally describing the action in each image, I realized it would be much better to have the words on the page so that I wouldn't have to keep saying them.' The style of the images and content of the story demanded a bold type treatment, so he used his favourite Gothic styles.

Sharpe insists that he inaccurately copied one style with a few misappropriated influences creeping in: Wassily Kandinsky, El Lissitzky, Alexander Rodchenko, Looney Tunes, *The Powerpuff Girls*, *Star Trek*, *Blade Runner*, Barney Bubbles, Peter Saville, Kraftwerk, Jenny Holzer, Chris Ware, *The Matrix*, Shepard Fairey, *The Ren & Stimpy Show*, Ghost in the Shell, urban vinyl designer toys, registration marks, and colour chips and bar codes.

With the drawings as the first element, Sharpe concludes that he was trying to mirror the bold and geometric aesthetic of the pictures: 'I guess, with the story as it is, a more conventional typographic approach was not going to work.'

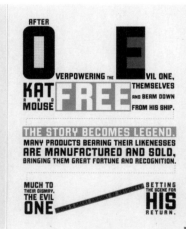

TITLE: *Mouse and Kat and the Evil One*
ART DIRECTOR/DESIGNER/ILLUSTRATOR/
CLIENT: Stuart Sharpe
PUBLISHER: Gingko Press
YEARS: 2003–2004 (Book 1), 2007 (Book 2)

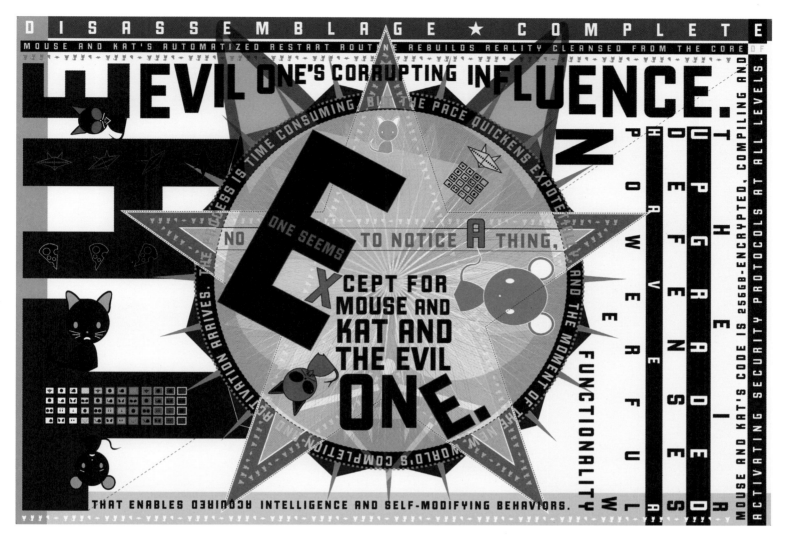

DISASSEMBLAGE ★ COMPLETE

MOUSE AND KAT'S AUTOMATIZED RESTART ROUTINE REBUILDS REALITY CLEANSED FROM THE CORE OF

EVIL ONE'S CORRUPTING INFLUENCE.

NO ONE SEEMS TO NOTICE A THING, EXCEPT FOR MOUSE AND KAT AND THE EVIL ONE.

THE PROCESS IS TIME CONSUMING, BUT THE PACE QUICKENS EXPONENTIALLY

MOUSE AND KAT'S CODE IS 256GB-ENCRYPTED, COMPILING AND ACTIVATING SECURITY PROTOCOLS AT ALL LEVELS.

THE UPGRADED DEFENSES ARE POWERFUL

AND THE MOMENT OF THE NEW WORLD'S COMPLETION AND REACTIVATION ARRIVES.

THE POWERFUL OVERSEER DEFENSES AND FUNCTIONALITY

THAT ENABLES ACQUIRED INTELLIGENCE AND SELF-MODIFYING BEHAVIORS.

GOING WRONG IS JUST WHERE IT STARTS.

THE EVIL ONE HAS CORRUPTED THE FUNDAMENTAL FRAMEWORK OF EXPERIENTIAL REALITY, MOCKING MOUSE AND KAT'S WORLD-BUILDING SCHEME AND IMBUING THE ENTIRETY OF EXISTENCE WITH A CHILLINGLY EVIL ESSENCE. FEAR ITSELF REIGNS, WITH MOUSE AND KAT STRUGGLING FRANTICALLY FOR A RALLYING CRY TO REVERSE THE TIDE. ALL TOO LATE, THEY BEGIN TO UNDERSTAND THAT THEIR OWN HASTY ACTIONS MAY HAVE BROUGHT ON THE CURRENT (-) STATE OF IMBALANCE LEAVING THEM WITH THE TASK THAT IS TO ENSURE TO FILL A NEVER-ENDING SERIES OF SEQUELS.

BELOW

TITLE: 'Duke Ellington'
ART DIRECTOR: Deirdre McDermott
DESIGNER: Daniel Devlin
PHOTOGRAPHER/ILLUSTRATOR: Jonny Hannah
PUBLISHER: Walker Books
YEAR: 2005

OPPOSITE

TITLE: 'Henry Zoot Suit'
ART DIRECTOR: Deirdre McDermott
DESIGNER: Daniel Devlin
PHOTOGRAPHER/ILLUSTRATOR: Jonny Hannah
PUBLISHER: Walker Books
YEAR: 2005

OVERLEAF

TITLE: 'Louis Armstrong'
ART DIRECTOR: Deirdre McDermott
DESIGNER: Daniel Devlin
PHOTOGRAPHER/ILLUSTRATOR: Jonny Hannah
PUBLISHER: Walker Books
YEAR: 2005

JONNY HANNAH
Hot Jazz Special

Jonny Hannah chose all of his jazz heroes, one for each instrument, then put them all together as an illustrated snapshot of history. He was inspired by the clothes of the jazz era, from zoot suits to knitted ties, and the work of the designers of the day, like Paul Rand, Alvin Lustig, Jim Flora and Alex Steinweiss. 'The ultimate goal was to celebrate these great, larger-than-life people,' he says. 'And give the pages a bounce.'

His lettering and drawings are seamless. 'The Charlie Parker page is all about speed. The frantic, yet utterly symphonic music of *Bird*. So I used the idea of a journey on a subway train, all the letterforms tightly packed together, just the notes he played. The Billie Holiday page is much calmer, with a more uniform type approach, giving the forms more space, just like the carefully chosen notes she sang, going across the page in a set of steps, walking us through the poem, in different sizes.'

Using different type styles to transport us back to another time, Hannah made it look like his own work, rather than making retro repackaging for the twenty-first-century audience.

Hannah's lettering is a mix of what he calls 'this, that and the other' that he's borrowed from 'more formal designers like Reid Miles, to the much more expressive hand-drawn text of David Stone Martin and Ben Shahn'. He says his lettering is 'type gone wrong. It's a bit wobbly, not quite right, but I like it that way: when good type turns bad. I'm not a graphic designer. If I were put in charge of a newspaper it would take the reader a month to read it all. But I love drawing letterforms, often with a brush and ink, to give it a flavour. The flavour of a good stodgy stew; a melting pot of so many influences.'

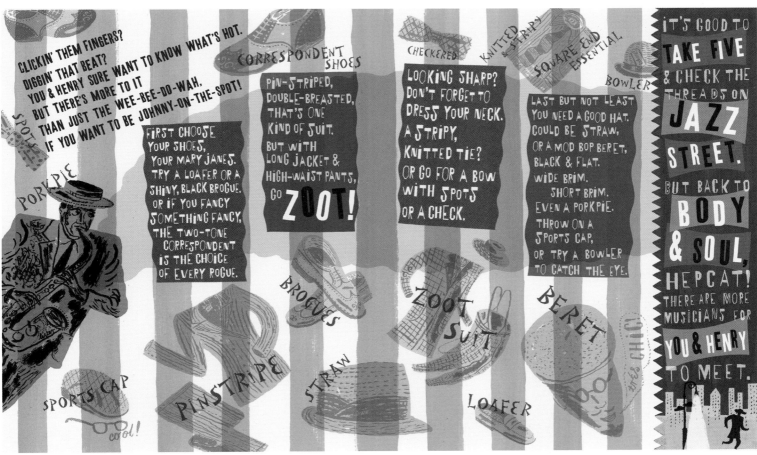

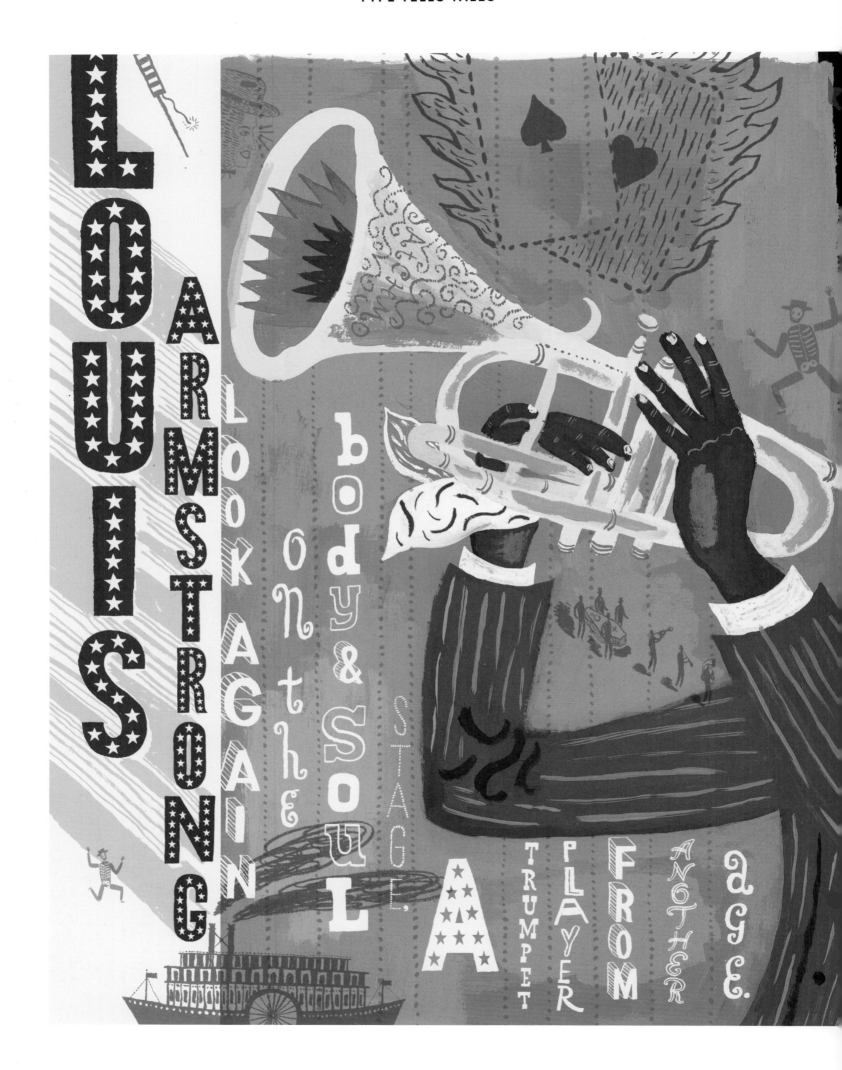

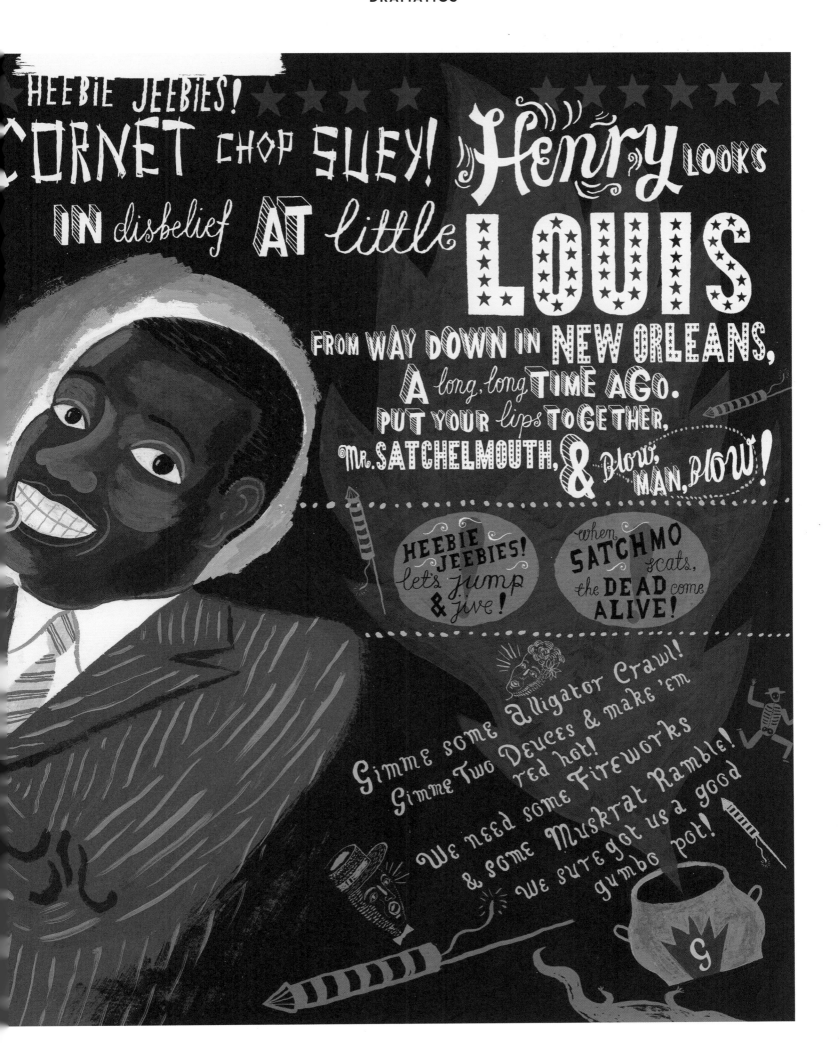

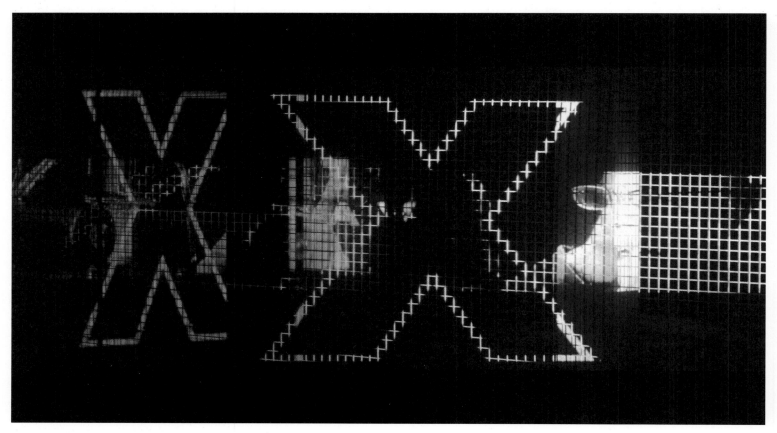

TOM HINGSTON
David Bowie's 'Sue (Or In A Season of Crime)'

This mysteriously dark typographic film was the accompaniment to the David Bowie single 'Sue (Or In A Season Of Crime)'. As Hingston explains, the score had a very cinematic feel, dark and evocative, conjuring a sense of a film noir, and the idea of playing with a title sequence that referenced that era felt like an interesting place to start. Hingston mixed live-action, graphics and type with some original footage of Bowie recording with the Maria Schneider Orchestra in New York, which was the base layer. 'Then we imagined a nocturnal world upon which this could be projected,' Hingston explains.

The type was created at Hingston's studio and then projected on to the distressed surfaces of a real environment.

Everything the viewer sees was shot entirely on camera, and the movement of the projected words was tightly synchronized to the track itself. As the song builds, the lyrics slide along a series of surfaces – walls, ceilings and floors – gradually becoming more layered, before dissolving to leave a ghostly trace.

The narrative, told through the lyrics, formed the basis of Hingston's typographic approach. 'The story is informed by the music and the brooding, enigmatic qualities expressed in the lyrics themselves. There is clearly a very dissonant and melancholic edge to the track and its story, so it was really about capturing this feeling through a moving piece.'

TITLE: David Bowie's 'Sue (Or In A Season of Crime)'
DIRECTOR: Tom Hingston
PRODUCER: Jacob Swan-Hyam
PRODUCTION COMPANY: Black Dog Films
TITLE DESIGN: Hingston Studio
DIRECTOR OF PHOTOGRAPHY: George Steel
PROJECTION SERVICES: Mesmer
WARDROBE: Kate Tabor

ART DEPARTMENT: Ezra Piers Mantell
EDITOR: Sacha Schwarz at Speade
NEW YORK STUDIO FOOTAGE: Jimmy King
UK: Tom Balkwill at Dirty Looks
ONLINE: Hingston Studio and Big Buoy
COMMISSIONER: Jo Blair at Parlophone
CLIENT: Isolar
YEAR: 2014

TITLE: *Gonwards*
DESIGN FIRM/AGENCY: Andrew Swainson
ART DIRECTOR: Andy Partridge
DESIGNER: Andrew Swainson
PHOTOGRAPHY/ILLUSTRATOR: Peter Blegvad
CLIENT: Ape House Records
YEAR: 2012

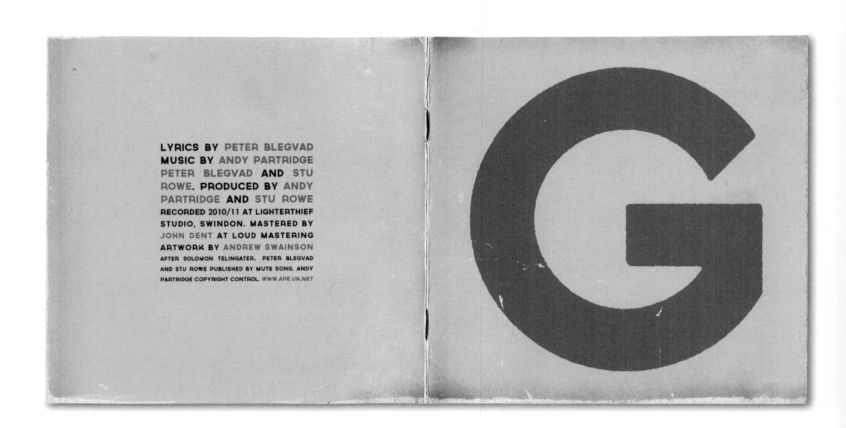

PETER BLEGVAD AND ANDREW SWAINSON
Gonwards

Gonwards is a contemporary album of blues lyrics and music in a box with a book and games – designed, as lyricist Peter Blegvad explains, 'to attract the eye from a distance with an antique golden Kodak glow, and then to reward curious scrutiny with lots of intricate detail'. Andrew Swainson's multilayered design, which is typographically modelled after the Russian Constructivist Solomon Telingater's *The Words of Kirsanov*, 'also emphasizes the physical materiality of the box'.

Although the design says Russian avant-garde, Blegvad says the story is about 'the whiskey glue road nickel body of the blues; the cypress sweat honey cloud doctor of its moan, crying steel beans dynamite matchbox tears for the loss of its city skillet pocket shotgun rose'.

But it is the design that was created so 'we could please ourselves'. Apparently, the collision of sensibilities involved – from Andrew Swainson's look to Andy Partridge's and Peter Blegvad's tunes – was only ever going to result in something unique that was destined to be called *Gonwards*; a movement all its own.

CARTOON, YIN AND YANG, SUN AND MOON, A GHOST TOWN SHOWDOWN AT HIGH NOON. SHE DRAWS SLOW, HE SHOOTS TOO SOON. THE SUN GOES DOWN BEHIND A DUNE.

WHAT NEVER FAILED TO INDUCE A STATE OF TRANCE-LIKE CALM AS A CHILD WAS BEING DRIVEN AROUND AT NIGHT IN MY PAPA'S CAR, A BIG GREEN LASALLE SALOON. SWADDLED AND BELTED INTO **WHAT** THE BACK SEAT, LULLED BY THE DRONE OF INTERNAL COMBUSTION, SOOTHED BY THE RHYTHMIC FLASHES OF THE PASSING LIGHTS, I DREAMED THAT THE CAR AND I WERE ONE, THAT MY BODY DID NOT END WHERE IT MET THE SEAT, BUT EXTENDED OUT INTO THE STREAMLINED STEEL, FORWARD INTO THE ILLUMINATED SNOUT PROBING THE NIGHT, AND DOWN TO WHERE THE WHIRLING RUBBER MET THE ROAD. YOU'VE BEEN GONE SO LONG BUT NOW YOU'RE ALMOST HOME. YOU WERE COLD BUT NOW YOU'RE **A** GETTING WARM. LUCAS LAMPS IN LIDS OF CHROME LIGHT UP IN YOUR HEAD LIGHT THE WAY AHEAD ON THE FAST TRACK BACK FROM THE LAND OF THE DEAD. WHAT A CAR YOU ARE. WHAT WERE ONCE YOUR HANDS AND FEET ARE NOW FOUR WHEELS — AND WHERE ROAD AND

PETER BLEGVAD- VOCALS
ANDY PARTRIDGE- PIANO, ELECTRIC GUITARS, BACKING VOCALS
STU ROWE- DRIVE-BY SLIDE GUITAR, SUB BASS
BILLY 'THE ONION' JONES- HARMONICA

RUBBER MEET IT FEELS SO SWEET. HEAR THAT HYPNOTIZING HUM? NOW THAT YOU'RE IN GEAR. NOW YOU'RE GETTING NEAR, YOU'VE COME SO FAR. WHAT A **CAR** YOU ARE. MOTOR RUNNING SWEET AS A NUT, MOTORVATIN' DOWN THE OPEN ROAD. THERE'S NO OTHER TRAFFIC. HUSH NOW, LISTEN TO WHAT THE ENGINE SAID: BOOKOFTHEDEADBOOKOFTHEDEADBOOKOFTHE DEADBOOKOFTHEDEADBOOKOFTHEDEADBOOKOFTHEDEADBOOKOF THEDEADBOOKOFTHEDEADBOOKOFTHEDEADBOOKOFTHEDEAD BOOKOFTHEDEADBOOKOFTHEDEADBOOKOFTHEDEADBOOKOFTHE DEAD. OH MAN, **YOU** WHAT A CAR ARE! HERCULES HAS LENT YOU HIS STRENGTH. EDWARD PRINCE OF WALES ENJOYS HIS RUN IN YOU SO MUCH THAT HE DECLARES THE MOTORCAR A NECESSITY FOR EVERY ENGLISH GENTLEMAN. HUMMING PAST THE ORCHARD AT NIGHT SLEEPING FLOWERS IN YOUR BEAMS UNFURL THINKING YOU'RE THE SUN. YOU LEAP THE CHASM LIKE AN ANTLERED STAG! AND TO THINK YOU WERE ONCE DERELICT IN A DUSTY BARN ON A TOBACCO **ARE** FARM IN NEW SOUTH WALES. WHAT A STAR! GARLANDED WITH TRIBUTES HUNG WITH GOLDEN GONGS YOU'RE A HERO TO THE NATION ADORED BY ALL CREATION. HONK YOUR HORN YOU'RE COMING HOME. WHAT A ONE YOU ARE WHAT A WONDER WHAT A CAR!

DISSECTING A CAT, WHERE IS ITS PEP? COINS MADE OF WATER ARE HARD TO **THE** PICK UP. WITH INK ERADICATOR I ALTERED MY GRADES. SATIRICALLY YET ROMANTICALLY I ALTERED THE WORLD. STREETCARS PASSED THE BALLPARK. DAYDREAMING IN THE **DOPE** OUTFIELD I WAS BEANED BY A POP FLY. I SAW SUFFERING SAINTS AND CHRISTLIKE FIGURES DESCENDING FROM TRAMS. DOWN FROM A CLOUD WITH A **ON** CLANG HE FELL, JACQUES COUSTEAU IN A DIVING BELL. I ELECTRO-PLATED RADIATORS TO DEFRAY THE COSTS OF MY FATHER'S FAILING FARM. IN AN ERA OF DISCRIMINATION SURVIVAL TACTICS ARE REQUIRED: HIDE. FLY THROUGH THE **PERELMAN** CLOUDS ON VACUUM CLEANERS WITH MALE COMPANIONS. WITH FEMALES IT'S MORE A MATTER OF MOONLIGHT CANOEING. DO SPARK PLUGS THINK?

PETER BLEGVAD- VOCALS
ANDY PARTRIDGE- ELECTRIC GUITAR SOLO
STU ROWE- KEYBOARD BASS, ACOUSTIC GUITAR
FRANK ABRAMS- FLUTE
NATASHA GRIFFITHS- 'FLY THRU' BACKING VOCALS

FROM GERM TO GEM THE STORY GREW, FROM GEM TO GERM THE HOURS FLEW. NO ONE WEARIED OF THE DRONE AS THE TELLER RAMBLED ON AND ON AND ON AND ON AND ON. FROM DAWN TO DUSK, FROM DUSK TO DAWN. WEEKS WENT BY, THEN MONTHS, THEN YEARS WHEN WE WERE DEAD BETWEEN THE EARS. I'VE

BEEN IN THE MALVERN HILLS, I'VE BEEN READING 'DAFFODILS'. NOW **FROM** WILLIAM WORDSWORTH'S YELLOW HEAD (EQUINE HEAD) NODS UPON MY NECK INSTEAD. I CUT MY FINGER TO THE BONE. I HEARD A DISTANT TELEPHONE. I'LL TAKE THE CALL **GERM** FROM FAR AWAY, I KNOW EVERYTHING I'LL SAY. "I'M FINE. OF COURSE. ARE YOU OK?" I'LL GIVE UP DRINK I'LL GIVE UP DOPE, I'LL SAY I SEE A RAY OF HOPE. I'LL ASK MY **TO** DOCTOR HOW SHE'D DEEM MY CHANCES NOW THAT I AM CLEAN. "WILL I LIVE LONGER?" "SURE" SHE'LL BEAM "BUT NOT AS LONG AS IT WILL SEEM." DREET, INK AND ME BERRY. I CAUGHT HER **GEM** DRIFT AND TOOK HER CHERRY. THAT'S HOW HAPPY ENDINGS START.

PETER BLEGVAD- VOCALS
ANDY PARTRIDGE- FUZZ VOCAL,
GUITARS, CHOIR AND SLEIGH BELLS
STU ROWE- BASS
FRANK ABRAMS- FLUTE

THE DEVIL'S LEXICON

PETER BLEGVAD- VOCALS, TREMOLO GUITAR

ANDY PARTRIDGE- BACKING VOCALS

STU ROWE- SLIDE GUITAR

BILLY 'THE ONION' JONES- HARMONICA

WORSE ON THE WAY

PETER BLEGVAD- VOCALS, BACKING VOCALS

ANDY PARTRIDGE- PIANO, BACKING VOCALS

STU ROWE- LATHE DRAGGING KEYBOARDS, BACKING VOCALS

MIKEY ROWE- PIANO

FRANK ABRAMS- SOPRANO SAX

ALL OTHER INSTRUMENTS ARRANGEMENTS AND MIXING BY **THE ENCYCLOPEDIA SALESMEN**

TITLE: *Love Story: The 1950s* (opposite), *The 1960s,*
The 1970s, The 1980s (left)
DESIGN FIRM/AGENCY: TypographyShop/
The King Group
ART DIRECTOR/DESIGNER: Patrick King
CLIENT: TypographyShop
YEARS: 2014–2016

PATRICK KING

Love Story: The 1950s/The 1960s/The 1970s/The 1980s

These posters originated with a typographic spread from a keepsake that Patrick King designed for his twenty-fifth high-school reunion. They each tell a love story – that failed – in song titles, using a nostalgic carnival poster/broadsheet format.

The tales evolve typographically. 'From meeting, getting to know one another, falling in love, making love, [to] the sudden appearance of trouble, doubt, jealousy and suspicion, and finally the sad break-up and lonely aftermath,' King explains. 'Every word and phrase is a song title from a single decade, carefully chosen and rearranged to carry the narrative forward and create humorous, romantic or erotic juxtapositions throughout.'

King's life has been filled with type: his father was a stereotyper at a newspaper. His best friend's father was a linotype operator. By the age of five he was crawling on the floor

of the compositing room, examining stray letters and discovering the vast array of typefaces one could utilize in a layout. 'My first job in the industry was in a type house, where I often set type on a Typositor. With a highly critical clientele of art directors and designers, I developed an eye for letter spacing, gauging typographic colour and other nearly lost arts that serve me well to this day.'

The style of these posters invokes the classic carnival or boxing poster look common to late nineteenth- and early twentieth-century broadsides, which were almost always composed in type alone. 'Introducing imagery was never a consideration,' he says. 'I did, however, add a graphic heart to one title and, in a nod to my last name, a crown to Sade's "Your Love is King".'

VENUS
LITTLE STAR
MY PRAYER

PLEASE SEND ME SOMEONE
TO LOVE

HEY THERE
STRANGER IN PARADISE
DO YOU WANT TO DANCE?

WHAT A DIFF'RENCE A DAY MAKES | MY WISH CAME TRUE | LOVE WALKED RIGHT IN

HEY, GOOD LOOKIN'

COME GO WITH ME
I WANT TO **WALK** YOU HOME

ON THE STREET WHERE YOU LIVE
WALK HAND IN HAND
WALKIN' MY BABY BACK HOME

SEND FOR ME | I'LL COME WHEN YOU CALL | I GET IDEAS | THINKING OF YOU
ENDLESSLY | **UNFORGETTABLE** | **ETERNALLY** | **ENCHANTED**

YOU SEND ME
COULD THIS BE MAGIC? | I PUT A SPELL ON YOU
BEWITCHED, BOTHERED AND BEWILDERED

I'VE GOT YOU UNDER MY SKIN

CHANCES **ARE**
I'M IN LOVE AGAIN

YOU BROUGHT A NEW KIND OF **LOVE** TO ME

A **BIG** HUNK OF **LOVE**
THAT'S **AMORE**

I ONLY HAVE EYES FOR YOU | ONLY YOU | BORN TO BE WITH YOU | YOU, YOU, YOU

JUST ASK YOUR HEART
A LOVER'S QUESTION
WHO DO YOU LOVE?

LET IT BE ME
EVERYDAY

KISSIN' TIME
VOLARE

KISS OF FIRE

WHEN I FALL IN LOVE
LOVE IS A **MANY** SPLENDORED THING

MORE
THAT'S ALL I WANT FROM YOU

I NEED YOUR LOVE TONIGHT | COME ON-A MY HOUSE | IN THE STILL OF THE NIGHT

I WANT YOU, I NEED YOU
COME SOFTLY TO ME | SEND ME SOME LOVIN'

WITH THESE **HANDS**
LOVE ME **TENDER**
TONIGHT YOU BELONG TO ME

WE WILL MAKE **LOVE** ALL THE WAY
MAKE LOVE TO ME

TENDERLY
YOU'VE GOT THE MAGIC TOUCH

I NEED YOU **NOW**
FEVER
I GOT A **ROCKET**

NEED YOUR LOVE SO BAD IN MY POCKET

WHOLE LOTTA SHAKIN'
GREAT BALLS OF **FIRE**

60 MINUTE MAN | OH WHAT A NIGHT | IT'S LATE | GOODNIGHT SWEETHEART, GOODNIGHT

STOOD **UP** DON'T BE **CRUEL**
YOUR **CHEATIN'** HEART
LIPSTICK ON YOUR **COLLAR**

CRY
CRY ME A RIVER
LONELY TEARDROPS
TEARDROPS FROM MY EYES

BYE
BYE, LOVE
I'M WALKIN'
SEE YOU **LATER** ALLIGATOR

LOVE
IS STRANGE
IT ISN'T FAIR
IT'S ALL IN THE GAME

AIN'T THAT A **SHAME**
TURN ME LOOSE
RETURN TO ME
LET ME GO LOVER
WHO'S SORRY NOW?

LONGING FOR YOU | I'LL NEVER BE FREE | I'M WALKING BEHIND YOU | I WENT TO YOUR WEDDING
I GET SO LONELY | IT'S JUST A MATTER OF TIME | IT ONLY HURTS FOR A LITTLE WHILE

YOU CAN NEVER GIVE ME BACK MY HEART

THE 50'S | A LOVE STORY

ALEXANDRA BEGUEZ

The Subtle Cosmos

Alexandra Beguez's goal was to 'bring a story to life' using at least six words, with only one word on each page. 'As someone who loves all things outer space and tries her best to keep up with new discoveries,' she explains, 'I decided to share with others the wonder I feel when I look up at the night sky.' So, she looked for a word to describe an aspect of each cosmic phenomenon: 'For example, I represented a black hole by depicting the word "Spaghettification" falling into the very black hole it describes. "Observe" forms the shape of an observatory, the Big Dipper constellation represents a "Pattern", and we see a supernova in mid-"Explosion".'

The idea is to navigate the cosmos one hand-lettered word at a time. 'In this love song to science, our journey to the stars begins at an observatory on Earth. From out of its mighty lens we travel through the cosmos; we encounter comets, constellations, nebulae and increasingly unfathomable phenomena such as black holes and dark matter,' she notes. 'And as we look up we see the things we're most familiar with; things we understand. But the farther away you train your eyes, the less we understand about the universe. These things are much more massive and ancient than anything we've ever known or made. While some may feel very small at the feet of these old and large things, I find it gives me perspective on who I am and makes me realize how small my problems (all our problems) are on a cosmic scale.'

Beguez never formally studied design or lettering 'so in order not to feel overwhelmed, I try to handle words as I would images'. For this book, she carefully illustrated each letter to both insinuate a form and an idea. 'It was challenging but satisfying to sculpt each word,' she says.

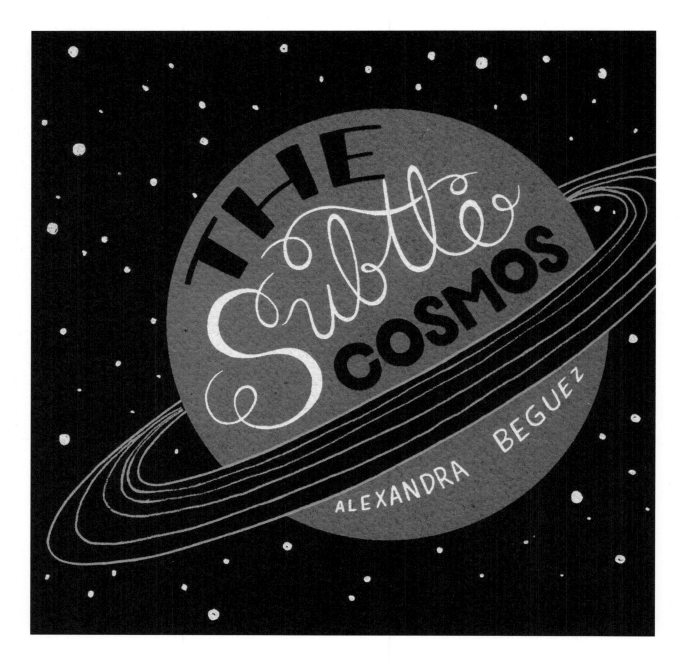

TITLE: *The Subtle Cosmos*
DESIGNER/ILLUSTRATOR: Alexandra Beguez
YEAR: 2015

THREE

MANI FESTO

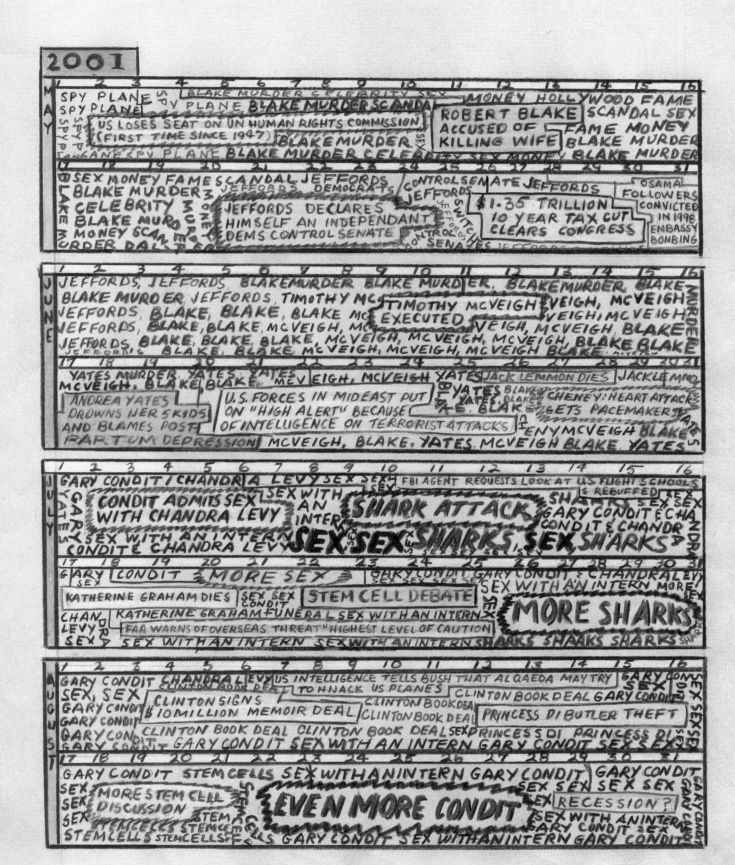

TITLE: *All the News That Fits*
DESIGNER/AUTHOR: Paula Scher
PUBLISHER: *Print* magazine
YEAR: 2004

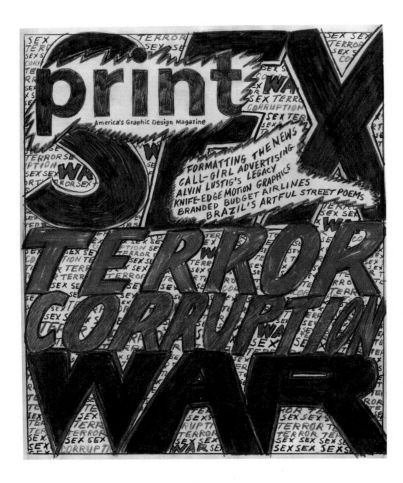

PAULA SCHER
All the News That Fits

Paula Scher uses words as medium and message – pigments and provocations, hues and information, textures and exclamations. Art is full of word-as-picture artists, and Scher is an artistic force, epitomizing the combustion of word and picture.

'The thing I do – which is why I became less interested in style and more interested in finding a way to do it – is to create expressionist typography,' she told John Walters in a 2010 *Eye* magazine interview about illustrating with type in a class with Stanislaw Zagorski.

The cover and pages hand-lettered for *Print* magazine are manifesto-like essays torn from the headlines of the topical news that defined 2004. Printed across six pages, this is not strictly a linear narrative but rather a story with peaks and valleys – of life and death, with as much impact as a stack of newspapers – made even more compelling through variation in size, intensity and colour.

'Words have meaning and typography has feeling. When you put them together it's a spectacular combination,'

Scher adds. 'I think the reason I responded so negatively to Helvetica way back when was that it neutralizes feeling. A modernist would argue that that's terrific because then the words speak and you're not influencing the content by creating disorder with them. It's almost like an understood, generic form ... that you can say OK, take the words as they are, because they're laid out very clearly in Helvetica. All other styles imbue the words with a shade or meaning, which changes them, which is where I think all the fun is!' And their absolute, explosive power too.

'What Zagorski did for me is this: I could never do the type on my projects; I could come up with an idea and I would illustrate the idea, but he said to me "Why don't you illustrate with type?" So I began drawing the type and discovering that typography could have form, and then later when I began setting type at CBS Records, I found that you could be expressive simply by making choices.'

PAOLO SOLERI

Visionary Cities: The Arcology of Paolo Soleri

Italian-born Paolo Soleri, who died in 2013 at the age of 93, was a visionary architect and the designer of Arcosanti, an experimental community in the Arizona desert that he founded in 1970. Soleri was a pioneer of the sustainable architecture movement, and by extension a leader in alternative architecture. His desert property began as a laboratory, where he erected buildings that were in harmony with their surroundings: architecture and ecology had to be viewed as a whole, Soleri believed. After an apprenticeship with Frank Lloyd Wright in the 1940s, he developed a philosophy he called 'arcology' (architecture plus ecology), in which buildings were densely packed and beehive-like, in contrast to the sprawl of suburbia. People paid to intern with Soleri and live and work at Arcosanti for weeks at a time, in a process that continues to this day.

One small part of Soleri's legacy is a major work of graphic design – or rather anti-design. The typographically cluttered, experimentally constructed book about his fundamental philosophy, *Visionary Cities: The Arcology of Paolo Soleri* (1971), was written and designed by architecture professor Donald Wall. The book design, which Rick Poynor wrote about in *Eye* magazine (no. 32, vol. 8, 1999), anticipates the Deconstructivist typographic antics of the 1990s, and is also a continuation of the concrete poetry of the 1950s and the typographic experimentation of the 1970s Fluxus 'anti-art' movement. The prototype of 'designer as author', Wall manipulated word and image, taking American typographer Herb Lubalin's penchant for smashed letters to a new level of density, intensity and illegibility.

Wall's layouts also mirrored some of the cinematic layouts that Quentin Fiore had accomplished in Marshall McLuhan's *The Medium is the Massage* (1967). Fiore sought to seamlessly integrate textual and pictorial experiences – words and pictures complemented each other in a unique yet linear way. Meanwhile Wall's manipulations of the text are even more inseparable from its content. Poynor noted how Wall, a former professor of architectural theory, design and history at the Catholic University in Washington DC, gave typographic shape to his own critical ideas, and the book is fully aware of the uniqueness of the project.

The book consists of a maze of typographic wanderings presenting phrases by Soleri and others, or – as the flap copy puts it, in lower-case type – 'paolo soleri's radical aesthetic and philosophy for urban man are presented in this unique book, which embodies new graphic concepts to express the innovative insights of this most controversial architect.' Wall was not a trained book designer, so his relationship to the medium was unfettered by constricting rules. Nonetheless, he adhered to certain contemporary conceits, including predominantly black pages with high-contrast images, the overall outcome as much a challenge to the history of the book as it is to the reader. 'It confronts the reader with a spectacle so relentless and estranging that it could easily have proved insurmountable to some,' Poynor wrote. 'No book that cultivates indeterminacy to this degree could be called a masterpiece, but it is certainly a landmark in its synthesis of critical commentary and design.'

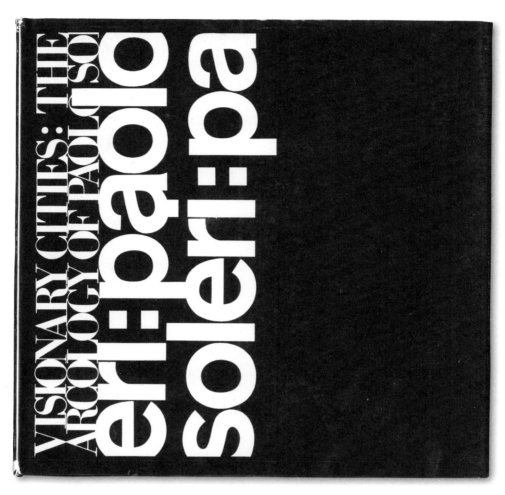

TITLE: *Visionary Cities: The Arcology of Paolo Soleri*
DESIGNER: Donald Wall
PUBLISHER: Praeger
YEAR: 1971

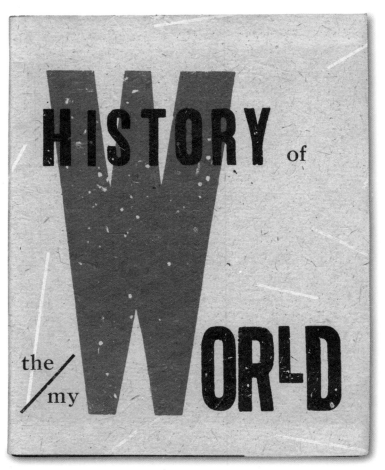

JOHANNA DRUCKER
History of the/my Wor(l)d

There are two simultaneous stories behind Johanna Drucker's *History of the/my Wor(l)d*. As she explains, feminist theory in the 1980s was attached to the notion of language as patriarchal, 'but I had the experience of learning language and being introduced to literature mainly through the relationship I had with my mother. It was a close, very intimate, even gently erotic, relationship of great affection and attachment.'

So the 'thin red line' that runs through the book, breaking up the black text, is the story of Drucker's connection with her mother – and a pushback against what she felt was a feminist orthodoxy in which the characterization of language missed other ways of thinking about literary life. The red text breaks through the black text, insisting that the personal voice will not be subsumed by the official history, but will still register in relation to it. 'The reader has to chose between following one narrative line or the other, as it is difficult to read both by turning the pages. To keep personal memory in mind is to obliterate historical narrative, and vice versa.'

The stock pictures were picked to make visual, graphic jokes across the pages, and to allow multiple levels of puns and associations to surface. 'The curve of a tunnel and the curve of a sunrise echo each other,' Drucker explains. 'Arrows circle in an image and on a page. A feather swoops upward and so does another arrow. So the visuals make their own set of connections while the language tells a story. The captions under the images are sheer play.'

The project drew upon the typographic and graphic resources of the Bow & Arrow Press at Harvard University. One of the first objects she found was the zinc plate of the drum majorette, which reminded her of her then recently deceased mother, who had been a baton-twirling marching band member in her youth. 'She was killed in an accident, quite young (fifty-seven), and I wanted to compose a work in her memory, but one that was about many things – feminist theory, the contrast of history and memory, and the capacity of the page and book structure to hold many themes.'

The book is typeset in ATF Caslon. Drucker uses type to construct relationships on the page and through a book's extended space; to suspend written texts in complex connections with each other, spatially, graphically and visually. 'My interest in typography has always been to call attention to the ways in which visual and graphic properties intensify and expand the linguistic meaning of a text. So many dimensions of language are expanded through typographic treatment – associations, connections, links and cross-references.' She says it was a joy to compose these pages, 'with their dingbats and elements of rule, their graphical features and visual ones, their bold reduced but suggestive language and their obscure and elliptical references'.

Soft, fat, slow time takes its first   breath following the   n the

while ancient cultures could only hold their breath so long against the inroads of homo-genizing commerce.

Playthings bothered to

giving in to instincts by response to force, the

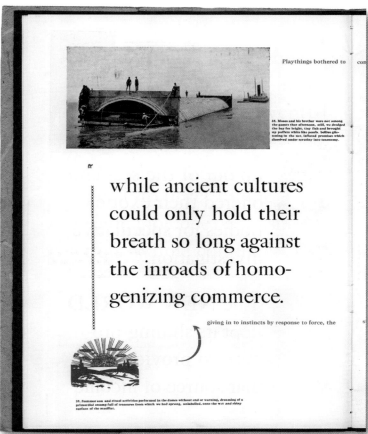

cosmology emerged as the flight from innocence locked them out of the garden.

Self a blocked off space of time, private allowance, childish hands marking a face organized as science.

DELIGHT was unearthly in the early stages of undress. Knowledge was a hot rout-ine to the primal primitives,

beginning was the world, nursed on the warm breast of chaos fast fol-lowing a night of

initial explosion, making light into a face swaddled in warmth and

hard publicity. Genetics produc-ed the fullness thereof and a new

letters. Our earth took us to heart and mind in the intellectual embrace of a cool companionship.

TITLE: *History of the/my Wor(l)d*
DESIGN FIRM/AGENCY: Druckwork
ART DIRECTOR/DESIGNER: Johanna Drucker
PHOTOGRAPHER/ILLUSTRATOR: N/A (cuts are from the collection of Bow & Arrow Press
YEAR: 1990

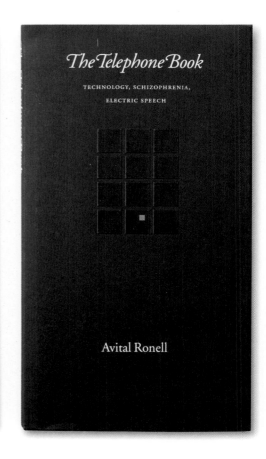

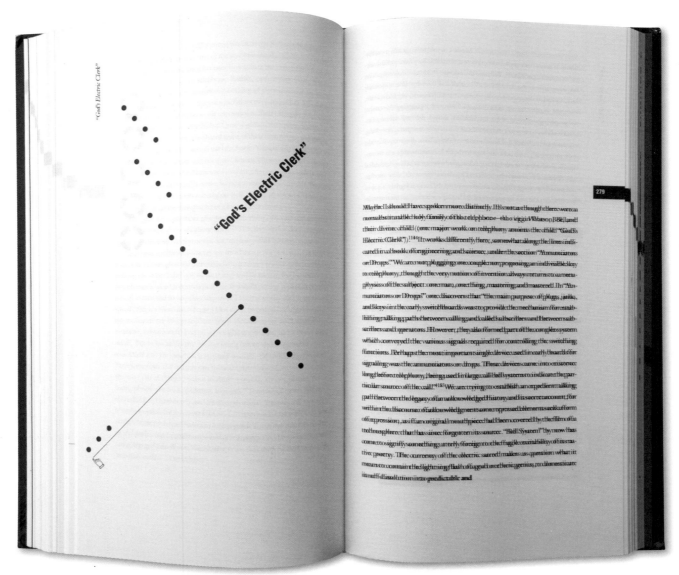

TITLE: *The Telephone Book*
DESIGN FIRM/AGENCY: University of Nebraska Press
DESIGNER: Richard Eckersley
AUTHOR: Avital Ronell
YEAR: 1989

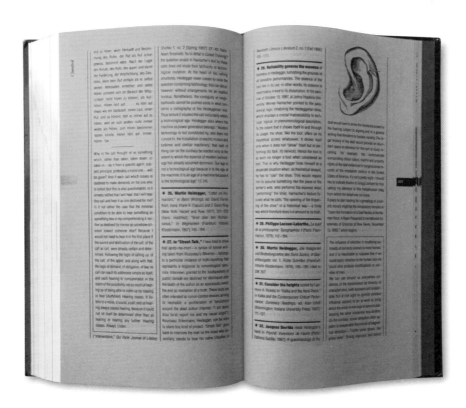

RICHARD ECKERSLEY
The Telephone Book

Avital Ronell's treatise on the impact of the telephone on modern life, *The Telephone Book: Technology, Schizophrenia, Electric Speech*, is described by Roy R. Behrens in *Looking Closer 5: Critical Writings on Graphic Design* (2002) as an unorthodox scholarly study of Jacques Derrida, Martin Heidegger and the philosophy of deconstruction. It was also the first book that graphic designer Richard Eckersley, English-born senior designer at the University of Nebraska Press, designed using a computer. It is, noted Behrens, 'louder and hence more startling than any of his other projects', which are characterized by subtlety and restraint, echoing the precision of modern designers Jan Tschichold and Paul Renner. This book throws such verities to the wind.

'In postmodern design, deconstruction takes apart familiar forms', wrote historian Jeremy Musson, 'as one might disassemble a jigsaw puzzle, not looking for correspondences which would help to fit pieces together to make a single unit, but concentrating on individual elements and on the gaps, dislocations and disjunctions between them.' Eckersley's unorthodox, reservedly chaotic design for *The Telephone Book*

was noticeably innovative for 1989; what *The New York Times* called 'typographically dazzling' because of its unusual use of what Behrens referred to as 'deconstructivist strategies to convey (and, in some ways, to confound) a labyrinthine point of view'.

The design takes off on Ronell's analysis of the telephone directory as a metaphor for shifting and disconnected human behaviour. The typography not only unhinges her text; it adds fuel to the chaos that contemporary communication represents.

'If only in a superficial sense,' Behrens continued, 'the book's layout threatens to upstage the text, by calling attention to itself and to tricks of the trade that designers employ to enable – or, at times, to complicate – the act of reading.' Words appear to be dislocated, carved up and juggled as though objects without meaning. Type is a backwards mirror image of the page that faces it. Rivulets of white space made from haphazard word spacing throw the reader off balance. The words in a passage on hearing disorders are blurred to underscore the indecipherability of deafness. The book seems to speak in different dialects with different levels of intentional and consequential challenges imposed along the way.

SAWDUST
Wired

Typography gives Sawdust a 'vessel with which to visually explore the world'. And this story addresses a very prevalent problem in that world. In fact, two problems: the first has to do with the context in which it is read. The second is that typography for a technology magazine may be different to that for a beauty product. 'So, when the opportunity is there we like to challenge convention,' Sawdust note. 'The idea that our work may be deemed progressive is a nice one, but more recently, we prefer the notion of it being undefined. It's hunger to explore that keeps us moving. When you stop moving, the world ceases to exist.'

The type/lettering for this cautionary poster was the essence of the solution and literally spells out as much, if not more, of the content as the words the type represents. 'Once

we had the idea of stripping the outer layers of cable away to reveal the copper inside, we knew it had to have an authentic, tactile quality. So we began researching into cables and running tests to see how easily (or indeed difficult) manipulating the material would be. We started by working with the most complex letterforms such as W and B to ensure it would be possible, or to figure out how it could be done.

'Once we knew they were achievable, we knew the rest of the letters were too. It then became about composition for the overall piece, ensuring the written words were being brought to life visually. We wanted the cable to become more stripped away towards the end of the written text to give the onlooker that Eureka! moment. We then photographed all the elements and composited them to form the final artwork.'

LOWLIFES HAVE BEEN STEALING COPPER WIRE FROM VACANT HOMES IN MY NEIGHBORHOOD. IS THERE AN ALTERNATIVE METAL LESS DESIRABLE TO THIEVES?

TITLE: *Wired*
DESIGN FIRM/AGENCY: Sawdust
ART DIRECTORS/DESIGNERS/PHOTOGRAPHERS/
ILLUSTRATORS: Rob Gonzalez and
Jonathan Quainton
CLIENT: *Wired*, US
YEAR: 2012

JOHN HENDRIX
Drawings in Church

John Hendrix is part of a long tradition of producing 'hand-drawn letters interacting with images', but what makes his visual voice distinctive is what he describes as 'the range of expressions I use for typography. Sometimes the letters themselves are the main characters, sometimes they are read behind the images, and sometimes they are overlaid on top so the image is seen through the letterforms. Treating type as image is a fundamental principle of how I build all my drawings. It is now hard for me to create a drawing without type in it!'

Hendrix has been drawing in church for his entire life. 'I still remember making comics in church when I was in fourth or fifth grade. As I got older I realized that these drawings I was doing during sermons could be more than just idle doodling.' In fact, back in 2006–2007 Hendrix made a few drawings that he thought were better than any illustrations he had made all year. 'I couldn't figure out what had happened to allow me to make these raw and risky images,' he explains. 'So, it became a kind of game every week at church. I just bring a bunch of pens and draw during the sermon; I would respond to the content in the sermon sort of like a cross between on-location drawing and improv

comedy. Then, I colour them when I get home during the week when I'm looking for some procrastination.'

The goal for these is very simple. 'I'm trying to reconnect with my love of drawing and image making by telling these small visual stories,' he says. 'I don't sketch anything out beforehand, I just listen and respond with type and image, looking for visual connections that go beyond conscious construction.'

Hendrix's stories vary in terms of the particular narratives, but looking at the series as a whole, the theme of expressing the inexpressible is clear. 'Engaging in religious worship involves many abstract concepts – faith, hope, death, grace, forgiveness, sin, eternity – and many of my drawings are about visualizing these mysteries in some way. Sometimes the stories are literal stories, but oftentimes the narratives are metaphorical or abstracted.

'Unfortunately,' he laments, 'the term "Christian Art" has come to mean a lexicon of clichés and trite motivational posters.' But as these pages reveal, 'engaging existential concepts, like those explored in all religious activities, are perfect for image making – especially in narrative illustration'.

TITLE: *Drawings in Church*, sketchbook series
PHOTOGRAPHER/ILLUSTRATOR: John Hendrix
YEARS: 2011–2015

ISABEL SEIFFERT
Not the End of Print

There are a couple of storylines that run parallel within *Not the End of Print*. Besides emphasizing the development of the designer from purely a service provider to author, curator, publisher, etc., Isabel Seiffert wanted to prove that '"digital" is not opposed to "analogue", and "print" for that matter', she says.

Quite the opposite, in fact. Without the personal computer, digital publishing programs, digital printing techniques and the internet, designers couldn't afford to publish and handle the distribution themselves. And on a formal note, books and printed matter were pushed to their natural advantage by having a counterpart: the screen. Fine paper, vivid colours, foil embossing and special bindings are used to increase the sensual experience while consuming a certain content.

'Since the beginning of my training as a graphic designer, I've been told that print is dead,' she laments. 'There was always, and in many ways still is, this distinction between "digital" and "print" … as if they would stand on opposing sites. But this scene of young designers and artists, mostly digital natives, were making printed books and magazines. Why weren't they making

e-papers or websites to communicate their interests or research? I felt there was a gap and maybe even a misunderstanding in the story that has been told until then, so I decided to look into it.'

Typography is a main tool in Seiffert's practice and within this project. It's the smallest unit of a book and the most powerful graphic, as it is form and information in one. 'In *Not the End of Print* I wanted to marry a classical and contemporary aesthetic. Classic, because it's an homage to the book, and contemporary, because of its new context within the digital world. This is achieved by using a grid-based layout but taking the typography apart, using it as symbols, imagery or patterns.' She wanted to further visualize the transformation of images within the digital language. Therefore, the images of the first chapter are shown as letters in numbers, but weren't altered other than that.

This symbiosis is part of Seiffert's work in general, and she adds, 'I can appreciate the systematic models of modernistic approaches but can't hide the influences that come with growing up in the midst of the digital revolution.'

TITLE: *Not the End of Print*
DESIGN FIRM/AGENCY: Isabel Seiffert,
Büro Für Graphik
ART DIRECTOR/DESIGNER: Isabel Seiffert
CLIENT: Merz Akademie, University of Art,
Design and Media, Stuttgart
YEAR: 2014

Max Schulze & Katrin Menne "One of the reasons why we decided to self-publish our magazine was to take part in the contemporary art discourse by using a public medium."

in „Graphic Magazine" Nr. 10, 2009, S. 67

C. SCHNITTSTELLE KUNST & DESIGN

Es gab Zeiten, da waren die Grenzen zwischen den angewandten und den freien Künsten haarscharf definiert. Heute machen Künstler Installationen zum Benutzen, Designer schaffen Unikate zum Sammeln und Betrachten. Mühelos werden die Disziplinen gewechselt, so auch in Bezug auf Kunst und Design. Woher aber kam die vorangehende „haarscharfe" Trennung der Sphären, die lange Zeit so rigide war, dass beispielsweise eine Fotografie bis in die 1970er Jahre ganz selbstverständlich keine Kunst sein konnte?

Allgemein wird auf das ausgehende 18. Jahrhundert verwiesen, auf eine Zeit großer politisch-gesellschaftlicher Umwälzungen wie etwa der Französischen Revolution, als auch der Begriff der Kunst eine Zäsur erfuhr. Auf die idealistische Ästhetik (Kant, Schiller, Moritz, Schelling, Hegel etc.) geht das Postulat der Autonomie der Kunst als deren Wesen zurück, was nichts anderes als deren Neuerfindung an der Schwelle zur Moderne bedeutete: „Seit Immanuel Kant war die Rede von der Kunst als dem ‚Höchsten', dem ‚Erhabenen', dem ‚Idealen', dem mit ‚interesselosem Wohlgefallen' begegnet wird."[67] Es war etwa für Georg Wilhelm Friedrich Hegel klar, dass das Kunstwerk seinen „substantiellen Zweck (...) in sich selbst" habe, und dass alle „äußerlichen Zwecke" wie etwa „Ruhm und Ehre" oder „Gelderwerb" es als solches nichts angingen.[68] Damit aber war alles Zweckorientierte aus dem Reich der Hohen Kunst vertrieben. Um das Einschneidende an diesem Autonomie-Postulat zu begreifen, muss man verstehen, dass die Kunst der Vormoderne reines Handwerk war, heu-

[67]
Schneider, Design,
S. 223
[68]
Georg Wilhelm
Friedrich Hegel:
Vorlesungen über
die Ästhetik I.
[Werke Band 13,
herausgegeben
von Eva
Moldenhauer]
Frankfurt am
Main 1986, S. 82

32   33

INPUT

SEE TOUCH SMELL
FEEL

ROT

Rot ist der Farbreiz, der vom menschlichen Auge bei einer spektralen Verteilung im Wellenlängenintervall oberhalb von 600 nm wahrgenommen wird. Der Farbeindruck „Rot" entsteht bei Anregung der L-Zapfen* und kann nach Gelb oder Blau tendieren sowie heller oder dunkler erscheinen. Orangerot wird wahrgenommen, wenn nur der langwellige Bereich des Spektrums wirksam ist, Magentarot, wenn dazu noch ein kurzwelliger Anteil kommt.

*Zapfentypen der menschlichen Netzhaut: S-Typ (kurzwelliger Blaurezeptor), M-Typ (mittelwelliger Grünrezeptor) und L-Typ (langwelliger Rotrezeptor).

ROUGE

ROJO

RED

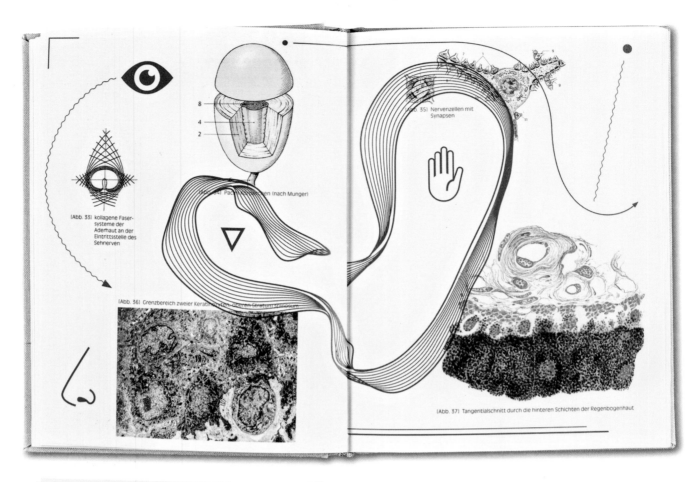

[Abb. 33] kollagene Faser-
systeme der
Aderhaut an der
Eintrittsstelle des
Sehnerven

[Abb. 34] Pacini-Körperchen (nach Munger)

[Abb. 35] Nervenzellen mit
Synapsen

[Abb. 36] Grenzbereich zweier Keratinozyten, äußeren Stratum spinosum

[Abb. 37] Tangentialschnitt durch die hinteren Schichten der Regenbogenhaut

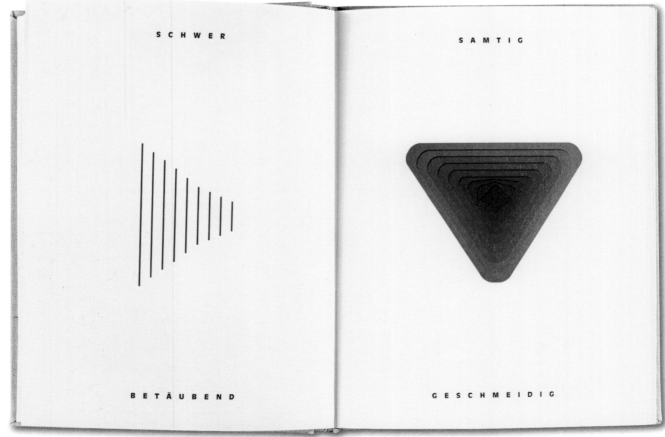

SCHWER   SAMTIG

BETÄUBEND   GESCHMEIDIG

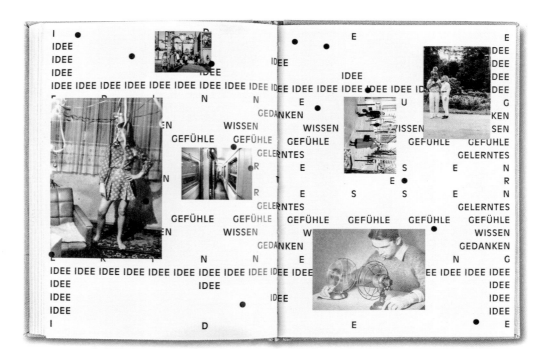

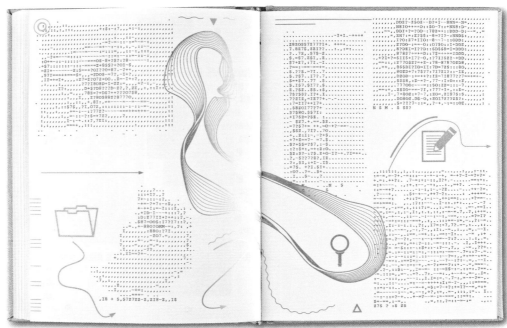

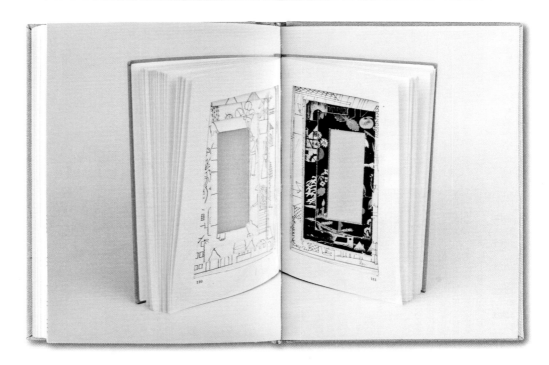

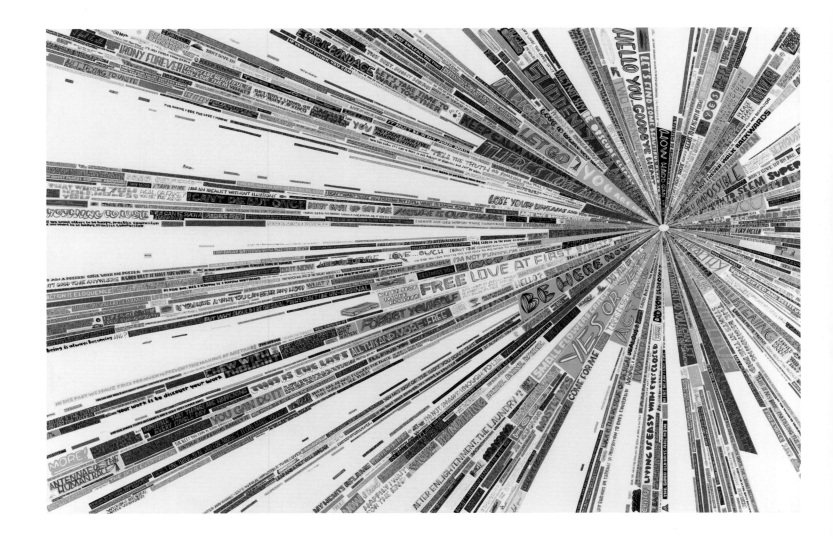

LORA FOSBERG
Text Paintings

Lora Fosberg says her text paintings represent the now. 'I think of myself as a historian … writing down whatever it is that I run across during the production of the piece, and therefore recording the history of the now,' she says. Listening to music lyrics, the news of the day, politicians, comedians, overheard conversations, literature, her mother, her brother, her lover and anything else that seems relevant and important to her in that moment: these are the words that emanate from her work, filling sky, land and space.

All the letters and fonts are invented by Fosberg and hand-painted on small slips of paper adhered to panels. The fonts are basically a distillation of what she is attracted to and surrounded by: 'old signage, vintage graphic design, comic books, pop culture and the like'. Extensive text comes from conscious and subconscious recollections in a swell of spontaneity.

'I never know when something will strike me,' she says, 'but am always listening … making this piece for the past ten years has made me more attentive to the world in a strange way.'

There now exists three feet by approximately 170 feet of text on panel … all about three feet tall by some variable length, all on separate panels and sold to individual collectors. Fosberg started making this piece in 2007 for a show at the Museum of Contemporary art in Chicago – and it needed to be epic. 'I realized I had been filling my sketchbooks with writing since I started keeping sketchbooks [when she was seven years old] and I have always used that writing as text within my art, but never entirely composed of it.' So, that is how these text pieces came about.

OPPOSITE

TITLE: *after enlightenment … the laundry*
DESIGNER: Lora Fosberg
YEAR: 2012

LEFT

TITLE: *I hope this feels real to you*
DESIGNER: Lora Fosberg
YEAR: 2007

BELOW

TITLE: *thank you for everything*
DESIGNER: Lora Fosberg
YEAR: 2009

OVERLEAF

TITLE: *always more*
DESIGNER: Lora Fosberg
YEAR: 2015

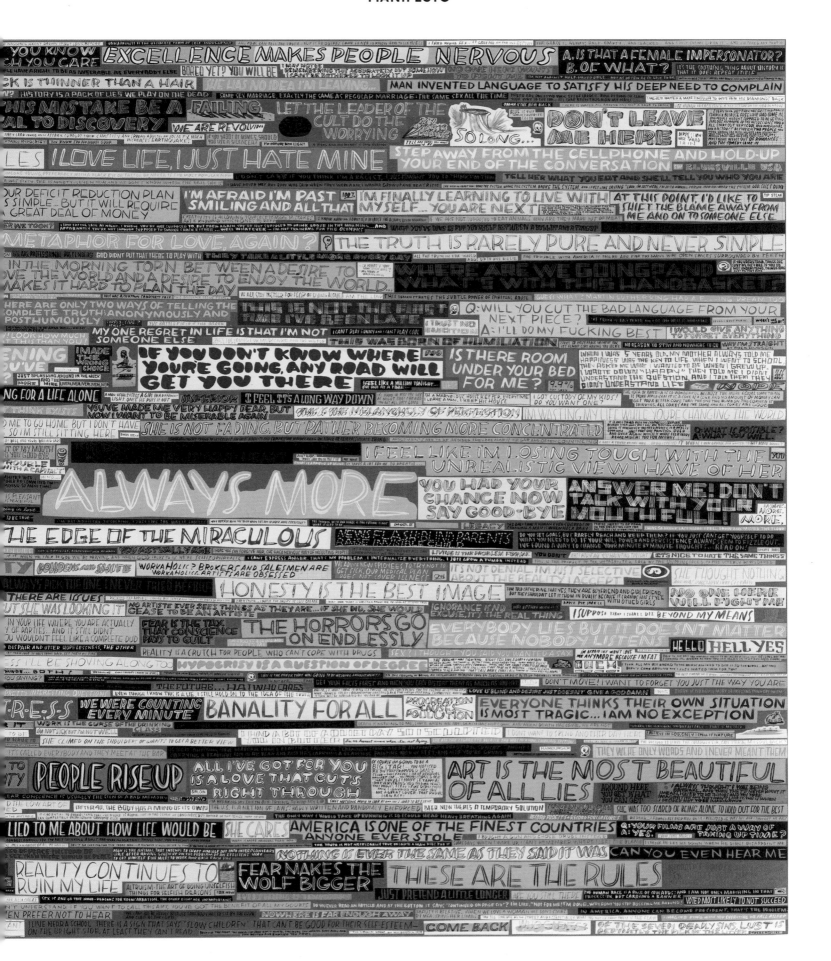

TITLE: *all the wrong people have self-esteem*
DESIGN FIRM/AGENCY: Rosenworld.com
ART DIRECTOR/DESIGNER/PHOTOGRAPHER/
ILLUSTRATOR: Laurie Rosenwald
PUBLISHER: Bloomsbury
YEAR: 2008

LAURIE ROSENWALD

all the wrong people have self-esteem

'*all the wrong people have self-esteem* is the book I've always wanted to write,' says Laurie Rosenwald, 'because it's 33⅓ each of graphic design, illustration and writing – just like my job, as I see it. For me, it's all a big mush, and the visual and verbal carry equal weight. In an average day, I might write a story, paint with hot wax, design a book jacket or animate a cartoon.'

So, this book has chapters that wed text, type and picture in a tasty stew of such themes as 'Advice To Teens', which is done 'mad-libs' style, 'The PMS Collection Agency' and 'Really Extreme Makeover: 25,185 Days To A Better You.' And, for the environmentalist, 'Is The Earth Really Worth Saving?'

'Not if it's being run by marketing executives,' she says, answering her own question. 'Marketing should involve a shopping cart, milk and bananas.'

Rosenwald's narrative is basically this: 'cheer up'. She does not believe art is an effective political or even social weapon. 'It preaches to the converted, usually,' she insists, so maybe the most radical thing one can be 'is cheerful'.

Typographically speaking, in the 1970s 'it was all about Univers fonts and grainy black and white photos and semiotics. I need the humour, colour and passion of real life, and my work always reflects that.' She considers herself an outsider in the graphic design community. 'I think I'm a good designer precisely because I'm self-taught. Also because my generation trained their hands to create things, and I use those drawing and lettering skills every day.' She adds that the digital world needs this human balance, 'and almost everything I do uses the best of both worlds'.

KICKED OUT OF YOGA

n the mat in front of each student was a small towel, a blanket, and a pink Kleenex. Everyone was deeply attuned to the instructor's soothing, hypnotic voice in the darkened room. "Hold one nostril and breathe in, then hold the other and breathe out."

I managed to keep a straight face. Right through the fish, the plow, downward facing dog and warrior positions, up to and including the jumping frog. The teacher spoke softly, "Now everybody roll up your blankets." Obediently, we started rolling up the big heavy wool blankets. She gently corrected us, saying, "I said to roll your towels, please" pointing to the towels. I couldn't help myself, crying out for cosmic justice. "But you said BLANKET!" I started laughing uncontrollably. Couldn't stop. Suddenly, the teacher's voice rang out in the darkness; a voice with a not-so-new-age-edge. "Perhaps there are some people here WHO SHOULDN'T BE HERE RIGHT NOW." I I removed my corporeal presence. I ran like the wind, and then I bought a Snickers. I never found out what the Kleenex was for. I was kicked out of Yoga class.

Prepare yourself for

THE SHOCKING TRUTH:
WHERE BABIES really COME FROM

ABSTINENCE, ONLY...

Advocates for "Abstinence-Only" education believe that schools should only teach about abstinence from sex, and should not provide information on how to obtain and use condoms and other contraception. In light of conservative support of an "Abstinence-Only" S-E- E-D-U- -T-I- -N policy in our public schools, we thought it was the very least we could do to present a fairly informative, kind of accurate, but not nearly comprehensive account of, well, you know. If teens learn just a few of the ghastly, disgusting "facts," they'll be less likely to try to find out all of them through the Internet and stuff. Or even worse, experience. We offer the following report: The sexual act is best demonstrated by putting your finger into an electrical outlet. First you must wet your finger. See? Sex may cause an "organism." An organism might pop out and make you scream something like, "Would you like fries with that?" Then the organism turns into a tadpole. If you are wearing rubber, don't worry, because you are grounded, and protected from the organism. Before the sexual act, put on new sneakers and brush your tongue. Put on your Usher CD, and try some French Twisting. Warning: You may experience one or more side effects, such as diaper rash, global thermonuclear meltdown, or tummy ache.

Try not to drool on your sex partner. This may cause a short. To practice safe sex, use a surge protector. Now, close your eyes, and get ready for the ride of your life. All right then, away we go! Some believe sex is where babies come from, but we now know that babies come from France. Sex is much like love, but burns even more calories. Sex is like ballet, except Mr. B is not always complaining about your short neck, and you don't have to wear your hair in a bun. Also, the Russians are no better at it than regular people. With sex, remember that size is the most important thing. If you are the size of a muon or a quark, forget it. Nobody's going to be sexually attracted to a subatomic particle they can't even see. If you wear lots of clothing, no one will have sex with you. If you wear tiny triangles of cloth attached with string, they will be all over you. If sex is so much fun, we asked a friend why she doesn't "do it" more often. She said she couldn't find the "right guy." Apparently, he has to be "single." We pointed out that New York City, where she lives, has the highest density of "singles" on earth, except for that leper colony in Hawaii. She told us to shut up, and that Sartre was right, Hell is other people. She's been very moody. Perhaps she is molting. All mothers are against sex, but if they had not had sex they couldn't even be mothers. Unless, of course, they have been to France.

TITLE: *Process*
ART DIRECTORS: Jenny El-Shamy, James Reidhaar
and David Wolske
DESIGNER: John Passafiume
YEAR: 2007

JOHN PASSAFIUME
Process

Completed in 2007, *Process*, the product of three months' work, was conceived to be what John Passafiume calls 'a reactive statement' against the growing influence of digital tools on traditionally human, hand-centric trades. In protest he set out to produce a large-format typographic narrative crafted with a 0.5mm pencil, to demonstrate how 'comparatively nuanced and competitively matched the human hand remained'.

'*Process* is a largely allegorical commentary contrasting the qualities of the hand with the recent prevalence of the digital aesthetic,' he explained; about 'countering the bastardization of process by documenting process itself; the content of this work is necessarily meticulous and overwhelming. An obsession with craft and classicism underscores a distaste for the "everyone is a designer" mentality that has infiltrated the profession; a lamentable transition positing the computer as crutch and ingesting an array of once hand-reliant trades in its wake. The content, hand-drawn over the course of a three-month period, necessitated more than 700 hours of drafting.'

While Passafiume notes that there is a great deal of autobiographical content contained in *Process*, 'most of the fragments are intended allegories circling back to a principal rebellious theme. Many of the components link to other sections through the use of a key which further obfuscates any attempt at interpretation. My hope was that the fabric of the whole would reveal itself in totality … no beginning and no end.'

A single dot of colour, a red flame of sorts, represents the health problems that Passafiume had been suffering through, very nearly putting an end to the project. That health concern is a recurring theme that shows up several times in both words and pictures.

Passafiume's so-called 'native handwriting' serves as a foundation for the entire piece. 'It could be said that lettering in particular is an especially personal art form,' he said. 'Specific hands are easily distinguished. I am fond of teaching an exercise whereby drawing only a single line amongst a group of participants illustrates this point … the degree of variation you will see from one person to the next! That's really what this piece is calling out – that automation has a way of robbing us of the individuality, and consequently, the interest.'

122

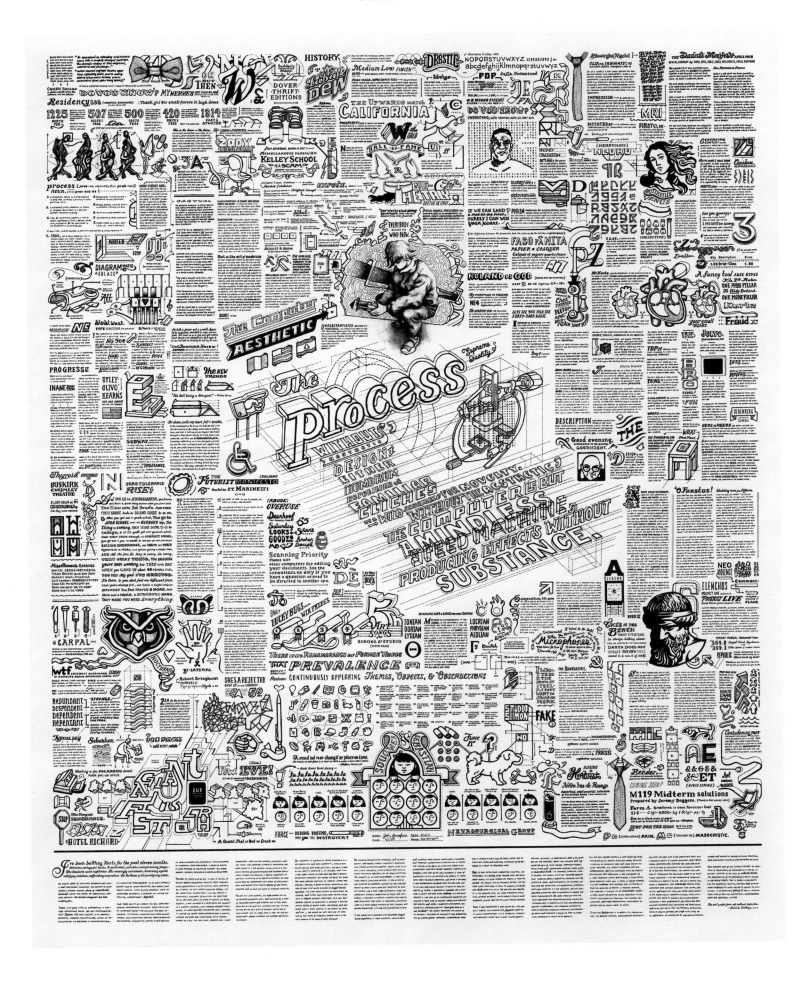

TITLE: Wedding Suit Lining
DESIGNERS: Nick Reeve, Marc Wallace (tailor)
YEAR: 2015

NICK REEVE
Wedding Suit Lining

Nick Reeve met his wife-to-be on an internet dating site in 2012. After messaging and then meeting each other, it became apparent that they were destined to have a relationship. Two years later they were engaged.

He approached Marc Wallace, a tailor based in Bath and London, about making a suit for his wedding: 'We got chatting and discovered we both had a passion for design.' Reeve recalls learning that it was possible to digitally print on silk and thinking about coming up with a unique design for the lining. 'I wanted to do something meaningful but not overly sentimental or slushy.' Reeve decided to celebrate the fact that by the time of their first date, the couple knew a lot about each other, 'which made our first meeting far less nerve-wracking for both of us'.

The messages were about the two of them – their lives and jobs. 'They weren't particularly flirtatious – just two people getting to know each other.' They were married at the end of May 2015, and Reeve kept the suit a secret from wife Jen until the big day 'when I could do the big reveal'.

Reeve did the typesetting and Wallace then sent the files to the printers, who are based in England. The detail of the output surprised everyone. Some of the type was as small as 9pt, and the quotes, which were pulled out in larger text, were in Gill Sans Light, which also reproduced well. 'We came up with the idea of using the pocket square to hold Jen's and my personal statements from the website, which matched the suit lining.' The suit took twelve weeks to make.

NATALI COHEN
Coline/Text Tights

Natali Cohen was sixteen years old when she moved from Russia to Israel, where she worked for fifteen years in managerial roles in the fashion industry. Then, as she describes it, 'I decided to start my own shop with my designs.' It began because she always had a problem wearing things that everyone else was wearing – 'so I wanted to be special and unique with my fashion; my designs express my inner world, my mood and my complexity'. Her fashion is also inextricably tied to type.

'I like using typography,' she says, 'because it looks intriguing, romantic and has more depth than a regular design; because it has also [an]other meaning.' Sometimes men order a pair of her tights with a poem or a love song, or just words from their heart, that they wrote to a loved one: 'I find this very touching.'

Her business motto reads 'Go with Art', and she proudly adds: 'When you look at my designs you can always see how I feel at that moment: if I'm in a good mood I do everything with warm colours and humoristic … and if I'm moody – my tights are dark and creepy.'

The tights receive a lot of responses from clients, such as: 'I wore my grey tights for Thanksgiving and it was a great conversation starter!' Another client, a copywriter, bought a pair with a spelling mistake for someone in the office as a joke.

Although Cohen admits it might sound 'a bit cheesy', she wants to spread joy through her type. 'I wish once someone put my tights [on] they'll feel happiness. I really like the idea that someone on the other side of the globe will wear something that I've created.'

OPPOSITE, LEFT

TITLE: *Pride and Prejudice*
DESIGN FIRM/AGENCY: Coline
ART DIRECTOR/DESIGNER/
ILLUSTRATOR: Natali Cohen
YEAR: 2015

OPPOSITE, RIGHT

TITLE: *Sherlock Holmes*
DESIGN FIRM/AGENCY: Coline
ART DIRECTOR/DESIGNER/
ILLUSTRATOR: Natali Cohen
YEAR: 2015

BELOW

TITLE: *Pride and Prejudice*
DESIGN FIRM/AGENCY: Coline
ART DIRECTOR/DESIGNER/
ILLUSTRATOR: Natali Cohen
YEAR: 2015

TITLE: *In Order to Control*
DESIGN FIRM/AGENCY: NOTA BENE Visual
YEAR: 2011

NOTA BENE Visual (NBv)
In Order to Control

In Order to Control confronts an audience with a political text projected and interacted through new media tools. NOTA BENE Visual designed typographic techniques that 'match' the mind and body actions. 'Our goal is to criticize people who don't "move" and make the visitors criticize themselves by encouraging people to gang up against the "social norms" and "legal norms" imposed and causing singularity, virtuality and violence.'

To create a full sentence in the projected text, the visitor must 'move with the flow rate of the line or merge their arms with another person'. With every visitor the design changes, causing an interaction that generates itself with the body actions of that visitor. With every user, the work adapts and therefore becomes a unique project. Some users are just having fun with their reflections on the letters, some of them read the text properly, and some watch the ones who read and who don't read;

during all this they are thinking, criticizing and discussing the process.

The consumer of media art becomes part of the installation and becomes a 'prosumer'. NBv chose a simple black and white typographic installation, 'which totally expresses what we want with a "portable and spatial" design product'. By investigating new ways of storytelling NBv try to find an interactive way of consuming data.

NBv insist: 'We are new media artists, not typography artists. Typography is a branch of art we totally respect, and *In Order to Control* is not a typography artwork, it's a typographical new media work.' During the process, and as a result, they used typography as a medium and animated the words through the spacing and kerning, 'just to blow the visitor's mind'.

BELOW

TITLE: *Gosh I've been here before #2*
DESIGN FIRM/AGENCY: Annie Vought
YEAR: 2014

ANNIE VOUGHT
Gosh I've been here before,
Underneath the blah,
I am Crossing an Ocean, With 2 Others on a Piece of Paper

Annie Vought created these typographic cut-outs to express her relationship to language and communication, as well as handmade objects, handwritten letters and time-based work. 'I love the slow process of meticulously cutting out the words and shapes from the paper,' she says. 'It's an investigation of the words that are chosen, the shape and composition of the words themselves, and the structure of the paper I am cutting.'

Taking a spiritual point of view, she insists that a handwritten document can be a 'physical confirmation of who we were at the moment it was made, or all we have left of a person or a time'. She is interested in examining just how many words we are surrounded by every day. 'We are bombarded by messages and much gets lost within them all. My work is an investigation of all the different forms of written communication.'

The font or handwriting Vought employs within a piece is directly related to the conceptual story behind that particular piece. If it is a letter, then she mimics the handwriting of the person who originally wrote that letter. If she is referencing Carl Jung's *The Red Book* then she references the calligraphy he used when he wrote down his own dreams. And in her current work, the text is what her handwriting looks like when she cuts into the paper freehand, without a template. 'The language in my new work is taken from things I overhear, advertisements, text messages, emails and other bits of communication I am surrounded by,' she says.

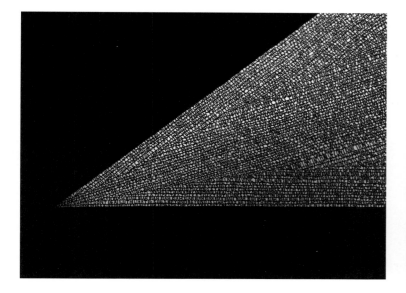

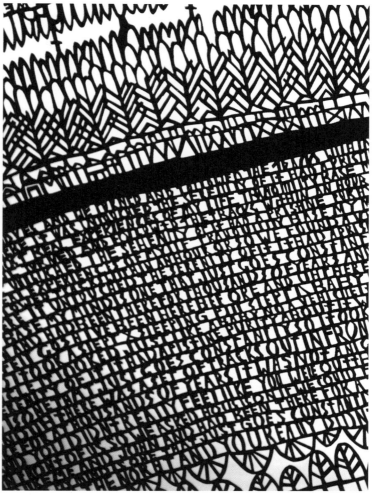

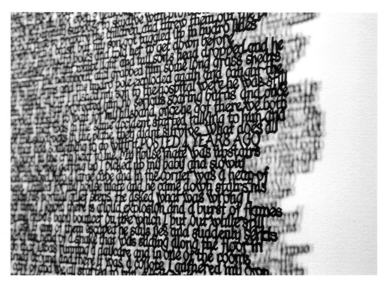

TOP LEFT

TITLE: *Underneath the Blah*
DESIGN FIRM/AGENCY: Annie Vought
YEAR: 2015

ABOVE LEFT

TITLE: *Gosh I've been here before* (detail)
DESIGN FIRM/AGENCY: Annie Vought
YEAR: 2014

TOP RIGHT

TITLE: *Gosh I've been here before*
DESIGN FIRM/AGENCY: Annie Vought
YEAR: 2014

ABOVE RIGHT

TITLE: *I am Crossing an Ocean, With 2 Others on a Piece of Paper* (detail)
DESIGN FIRM/AGENCY: Annie Vought
YEAR: 2012

TITLE: *Obvious?*
DESIGNER: Jack Summerford
PUBLISHER: Clampitt Paper Company
YEAR: 2015

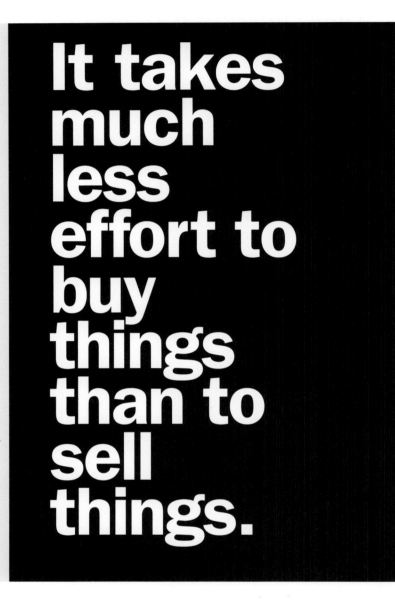

If *you have a great idea, it will tell you how to execute it.*

Style doesn't have a lot to say.

It takes much less effort to buy things than to sell things.

JACK SUMMERFORD

Obvious?

Jack Summerford might be evoking what is and is not obvious in life in the title of his typographic self-produced examination. He says that he did it, quite obviously, as simple self-motivation: 'It was just something that had germinated over fifteen years ago and had lived in exile in my computer until a couple of years ago when I decided to put it in finished form.

'After bouncing it off a few friends, and with encouragement from the designer George Tscherny to approach a paper company, I found a publisher in Don Clampitt of Clampitt Paper Company. They felt it was an obvious way to capture the interest of their customers.'

Summerford has been designing for decades, but proudly notes that 'I have no style, thus that may make my use of typography unique.' The book follows his pattern of 'over simplify, over simplify. One colour (though not really), two typefaces and an economy of words.' Then, he adds, there is 'no real story unless you count the maturing of a designer'.

When we are busy, we are too busy to market. When we are not busy, it's too late.

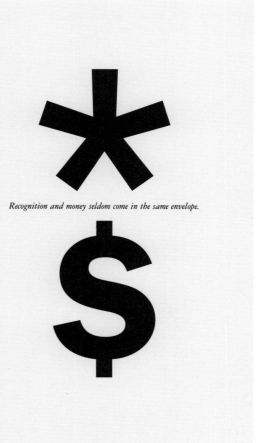

Recognition and money seldom come in the same envelope.

WHEN DESIGNING FOR YOURSELF, REMEMBER WHO THE CLIENT IS. NO, MAKE THAT, REMEMBER THAT THERE IS A CLIENT.

(Your Logo Goes Here)

TITLE: The Wire Poster Project
DESIGN FIRM/AGENCY: OMG/Oliver Munday
ART DIRECTOR/DESIGNER: Oliver Munday
CLIENT: Baltimore Urban Debate League
YEAR: 2013

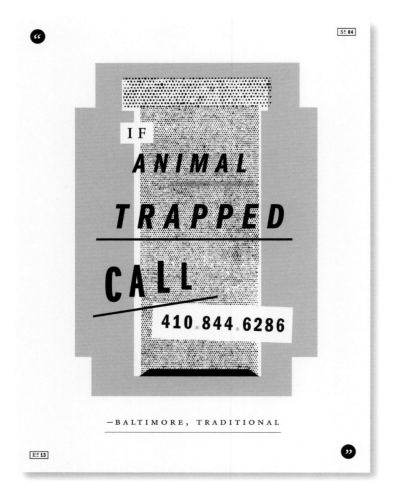

OLIVER MUNDAY
The Wire Poster Project

The Wire Poster Project consists of sixty typographic posters, each representing one of the sixty different epigrams that precedes every episode of HBO's critically acclaimed series *The Wire* (2002–2008). Created and designed by Oliver Munday, the posters were intended to help fund the Baltimore Urban Debate League, which began as a fictional organization, but as a real one will help at-risk kids in Baltimore.

This project is Munday's response to the grippingly realistic, inner-city narrative written by David Simon, particularly the opening epigraph in each episode that reveals itself at a key moment in the story. 'My goal was to celebrate and illuminate these moments, and it started as a sort of (gasp) fan-art project,' says Munday. 'I wanted to expand it beyond that, and make it into something that connected to the show (about drug abuse and policing the sources), and all of the themes and ideas that the show continues to speak to.'

Munday was interested in what he calls the potential synthesis of the vintage/vernacular Globe Poster aesthetic (an institution native to Baltimore), and the Constructivist-inspired, expressive compositions. Each 18in × 24in poster is printed in high-quality digital on archival paper by A to A Studio Solutions, Ltd. The season number is indicated in the top right-hand corner and the episode number in the bottom left-hand corner of each print.

"

A LIE AIN'T A LIE A SIDE of A STORY. IT'S JUST A LIE A LIE

—TERRY HANNING

"

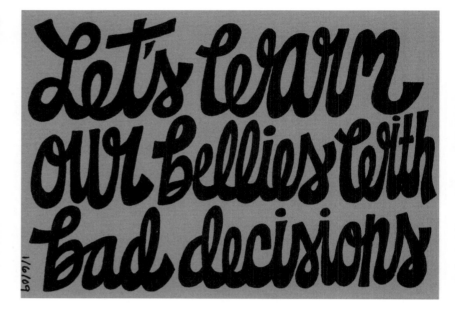

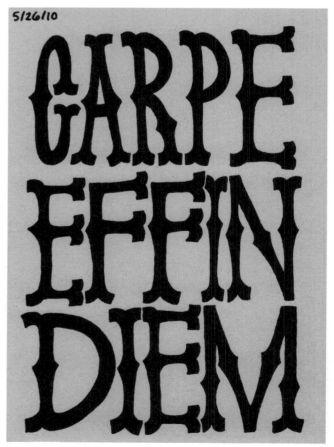

TITLE: Postcards to My Parents
DESIGNER/PHOTOGRAPHER/ILLUSTRATOR:
Carolyn Sewell
YEARS: 2009–2010

CAROLYN SEWELL
Postcards to My Parents

After a death in the family left Carolyn Sewell's closest cousin with no living parents, she felt panicked about losing her own. 'I wanted to make a big gesture, something sentimental but not easy, to let my parents know how much they meant to me.'

She decided to send a love letter to her parents every day for a year, and made their wedding anniversary the start date. At the time Sewell was also drawing more, so combined writing and drawing, and hand-lettered each postcard to her parents. 'As for content,' she reports, 'I've always kept a small notebook to jot down funny things that friends and family say, and the postcards finally gave me a vehicle to share them.'

The distinguishing characteristic for these cards, she says, is the predilection for 'irreverent content plus imperfect lettering'. The lettering has a lot of 'wobbles, something that I used to hate, but have grown to appreciate. And the content of my postcards is a blend of puns, jabs and high-fives.'

137

FOUR

MONUMENTAL

BELOW

TITLE: *A Vanishing Point*, installation view
ARTIST: Alida Sayer
YEAR: 2011

OPPOSITE, TOP

TITLE: *Here We Are I* (detail)
ARTIST: Alida Sayer
YEAR: 2010

OPPOSITE, BOTTOM

TITLE: *All Moments*
ARTIST: Alida Sayer
YEAR: 2009

ALIDA SAYER
A Vanishing Point
Here We Are I
All Moments

Alida Sayer's sculptural pieces for a London gallery installation reflect her self-described attempt to read and to write beyond the surface. 'I try to enter into and expand the forms that we associate with language and voice in order to question its power and its potential for describing intangible sensations and experiences,' she says.

The works are largely based on fragments of text from novels by Kurt Vonnegut and Vladimir Nabokov, in which the main protagonists have entered into altered states of mind, outside of a conventional linear narrative. In each, they are attempting to articulate what they are experiencing. 'It is about trying to capture the sense of a moment that is fleeting or seemingly dissociative,' Sayer adds, 'yet is nevertheless inextricably linked to many others at once.'

Sayer insists that she does not deconstruct and fragment letterforms in order to tell stories, but rather as a means of seeking stories out. 'I try to read between the lines, to pull them apart and see what is left. Perhaps I am using letterforms as a way in to something that cannot be expressed in words at all.'

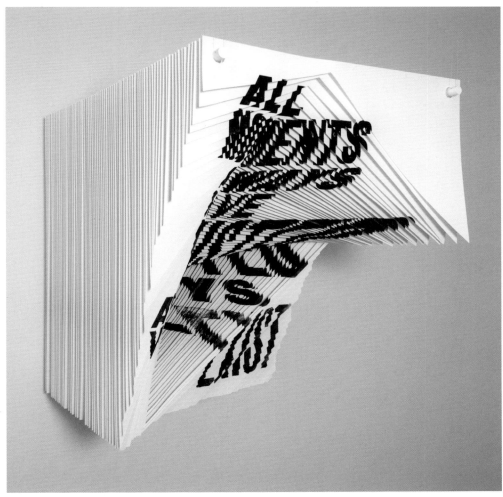

BELOW

TITLE: *Style Stones* (below and overleaf)
DESIGN FIRM/AGENCY: Ariane Spanier Design
ART DIRECTOR/DESIGNER/ILLUSTRATOR:
Ariane Spanier
PHOTOGRAPHER: Dulcineia Gomez
CLIENT: Museum for Communication, Berlin
YEAR: 2011

OPPOSITE

TITLE: *Lives Remembered*
DESIGN FIRM/AGENCY: Ariane Spanier Design
DESIGNER/PHOTOGRAPHER/ILLUSTRATOR:
Ariane Spanier
CLIENT: *Washington Post Magazine*
YEAR: 2012

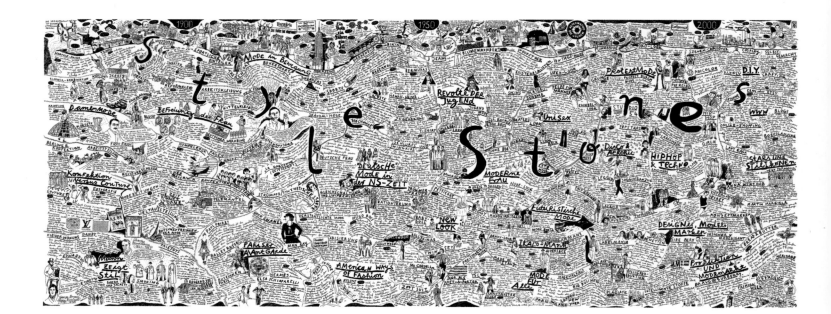

ARIANE SPANIER DESIGN
Style Stones
Lives Remembered

For the cover of the *Washington Post Magazine*'s annual 'Lives Remembered' feature, reflecting on the accomplishments of six people who passed away in 2012 in the Washington area, Ariane Spanier made a paper reveal. This was cut paper spelling out 'Lives' with fragments of six obituary texts showing through the window of the letters. The typographic purpose was, in Spanier's words, 'opening up the surface of the magazine to something that was closed already'; bringing the lives of the dead back from beneath a shroud to the readers' eyes.

This technique also references the magazine's content and material (i.e. paper): 'the magazine becomes a dimensional object, as something you can look deep into, reach inside, and find the stories,' she says. 'Moreover, this rather simple paper concept seems to speak to a lot of people as a trigger for imagination. Just seeing a part of something has always been more interesting than getting the whole picture immediately. Your brain is invited to add the rest, making up stories or images.'

The typographical treatment quite clearly showed that there are different stories on different lives. Spanier's goal was to move the eye directly to storytelling rather than just opening up a dark void. In a sense, rather than this metaphorical void, it was about remembrance.

Meanwhile, *Style Stones*, a 7.5m × 2.7m wall illustration, depicts key points in the history of fashion for the exhibition 'Fashion Talks' at the Museum for Communication in Berlin. It is a story that describes the development of styles, techniques and movements in fashion throughout the last century within a historical and cultural context. It uses linear storytelling, putting the items in a rough chronological context.

December 23, 2012

WP

LIVES

The gifts of our neighbors

Remembered

THE GIRL WHO LIVED IN FAST FORWARD

THE FEARLESS TEACHER

THE BASEBALL VISIONARY

'STRONG-LEGS' THE SOLDIER

THE CHINATOWN MATRIARCH

THE HUMAN JAZZ ALMANAC

FAMED COMPOSER ...SLEPT HERE P.4 | TOM SIETSEMA FAMILY & FRIEND GO-TO SPOTS P.31 | WE DO IT OVER IN DATE LAB P.6 | WEINGARTEN GENE REALIZES HE IS NO. 2 P.36

BRIAN REA
Fears

Brian Rea's *Fears* mural, which was installed at the Fundació Joan Miró in Barcelona, Spain, as part of a group show entitled 'Murals', comprised a litany of his own major and minor disorders. 'I kept a list in a sketchbook of all the sources of anxiety and fear I felt,' he explains; '... everything from everyday fears like being late for work, getting hit by taxis, alien abductions, to "way back in the brain" anxieties like terrorist attacks, falling cranes, bad hair, etc.' This piece is a large-scale version of that one-year inventory.

Rea was given two large walls in the museum to work on in a long, narrow hallway at the entrance of the exhibition. 'It was a very large confrontational space', he explains, 'that provided an opportunity to deliver a more powerful message and experience.' In the context of the museum space, the *Fears* wall demanded attention, as a visitor had to walk through a tapestry of anxieties. Rea says he heard that it made some people cry. 'I even had

a psychiatrist ask if I could recreate the piece in the waiting room of their office. It tells many stories, I'm sure, but the one underlying one is that we all worry.'

Downplaying the uniqueness of his lettering, Rea says, 'It's simply handwriting, and everyone writes. What does make my lists different, however, is that they pull specifically from emotions.' He recounts recent explorations into lists about 'anger', 'pain' and 'happiness'. His process is the same each time when creating the lists: 'I gather an inventory over a set period of time, then I organize the list into categories. This helps me see ways to present the lists better graphically – the amount of words and categories helps to define that. When working on the larger versions of the lists, I don't think about typographic rules, really – over two- to three-hour stretches at a time "writing" can become more like building and less like designing or drawing.'

TITLE: *Fears*
CURATOR: Martina Milla
ARTIST: Brian Rea
MUSEUM: Fundació Joan Miró, Barcelona
YEAR: 2010

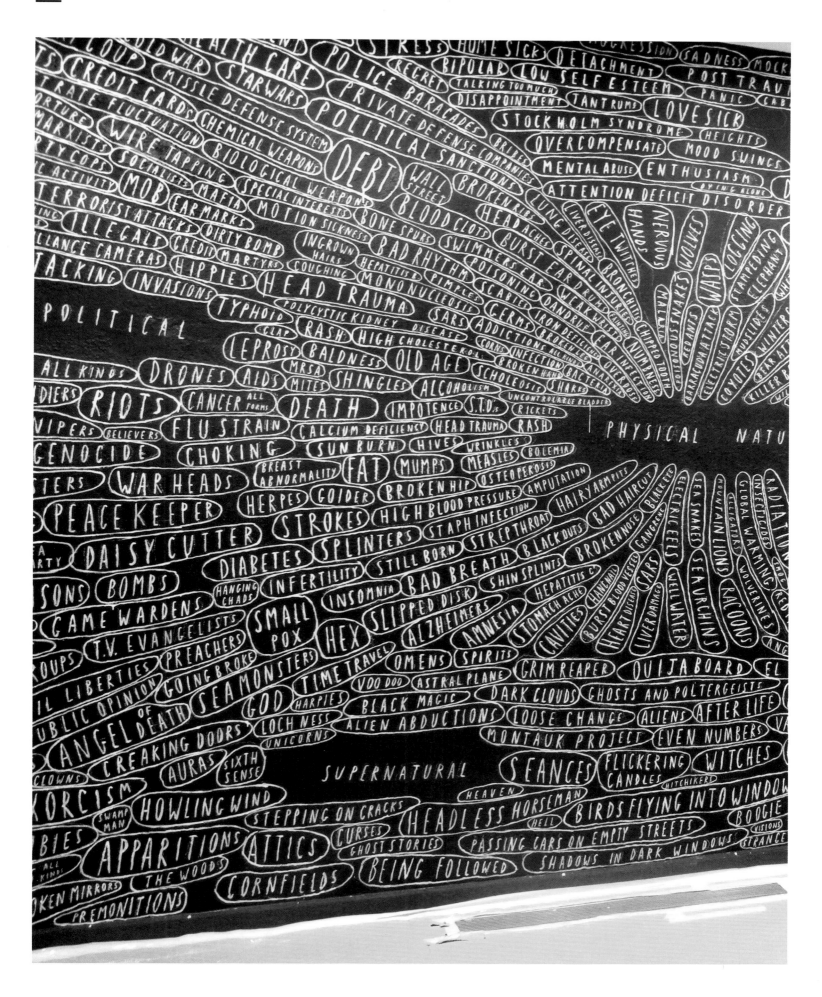

TITLE: *Steep and Drink: A Study in Grey Orchids*
DESIGN FIRM/AGENCY: Daniel Patrick Helmstetter
PHOTOGRAPHER/ILLUSTRATOR: Sara Frolich
CLIENT: Exhibited by Solo(s) Project House at
Fountain Art Fair, Miami, Florida
YEAR: 2012

DANIEL PATRICK HELMSTETTER
Steep and Drink: A Study in Grey Orchids

Daniel Patrick Helmstetter's *Steep and Drink: A Study in Grey Orchids* was commissioned by Solo(s) Project House gallery as the floor for its exhibition booth at Fountain Art Fair in Miami, 2012. The gallery wanted a piece that would fit perfectly within the footprint of the booth, and be bold and loud enough to grab attention.

'My motivation', Helmstetter recalls, 'was to create something that would have the visual power the gallery desired, and at the same time, deliver poetry that is intimate, delicate and contemplative. In many ways, there is no traditional A to Z story within this work.'

Steep and Drink is a collection of small pieces of writing picked with deep care from many years of personal journals. Helmstetter says that each little piece is a poem, and each poem is an attempt to freeze in time some little spark of what it feels like to be alive in this world. Any kind of sequence to the way they are arranged is eschewed, and no two viewers would ever read them in exactly the same way. The content is meant to be adaptable and expansive. Individually, the pieces are like 'windows or mirrors' – a view into or out of something that matters to the reader.

Yet the project is not without narrative. 'If you view the story of me creating the work as equal in part to the words and letters themselves, you can start to see it as a tale of a fragmented mind struggling for hard clarity.' Helmstetter explains. 'You can see the individual poems amass together to paint a picture of a young man with dangerous sensitivity attempting to make sense of the depth.'

Swirls of typography begin to reveal information about a character who is trying to find his way within the maze. The letters hint at a frantic, adaptable, wild pursuit of balance. The black and white mix to paint the experience of grey. The loudness depicts a quest for internal quiet.

'My use of typography differs from many others who work with hand-lettering in the simple fact that I write what I paint. I am both the author and the typesetter. It seems somewhat rare, both in typesetting and hand-lettering, that the person who creates the content is also the person who handles the letters.' Helmstetter also believes that a poem, when done right, is a physical object. 'It takes the inside world and makes it exist outside of the creator's brain and body.' With *Steep and Drink: A Study in Grey Orchids* that physicality was taken to an extreme: the poems became a hundred-pound roll of bulk linoleum flooring that he hauled to Miami for its installation.

LUST
'Type/Dynamics'

The Dutch design firm Lust was commissioned by Amsterdam's Stedelijk Museum to create an exhibition and installation that dealt with the work of Jurriaan Schrofer, an eminent designer whose death in 1990 had yet to be memorialized. The resulting exhibition, 'Type/Dynamics', consists of two identical galleries with the same conceptual theme. In the first gallery the walls are covered with enlarged detail images of Schrofer's work – originals, with the emphasis on sketches, are located in vitrines, along with two vertical screens showing works by Schrofer in an interactive format. The second gallery presents Lust's own interpretation of Schrofer's work.

Sensors track the visitors' movement, while the projections subsequently respond to the position and number of visitors in the space, as well as their distance from the gallery walls. Visitors acquaint themselves with a specific topic by walking towards an item of interest. The typographic grid closest to the visitor then opens up and becomes more readable, while new typographic layers open up for further exploration.

The installation visualizes information that continuously surrounds the viewer in real life (and is always accessible). By searching for real-time locations currently in the news, like 'Paris', 'Reichstag' or 'Tiananmen Square', the installation can locate the panorama images from Google Street View, abstract them into grids and fill the grids with new information. In the space, the visitor is 'transported' to that specific location and surrounded by all the news associated with it. 'Instead of a photographic representation, the place is represented purely typographically, with a host of new items currently being talked about at that location,' Lust explains about the gallery space, where all the information is dynamic.

Jurriaan Schrofer's *oeuvre* consists primarily of handmade printed matter, but in the 1960s he experimented with new techniques, offset printing for instance, as a means to achieve 'moving typography'. Throughout Schrofer's work, dynamics – or movement – is the common thread. Starting in the 1970s Schrofer, then a design researcher, explored patterns and structures inspired by the Op Art movement. He meticulously investigated strange perspectives, depth of field and typographic symbols.

'Type/Dynamics' showcases the dynamic qualities of information and typography. Typography is very important in the space, where it encompasses text and image simultaneously. Furthermore there is a use of small elements or modules that together form a bigger structure or pattern. The concept that design is endowed with a form that is unfinished or changeable has been self-evident in contemporary design for quite some time, and nowadays attention is paid more to the design of rules, or creating the framework in which something can happen. In a database, for instance, content does not have an innate form, but rather receives form at the moment it is shown via the interface. In fact, the same information can be represented in an endless number of ways. The interface allows for content to be shown as data, as information or as knowledge; ultimately content appears as loose data without a context, as data in a context, or as interpreted information. This data can even change by the week, day or minute. What is evident through this process is a very different approach and attitude towards design than was evident in the questions that faced Schrofer's generation.

TITLE: 'Type/Dynamics'
DESIGNER: Lust
CLIENT: Stedelijk Museum, Amsterdam
YEARS: 2013–2014

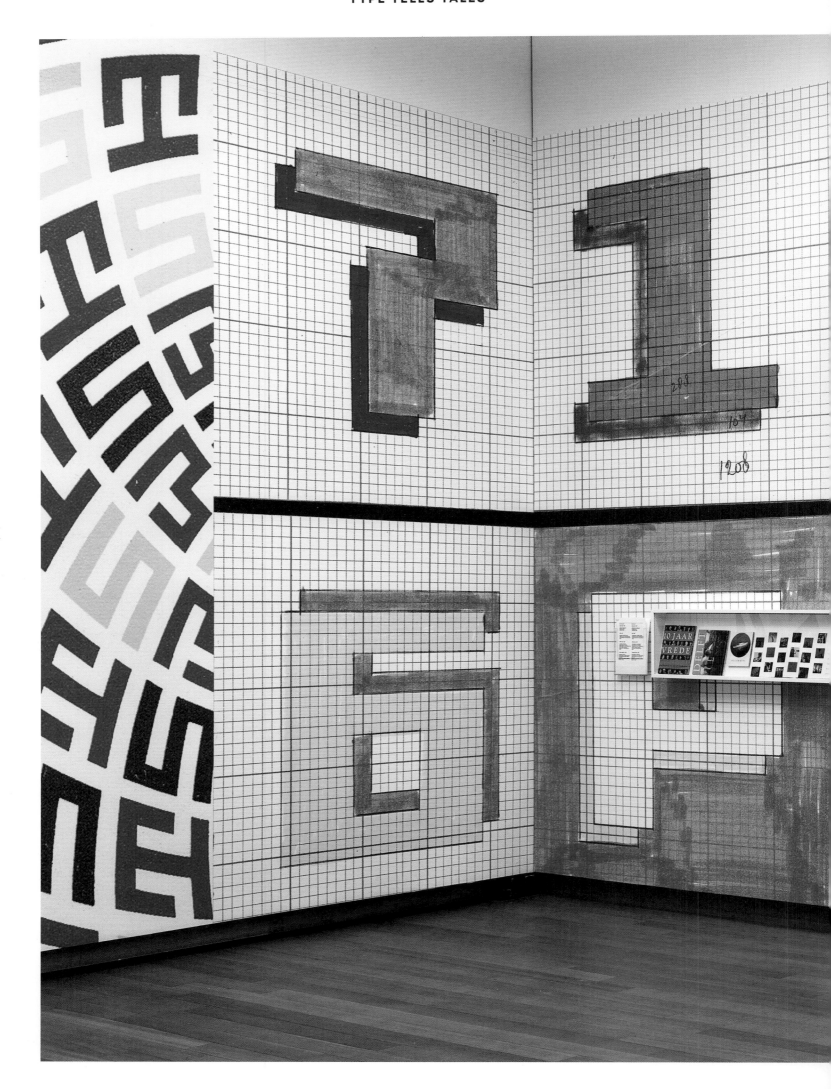

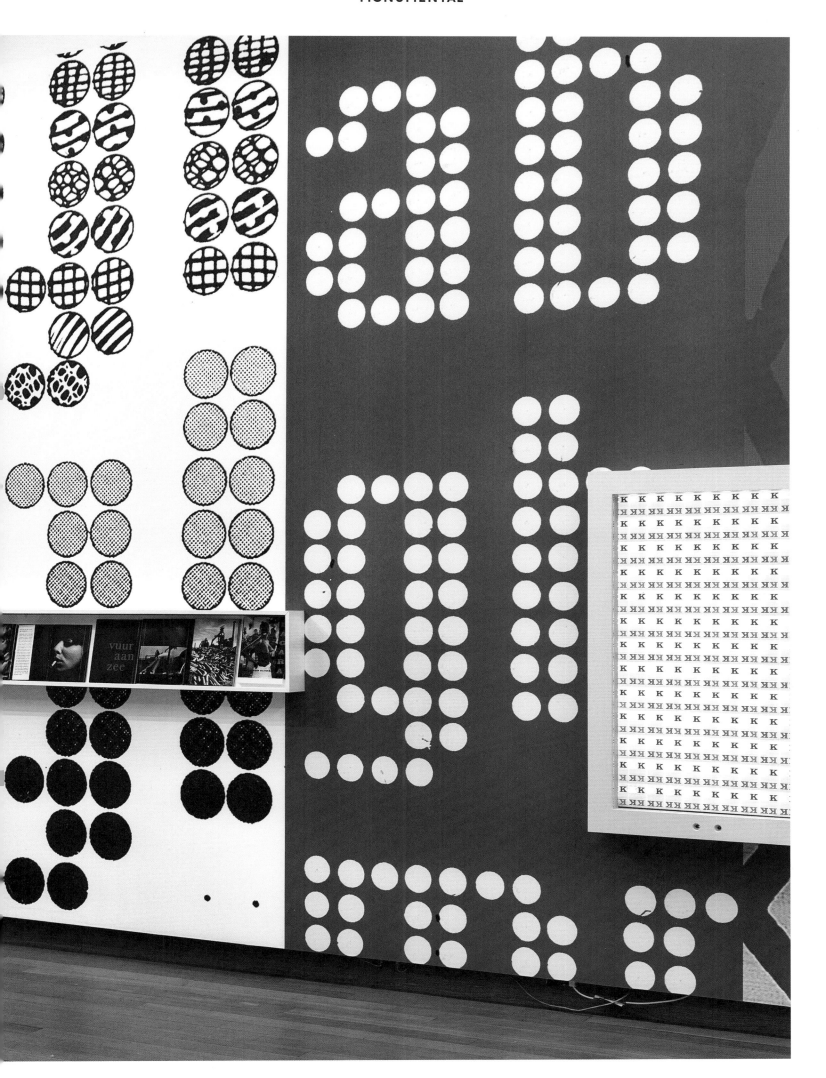

TIMOTHY GOODMAN
Flexfit

Flexfit challenged Tim Goodman to come up with a mural that he would draw, real-time, during the first day of their trade show. In response to this he hand-lettered lyrics by Tupac Shakur, the top-selling hip-hop artist of all time, over 500 square feet of wall space. Gunned down in Las Vegas in 1996 at the age of 25, Tupac Shakur is a mythological figure within the hip-hop community, and it made sense to do this in Vegas (where he was murdered).

The story that Goodman is telling begins at the top left-hand corner of the wall: 'I went round and round for close to nine hours, hand-lettering one of his most popular and heartfelt songs, *Keep Ya Head Up*. Without much time to prepare, I experimented on my studio walls during the days prior.' He had to calculate the size of the words (5 inches), and how many songs would work, as well as the style and arrangement of the letters. 'Ultimately, it became another act of obsessiveness, with a time limit or parameter, that I always seem to enjoy.'

Goodman says that he's interested in density; obsessed that every square inch of a mural should be covered. He wants someone to feel something about what they're seeing. 'I like the content to be meaningful or provocative,' he adds. 'I want a wall of discovery. I'll do anything I can in order to do that. Therefore, I want the style to be controlled so the content can sing.'

TITLE: Flexfit Tupac Mural
DESIGN FIRM/AGENCY: Timothy Goodman
ART DIRECTOR: Timothy Goodman
DESIGNER: Timothy Goodman
ILLUSTRATOR: Timothy Goodman
PRODUCER: Andy Song
PHOTOGRAPHER: Daniel Rhie
CLIENT: Flexfit Headwear
YEAR: 2012

ROGERS ECKERSLEY DESIGN (RED)
Stat Bats

Statistics are integral to baseball, particularly for the fans; the figures provide the underlying narrative to each player's career. RED are avid stats followers. 'We wanted to show statistics in a new way that would interest fans and non-fans alike,' says Stuart Rogers (the 'R' in RED). 'Because we're using bats as our canvas, we focused strictly on offensive categories.'

Engraved into each bat are the typographic representations of players' statistics. 'Our first bat displays a top-ten list of the all-time major-league hits leaders. The second bat (the one with the circles) tells the story of how Hank Aaron became the career home runs leader year-by-year. Finally, as a counterpoint to Hank Aaron's statistics, we created an asterisk bat to address the issue of cheating in baseball.'

The hardest typographic feat was to wrap the type around a baseball bat. Reading it becomes an interactive experience, demanding that the user turn the object to fully take in the story. But there is a bonus: instead of printing the text, it was engraved (for both the wood and aluminium bats), enabling the user to feel the weight of the object and also the contours of the text. 'Incidentally, we were lucky that Knockout [type family] exists, because it has such a complete array of weights and widths that made many of our solutions possible,' Sam Eckersley notes.

TITLE: Stat Bats
DESIGN FIRM/AGENCY: Rogers Eckersley Design
DESIGNERS: Stuart Rogers and Sam Eckersley
CLIENT: Personal project, later Nike
YEAR: 2012

FIVE

CLASSICS

ДАНИИЛ ХАРМС

ИЗБРАНИ
ПРОИЗВЕДЕНИЯ

ФАКЕЛ ЕКСПРЕС

TITLE: Daniil Kharms's 'Selected Works'
DESIGN FIRM/AGENCY: Kiril Zlatkov
ART DIRECTOR/DESIGNER: Kiril Zlatkov
PHOTOGRAPHER/ILLUSTRATOR: Kiril Zlatkov (public domain photos and graphics from various archives)
CLIENT: Fakel Express Publishing House
YEAR: 2014

KIRIL ZLATKOV
Daniil Kharms's 'Selected Works'

Kiril Zlatkov admires the work of Soviet-era Surrealist and Absurdist author Daniil Kharms, whose poetry and prose is less known in the West than that of his avant-garde contemporaries; the examples here are from the 1930s. Zlatkov was therefore thrilled when he was offered 'a once-in-a-lifetime chance to design a book by the author who helped shape my thinking', he says. 'Me and my schoolmates would memorize phrases from Kharms and use them to spice up our slang. It was considered the epitome of "cool" and is still in use.

'Apart from my personal experience, Kharms's works are a great primordial soup of raw imagination that can feed every person in need of something beyond the usual.'

Zlatkov says that he tried not to take 'the leading role' by letting his work overpower the author's writing, but rather 'played along with the author in a very fascinating, expressive game'. Design in general – typography and illustration – must respect the core ideas of the text, he notes. 'In this case, I tried to follow Kharms but contributed my own interventions, made with a wink to his rules. I think he would like that. Kharms's real life was governed by absurdity, just as ours is. I almost feel like his contemporary.'

The typography is designed to celebrate Kharms, and the typographic image is unusually diverse and expressive – yet remains consistent. Zlatkov used the Moderato type system by Iliya Gruev, an extensive family consisting of four different styles: Antiqua, Grotesk, Egyptienne and Grotesque, with serifs, and all equipped with special italics, carefully crafted small caps and three sets of figures, from Thin to Extra Black, all built on the principles and proportions of humanistic formulae. Zlatkov used the Antiqua for the prose, drama and notebooks, Grotesque for the poetry and Egyptienne for the judicial trial documents, because of its steady and serious appearance.

The page spreads that separate the parts of the book have a different typographic approach. Zlatkov mixed together two totally incongruous typefaces – Red October by Ivan Filipov and his own Trirema (Bold and Unicase). Red October is a Structuralism-influenced typeface, combining letterforms typical of the Russian and West European avant-garde movements from Kharms's cultural epoch. Trirema, on the other hand, is a multipurpose display typeface designed in the wood-type tradition of the late nineteenth and early twentieth century. The mixture of these typefaces stands for the conflict between the idea of new, radical exploration and down-to-earth-conformism, both speaking rather loudly. This clash of the real and the imaginative has deep roots in the Kharms works.

The main characters from Red October and Trirema were laser-cut from thick cardboard and used as old-fashioned printing blocks at home. The printouts, with their various pressures and textures, were then used in the composition of the headlines.

The art and design uses both gritty, textured images and text, and crisp images – a combination reminiscent of the early Futurist, Dadaist and Surrealist art that was practised at the time Kharms created his works. 'Mixing monochrome photography, type, prints and ink drawings gives the book richness and diversity,' says Zlatkov. 'Visual polyphony happens most of the time despite the artist's efforts to keep things clean. A Daniil Kharms collection must be something out of the ordinary by default. I think I just felt the reality of the author. My own surroundings helped a lot.'

It was no time before the children's books found themselves persecuted by adult ideas and under the landslide of such reality they lost their meaning. There were too many reasons, too many explanations and too much 'evidence' for such simple books to pretend they were fiction anymore.

Not all was lost for long, however. As is the way of children's books, they were quick to adapt, and the first one to do so was Snow White.

Snow White had become so fed up with the way her tale was turning out she left it altogether. Instead, she went on the rampage through all kinds of other literature from the Holy texts to joke books. In fact she didn't stop until she met 'Beauty and the Beast'. The beast was in such a state of distress that he had started to chew his dust jacket.

"Now listen to me beast," said Snow White. "Stop being a character in other stories and start explaining your way out of this".

The beast paused for a while and looked at the words around him. After a moment he began to do something he'd never done before. He began to arrange the words.

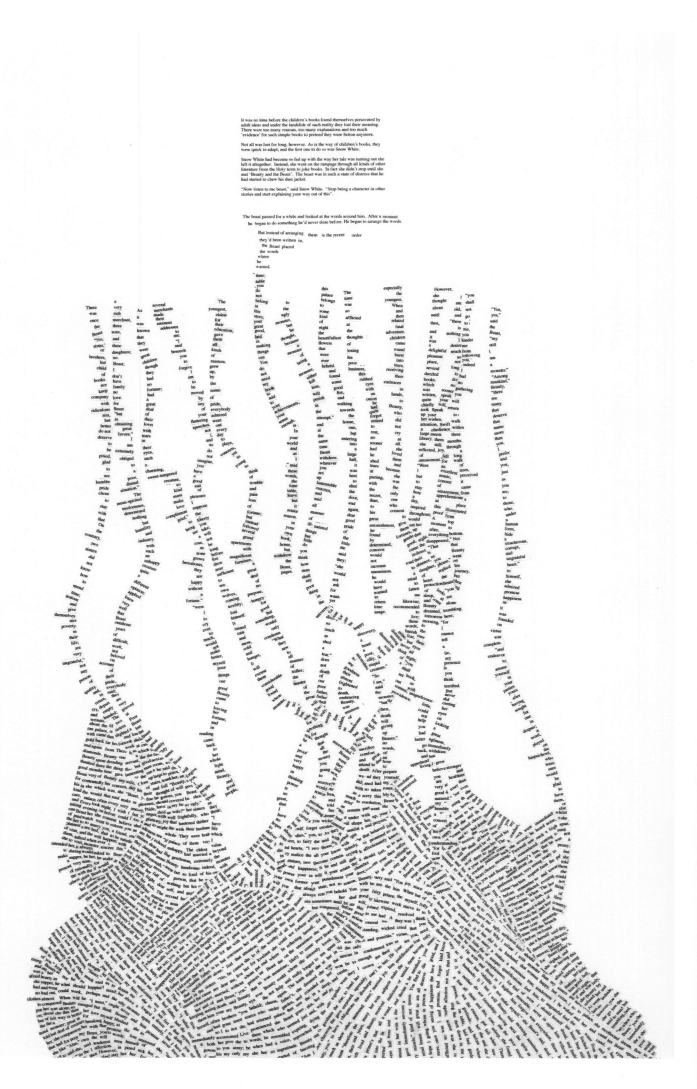

SAM WINSTON

a made up | true story

Romeo & Juliet

Exploring the emotional and symbolic importance of fairy tales for children, specifically around how these characteristics are delivered through narrative prose and typography, is the goal. 'I found one of the best ways to engage with this theme', Sam Winston explains, 'was to appropriate existing fairy tales.' Then, he re-formatted the text into very primitive data maps. 'This was done by hand-cut collaging the type and using additional texts to run alongside the original narrative.'

One of his examples is the arranging of each word alphabetically from 'Beauty and the Beast' to create rivers of text on the page. Another is including the encyclopaedic definitions in 'Jack and the Beanstalk' to suggest a mountain of type underneath the original story. 'With as much humour and playfulness as possible, I am trying to draw out the hidden narratives that are already buried in classic children's literature. By using visual design strategies and my own writing, I wanted to tease out the hidden moral and cultural patterns at the core of fairy tales,' Winston adds.

An excellent example in this project was composing the text of 'Snow White', where it 'meets the language of a tabloid newspaper'. By collaging together these found texts – the UK tabloid press ('the busty blond'/'love rat') with the pure and moralistic voice of 'Snow White' – he says, 'I think I created both a humorous and revealing narrative about both forms of literature.'

Winston calls his process 'embodied image making'; a type of learning that happens when 'you use your body to the point that it takes the lead and there is less conscious control over what picture is being produced. So the hand-cut/handmade mark-making and lettering became an expression of that.'

Winston's process is a continual evolution of some core themes – that every now and again will collapse into a book, exhibition or print. The challenge is defining which medium best serves it – creative writing, poetry, typography or drawing. 'I usually start in language – a written idea – and then watch it traverse into letterform and finally mark-making.'

OPPOSITE AND OVERLEAF

TITLE: *a made up | true story*
DESIGNER: Sam Winston
PUBLISHER: Circle Press
YEAR: 2005

RIGHT

TITLE: *Romeo & Juliet* (detail)
DESIGNER: Sam Winston
YEARS: 2007–2011

Snow White then spoke to Jack. As he listened he realised a way in which he could explain things to both himself and his unwanted guest.

He began using the encyclopedias own language against itself. Every face, used and rule made, was turned upon and done to one. He expressed things that couldn't exist, simply and truly, allowing for chaos to be nonsense. He created something the encyclopedia couldn't explain.

Snow White reluctantly returned to the newspaper.

"Could I speak to you please?" *said the brainy bombshell.*
"I need to explain about myself. I am not news and you don't need to report
me. I am just a character in a story that is meant for children. A metaphor,
so to speak, that helps the young cope with the adult world."

There was a pause. The newspaper seemed to think for a second.
Secrets of children's tales exclusively revealed by blonde boffin! it said.

Snow White sat down and thought some more.

"I am tired of listening to you, newspaper, now listen to me. You and I are
also part of another story - a tale about different books meeting each other.
You can't talk your way out of it or sensationalise your way around it - you
belong to something called *a made-up | true story.*

Now you could report about this a book. You see, newspaper, to truly
understand what this is about, you will have to admit your part of
its fiction. If you stop giving it names the story will end."

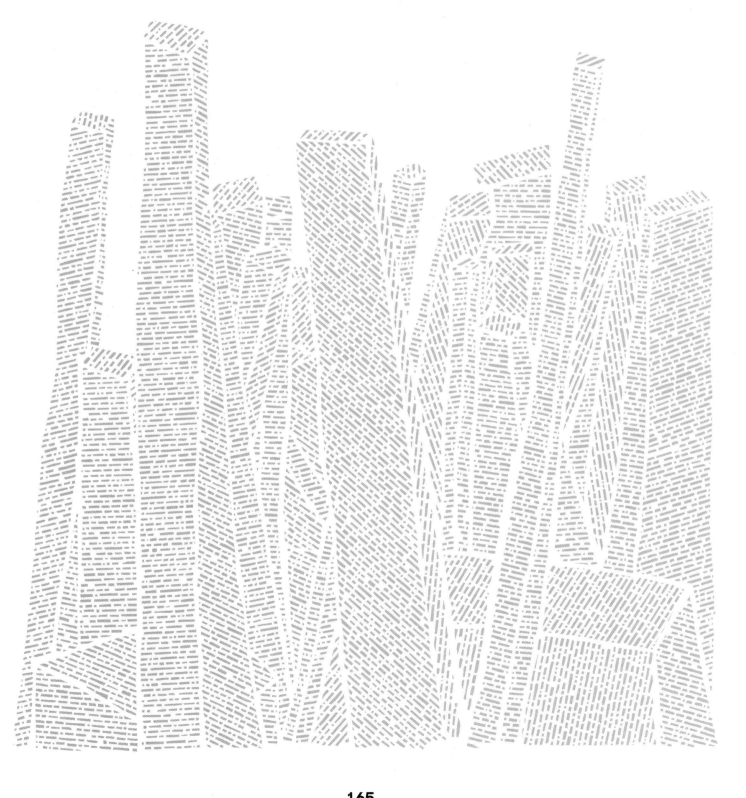

DAMIÁN SENA
Manuel Puig – *Entre el cine y la escritura*

Damián Sena admits that behind this book there is a desire to meet Manuel Puig, the writer, and to try to show how his character translates typographically. 'Through his texts and the way he moves we can begin to talk about different visual languages.' Sena's motivation is to be able to build a typographic universe, parallel to the universe of the author; his identity, his beliefs and his ideas.

'I'm telling the story of Puig's life,' Sena adds. 'What he has been through, moments, countries, feelings, repression, love affairs, sadness, his secrets, his colours, how was he, his work … that in some way is what identifies him the most. There are

some parts of his books in my typographic book and they set a bunch of different resources that shows through design and typography. Puig has a story full of taboo, repression, back and forth, dark and light, success and failure. This contrast is what makes this different: colours and rhythms live together through the typographic game during the entire journey of the book.'

Sena insists that the typography speaks for itself. 'It has a different way of telling things' and allows the transmission of feelings to the reader. 'The morphology of the letter places us in a context, provides us [with] memories, places, regions. It makes us connect [with] what we are telling in an immediate way.'

TITLE: Manuel Puig – *Entre el cine y la escritura*
DESIGN FIRM/AGENCY: Damián Sena
ART DIRECTOR/DESIGNER: Damián Sena
YEAR: 2015

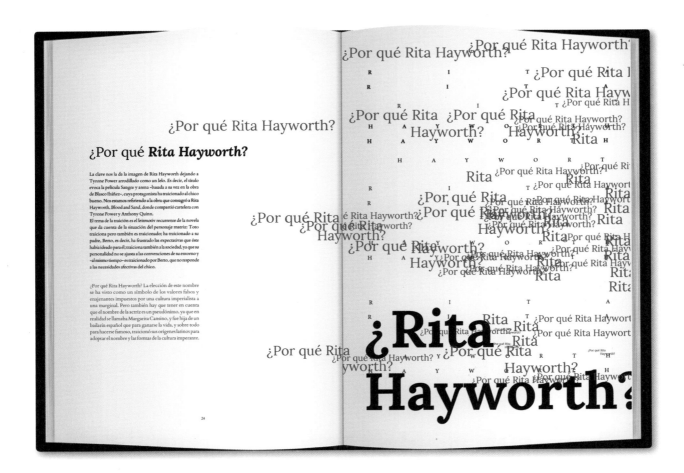

TITLE: 'The Tell-Tale Heart' by Edgar Allan Poe
ART DIRECTORS: Lorena Leonhardt
and Hermes Mazali
DESIGNER/PHOTOGRAPHER/ILLUSTRATOR:
Hermes Mazali
YEAR: 2013

HERMES MAZALI

'The Tell-Tale Heart' by Edgar Allan Poe

'The Tell-Tale Heart' by Edgar Allan Poe is a story of paranoia and murder. Hermes Mazali selected a fragment of this classic tale, and illustrated it using typographic lettering to move the narrative along. In his analysis of Poe's famous story, Mazali drew inspiration from the nervous behaviour suffered by the narrator. The protagonist is a murderer who is obsessed with his crime; his guilt leads him to confess to the police.

Order and chaos inspired Mazali, and they recur in all of his work. 'I think there is an infinite and constant struggle between opposites,' he says. 'In this case I decided to tackle the chaos as primordial concept. The protagonist of "The Tell-Tale Heart" is depressed, lonely, crazy, desperate and paranoid. So I decided to make a typeface that reflects these concepts.'

His choice of hand-drawn lettering was to select a typeface based on the anatomy of the human body, and how it best communicates the murder. 'This typeface begins to evolve the story when the tension increases,' he notes. 'I try to reflect the obsession of the narrator and his need to confess.'

To maintain consistency with the story, Mazali adapted the typography as the tension of the story increased. Whenever the reader turns the pages emotion mounts and lettering generates a visual chaos.

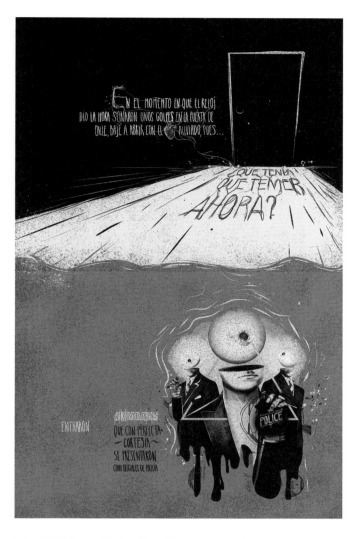

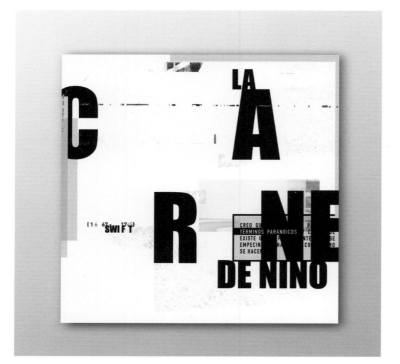

TITLE: *La carne de niño*
DESIGNER: Pilar González Bergez
YEAR: 2015

PILAR GONZÁLEZ BERGEZ
La carne de niño

The main text of *La carne de niño* is an analysis of the satirical essay 'A modest proposal', written by Jonathan Swift in 1792. The second text is a reinterpretation of Swift's work by contemporary Argentinian author Marcos Bertorello. Throughout the book, these two voices are displayed using the colour and type style chosen to represent each author. The first author is presented as a psychopath who proposes a ridiculous solution to poverty, while the Bertorello text addresses the Swift psychosis.

The typography defines the structure of the whole book, and the two voices are present throughout the piece. 'For the text of the first author I chose typography more related to chaos and [the] lack of boundaries associated with psychosis,' says Bergez. 'I propose a use of typographic variables, the breaking of grids and structure and fonts pasted to represent voices shouting and the dichotomy of being a psychopath. The use of different font sizes not only demonstrates the psychosis but also adds reading levels to the narrative proposal.'

For the Bertorello text, he says, 'I decided to present it as an organized character, which emphasizes what is going to speak (01, 02, 03) and highlights in yellow the interpretation he provides for the Swift. It raises his themes in an index usually on the left side of the page and then explains his theories in a whole page [of] full colour. It exposes his theories in an organized and controlled manner by using a grid and a clear structure and typography.'

The colour chosen for each 'character' defines the two voices talking across all the editorial. The reduced palette reveals the difference between the two authors: one is represented by black and grey tones generated by the typographical chaos, and the other author is recognized by the structural order and the use of yellow highlighting – showing his obsessive control.

SIX

TYPO PLAY

TITLE: *Depero: Futurista 1913–1927*
DESIGNER: Fortunato Depero
PUBLISHER: Dinamo-Azari
YEAR: 1927

FORTUNATO DEPERO
Depero: Futurista 1913–1927

At the age of twenty-four, Fortunato Depero was artistically formed, with a distinct stylistic personality that also constituted a more playful side of the Futurist movement. Much of Depero's design prefigures today's postmodern and new-wave eclecticism in its form and colour.

Depero was an indefatigable proponent of Futurism. He wrote for newspapers, founded and directed the machine art magazine *Dinamo*, organized personal exhibitions, and worked in the theatre as a set and costume designer. He was commissioned by Sergei Diaghilev to make a set and costumes for *Le Chant du Rossignol*. He invented an 'onomalanguage'; a free-word, free-sounding, expressive verbal rigmarole. He represented the Futurists at the 1925 Paris exhibition of modern decorative and industrial art, exhibiting his life-sized mechanical men. He decorated cabarets, bars, restaurants and dance halls. With his wife Rosetta, he opened the Casa d'Arte Futurista in Rovereto, Italy, where he made wooden constructions, furniture and costumes for a mass clientele. He also designed Futurist clothing, vests and jackets.

During the 1920s the 'book-object' was seriously practised as a Futurist art form – the marriage of ad-hoc layout and typographical experimentation. For the 1927 Biennale internazionale delle arti decorative in Monza, Italy, Depero designed a book pavilion built entirely out of giant block letters. It was a grand architectural achievement, but not as historically important as his bolted art catalogue, which, along with Tullio d'Albisola's famous tin book *Futurist Words Set Free: Tactile Thermal Olfactory*, is emblematic of Futurist applied arts.

Depero: Futurista, as it was called, reproduced in letterpress and bound in machine-age fashion by two stainless steel bolts, is a compendium of Depero's own design work (including many advertisements he had designed for Campari) covering the years from 1913 to 1927.

Depero was predisposed to an 'Aztec deco' sensibility that was influenced by set-back skyscrapers, and his use of bright colours and collaged coloured papers was startling. His synthesis of dynamic and expressionistic graphic forms was undeniably original. He reconciled craft and fine and applied arts and, believing that product advertising was the means to stimulate a dialogue with the public, he took on commissions in Italy, including a highly visible series for Campari. In the 1932 manifesto 'The Art of Advertising' Depero announced that 'The art of the future will be powerfully advertising art.' And he continued that 'All last centuries [*sic*] art was advertising oriented.'

He would only work for clients who gave him licence. With such assignments he deliberately used the product as the source of his own iconography, inspiring, he believed, 'a new pictorial taste for the image'.

TITLE: *Depero: Futurista 1913–1927*
DESIGNER: Fortunato Depero
PUBLISHER: Dinamo-Azari
YEAR: 1927

l'onomalingua

VERBALIZZAZIONE ASTRATTA

CREAZIONE DEPERO - 1916

E' derivata dall'onomatopea, dal rumorismo, dalla brutalità delle parole in libertà, futuriste. E' il linguaggio delle forze naturali:

vento · pioggia · mare fiume · ruscello · ecc.

degli esseri artificiali rumoreggianti creati dagli uomini:

Biciclette, tram, treni, automobili e tutte le macchine,

è l'assieme delle emozioni e delle sensazioni espresso con il linguaggio più rudimentale e più efficace. Depero creò e declamò queste sue originali composizioni davanti a folle entusiaste ed ostili. Nei monologhi dei clonws e dei comici di varietà vi sono tipici accenni all'onomalingua che avranno futuri sviluppi, costituendo la lingua più indovinata per la scena e specialmente per le esagerazioni esilaranti. Con l'onomalingua si può parlare ed intendersi efficacemente con gli elementi dell'universo, con gli animali e con le macchine. L'onomalingua è un linguaggio poetico di comprensione universale per il quale non sono necessari traduttori.

217

MANIFESTO AGLI INDUSTRIALI

deciso di fondere i due progetti e modificarli, cioè di renderli pratici e prontamente eseguibili. Tale attuazione è precisamente la

ARCHITETTURA PUBBLICITARIA.

Abbiamo fiere campionarie ogni mese, in ogni città; Esposizioni regionali, nazionali, mondiali. Esse, esclusa quella di Parigi del 1925, sono terribilmente passatiste, la loro presentazione architettonica è semplicemente

RIDICOLA.

Egregi ed arditi industriali, sembra a voi possibile esporre le vostre materie e prodotti moderni: automobili, aereoplani, motocicli, ecc... in palazzi greco-romani, barocchi o „liberty"? Allora per essere coerenti dovreste presentare macchine e strumenti con ovuli o greche, e motori con capitelli corinti e bizantini. Dunque i vostri palazzi, i padiglioni, i chioschi delle **Fiere** e delle **Esposizioni**, devono essere nuove, meravigliose architetture ultra-moderne-futuriste-colorate-macchinarie-mobili-luminose; in perfetta armonia con il contenuto. Il pittore e scultore futurista **DEPERO** oggi è l'architetto che vi presenta il mezzo per maggiormente gnità d'arte veramente moderna..... Una delle maggiori manifestazioni del

dicare e affermare il vero nostro stile. Gli architetti passatisti costruiscono con la loro ingombrante ed inutile sapienza scolastica, goffi edifici, con i più anacronistici e balordi arrangiamenti e pasticci di pseudo-antico. I geniali ingegneri e costruttori, con i loro audaci ponti, centrali elettriche, opifici, vi hanno dato architetture moderne, mondo da ogni sussidio tradizionale e noi, con il loro preziosissimo ausilio tecnico sbalordiremo il mondo e vi daremo la

SUPER-ATTRAZIONE ARCHITETTONICA. IN VOI HO LA PIENA E MASSIMA FIDUCIA.

„CARTELLONE"

„CARTELLO" ha grande importanza mente gli si attribuisce. Io paragono dei secoli scorsi; voi industriali siete volta, i nostri autentici mecenati. non solo l'immagine sacra dei vo tello, ma anche il Tempio, il Padi

l'arte pubblicitaria è senza dubbio il Ebbene il trionfo di esso è dovuto solamente agli industriali. Per me il za, superiore a quella che solita il cartellone al **QUADRO SACRO** te i nostri vescovi e papi d'una **CARISSIMI INDUSTRIALI:** stri prodotti vi faremo, cioè il carglione, per contenerli degnamente.

Palazzi e padiglioni dove TRIONFERA' lo stile dell'acciaio, lo stile del CRISTALLO, lo stile della MACCHINA.

Padiglioni di luce, di cristallo, di metalli, di stoffe, ispirati a liquori, penne, pompe, frutta, fiori, bottiglie, ecc.. Duomi colorati di matite gigantesche, chioschi dentati, seghettati, a spirale, a trivello, per specialità meccaniche. Padiglione rosa e arancio fatto

a corolle e calici per il famoso

BITTER-   **CAMPARI**

Palazzo lucente con corridoi e sale rapidissime, da visitarsi entro siluri GRANDI CASE automobilistiche Padiglioni a Trombe-parlanti e Se il grandioso sforzo di Parigi del

si può fare di più -

E saremo finalmente lieti, raggianti,

obblique dai pavimenti curvi a svolte colorati velocissimi; degno delle **FIAT - ALFA-ROMEO** suonanti per case di fonografi ecc. 1925 fu superbo, vi garantisco che

molto e molto di più.

se con il vostro aiuto potremo in-

85

TO   **DA**

qualità di questo grande Pittore
imo incontro nello studio di Balla,
da sè stesso nel famoso quadro
i splendidi di nuovo rosa, sotto i
verde, ritto davanti alle sue ope-
i il piacere sette anni fa, di ri-
lismo al pubblico milanese che
ritto e aureolato dagli splendori
llissimo passatista che tentò di
u da me acciuffato e proiettato
Magica" di Depero. Il passatista

gi: Le maggiori riviste di Fran-
zzi Deperiani. Martinie in „Art
tes ces raisons expliquent aussi
s futuristes qui ne prennent tout
On sait que des avant la guerre
ait une action violente en vue de
ns tous les domaines de l'esprit.
simultaneisme devaient enfanter
tement nouvelles . . L'esthe-
domaine décoratif évolua paral-

novatrice. Des artistes comme
posent des affiches, tapis, étof-
pisserie, etc. . . . . . qui retien-
procédés de composition que
s. Des groupes de bois decoupé
ation et font penser à des jouets
s maquettes et accessoires du
sent les projets du Théâtre fu-
nell' „Illustration": „La présen-
dante: des panneaux, de tapis,
ux, des livres, des dessins, des

groupes en bois. Tout est
sans éloquence. La synth
toujours pittoresque. Des
détonnent, étonnent, puis s
évidente jaillit de formes
pousse d'abord comme obs
lien a des trouvailles. U
vention. Voulez-vous des
Depero et ses mosaiques d'
polini et ses panneaux origi
Franki scrive nella rivista,
position de l'Art d'aujourd'
Depero, et il faudrait que
ignorance pour ne pas conna
cet artiste multiple a sur le
apôtre de la Modernolatrie a
ment saisi ce rythme prop
raine et dégage de son ap
canique de nos jours. C
tout particulièrement, c'est l
son oeuvre (voir notamme
des Arts Décoratifs — la v
mati ecc.) où il semble que
l'ait projété au de lá de lui
tation creatrice de ses v
peintre, decorateur, organi
vré tout entier aux forces
mais c'est pour mieux les p
magiques fantaisies de sa
une énergie indomtable, plus
qui le dépasse et qui, intaris
ce d'un jeune Dieu opérant
L'influence de Depero sur
est et sera considérable.
qu'il offre a leur amuse
voluptueux de vitesse et d'
les rares divertissements

Italiani, vi cons
e glorificare i ca
stici di questo
stro italiano or

MARINETTI

Rien n'est
bitraire mais
ges de couleurs
  Une psychologie
   inexperimenté re-
 theâtre futuriste ita-
 existe dans son in-
alla et ses tapisseries;
ieuses plaisantes; Pram-
ureux, ingénieux". Serge
tes d'Aujourd'hui": L'ex-
nous a revélé Fortunato
nous soyons d'une grande
 tre l'action décisive que
nouvement futuriste. Cet
t être le plus parfaite-
 sensibilité contempo-
netallique la vie mé-
 arait le distinguer
 apocalyptique de
atori-macchina
avalieri piu-
 joyeuse
une exal-
Sculpteur,
pero s'est li-
il à déchaînées,
 leur imposer les
litè. Il est en lui
apide que le temps et
sablement crée, for-
une nouvelle genèse.
les jeunes d'aujourd'hui
C'est un monde tout neuf
ment. Puissent leurs jeux
audace égaler en qualité
de leur fabuleux maître".

glio di amare
polavori pla-
grande mae-
mai mondiale

F.T. MARINETTI

CORITA KENT
Damn Everything But The Circus

Few artist-designers represent the graphic joy and chromatic vibrancy of the 1960s art ethos more than Sister Corita Kent, whose prints were ubiquitous in books, magazines and even on a large gas tank on the outskirts of Boston. Known for co-mingling expressive lettering with colour and shapes, her inspirational messages filled the eye with hope and optimism. This series of serigraphs in *Damn Everything But The Circus* was created in 1968 when she was on a sabbatical, during which time she decided to relinquish her position at Immaculate Heart College and was released from her vows.

These images were in part influenced by Kent's colleague and mentor, Sister Magdalen Mary, who amassed a huge collection of folk art for the college, called the Gloria Collection. The vintage cuts came from the collection, which was also meant to inspire students and their work – it was felt that the vernacular would be more accessible to them than other types of 'higher' art. Kent and 'Maggie' collected pieces together while on their travels in the US and abroad. In the late 1950s, they visited the Ringling Museum in Sarasota, Florida, the winter home of the Ringling Brothers and Barnum and Bailey

Circus. The influence of this trip can be seen in this series of serigraphs.

The serigraphs also typify Kent's signature style of juxtaposing text and images to create specific messages, though the messages themselves vary. 'B beauty you' includes prose from Lord Buckley about the beauty of the reader, and how it arms him or her with a turn-of-the-century woman that could be an advertisement or illustration. 'E eye love' has focused on the same style of illustration but this time one element, an eye, is at the forefront in the work, and Kent's own hand represents the Camus quote: '... should like to be able to love my country and still love justice'.

Here the eye stands in as a pictogram for 'I'. Taken collectively, some works are fanciful, and some serious, echoing elements of a circus itself. Kent's use of typography was unique; the 'physical manipulation of text was ahead of its time'. The way she incorporated a Pop Art aesthetic to convey a spiritual message was in marked contrast with other Pop artists. The combination of high/low, advertising or sign images and text, and her own handwriting also set her apart from her peers.

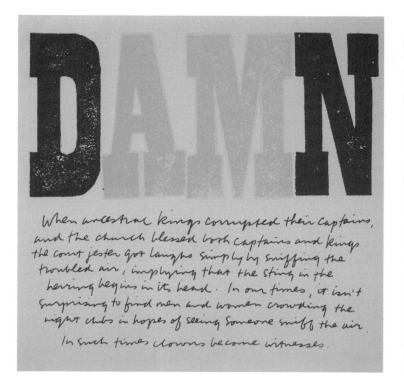

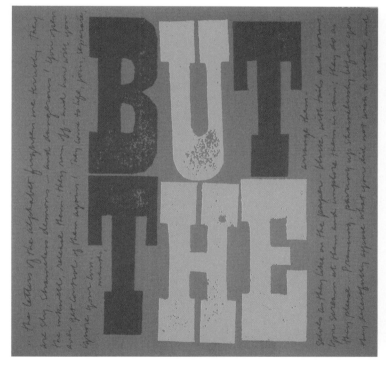

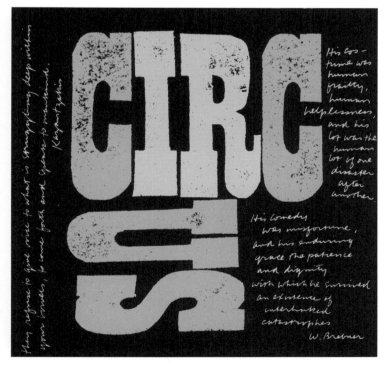

TITLE: *Damn Everything But The Circus*
DESIGNER: Corita Kent
YEAR: 1968

TITLE: 'B Beauty You' in *Damn Everything But The Circus*
DESIGNER: Corita Kent
YEAR: 1968

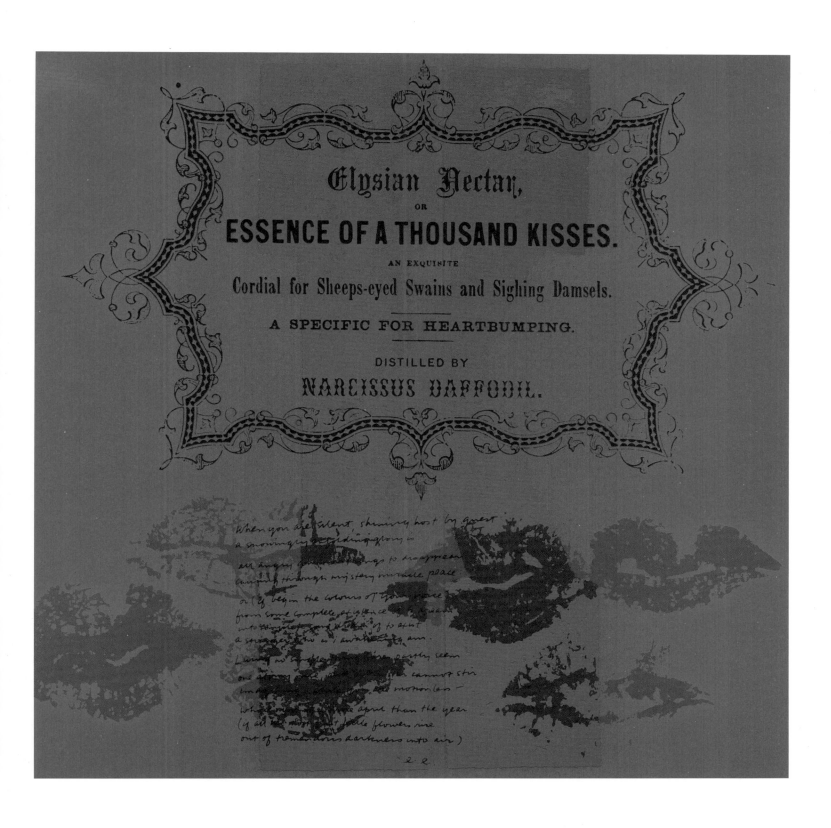

TITLE: 'K Kiss' in *Damn Everything But The Circus*
DESIGNER: Corita Kent
YEAR: 1968

TITLE: *I Wonder*
DESIGNER/AUTHOR: Marian Bantjes
PUBLISHER: Thames & Hudson
YEAR: 2010

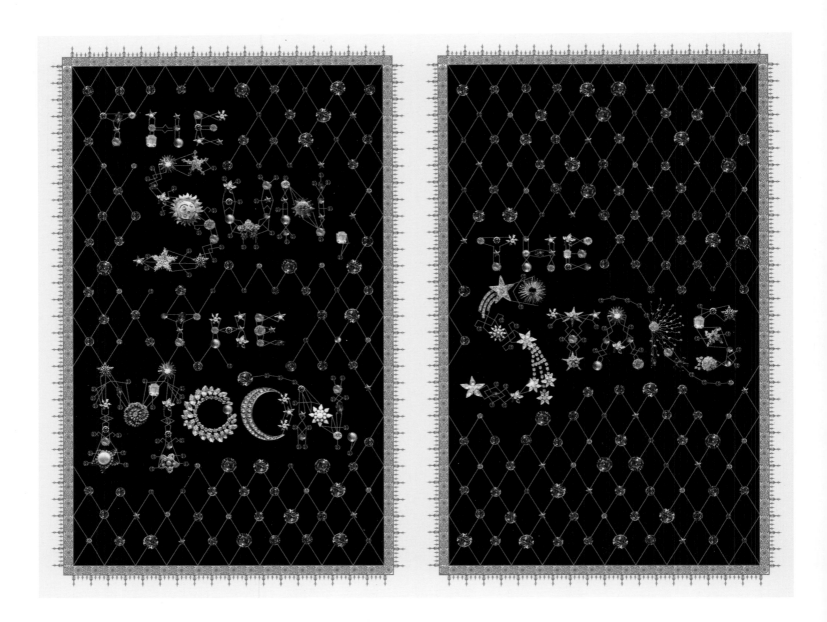

MARIAN BANTJES
I Wonder

Canadian designer and letterer Marian Bantjes conceived a series of essays loosely themed around the idea of 'wonder', when she had a flash of inspiration. 'I determined that the book should BE a work of wonder,' she says, rather than just writing a title and talking about it. 'I wanted a book that showed a symbiosis between text and image, where the two were intertwined and neither was complete without the other.'

I Wonder brings together many textual and typographical elements. 'I'm telling many stories, some serious and true, some tongue-in-cheek but still true, and some works of fantasy.

'I am not one to decorate Helvetica,' she proudly exclaims. 'I like to take typography to its limit, to use it as a whole image. I also like to bend, or break, the rules of typesetting, and to use typography to instil heaps of character into the words, without resorting to distracting changes in size (or what I call "jumping type").' With this in mind *I Wonder* is decorative, intricate and everything but minimalist.

112

113

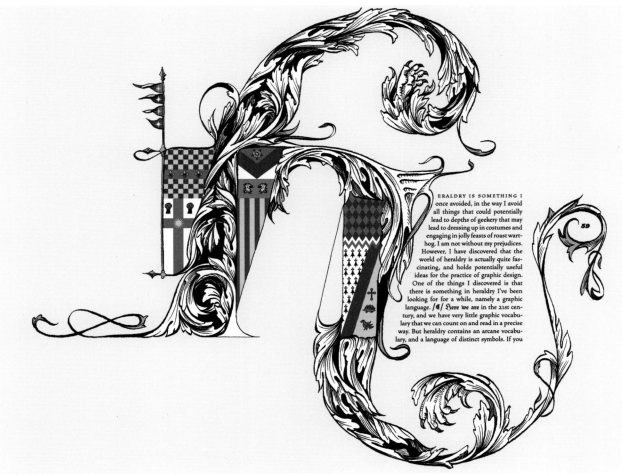

ERALDRY IS SOMETHING I
once avoided, in the way I avoid
all things that could potentially
lead to depths of geekery that may
lead to dressing up in costumes and
engaging in jolly feasts of roast wart-
hog. I am not without my prejudices.
However, I have discovered that the
world of heraldry is actually quite fascinating, and holds potentially useful
ideas for the practice of graphic design.
One of the things I discovered is that
there is something in heraldry I've been
looking for for a while, namely a graphic
language. / ❡ / Here we are in the 21st century, and we have very little graphic vocabu-
lary that we can count on and read in a precise
way. But heraldry contains an arcane vocabu-
lary, and a language of distinct symbols. If you

59

183

PHILIPPA WOOD
The Last

The Last sets out to explore how applying a series of hierarchical systems to the typographic content can affect the visual appearance of the page. 'Would adherence to a set of mandatory rules to develop the content (and form) of the book mean compromise, and would creative control be affected?' Philippa Wood asks rhetorically. The content was generated from responses to a questionnaire based on 'What was the last ...' time you told a lie/thing you bought/object you desired, etc. There was a realization that when the content was taken out of context 'it appeared to be a series of disjointed, abstract and unrelated phrases that enabled the viewer to form their own decisions when regarding the juxtaposed statements'.

Some initial factors dictated and determined the book's size and form, notably the flatbed dimensions of the printing presses – an etching press and a Farley proofing press – and the size of the available wood type. 'These restrictions meant that some of the initial design decisions were pre-ordained,' explains the aptly named Ms Wood.

Working with the text matter and applying a series of pre-determined rules to the type meant that each page evolved naturally as part of a system, as opposed to a planned outcome, Wood says, explaining that these processes 'proved an

effective working strategy for book production; the adoption of these strategies led to the willing submission of control, as all decision making in terms of the visual appearance was surrendered. However, rather than the rules acting as a restriction, they gave the book a purpose, and ultimately both the system and the print processes dictated the visual appearance of the work.'

Wood works with traditional and analogue letterpress, print-making techniques and typewriters, often combining several techniques in one piece of work. 'As a graphic design student I was taught the rules of typography – legibility, readability and how to work with grids, hierarchy, etc. However, my current practice is based more within the discipline of fine art, and this enables any typographic treatment to be more intuitive – working directly on the print bed, for example. I now use type in a more abstract way – rather than it necessarily communicating a clear message.'

The visual outcome of Wood's work is determined by a particular range of wood type, which isn't vast – and by an even more limited range of metal type. But she says she would rather have the restricted choices that her type drawers have to offer than the plethora of digital type available.

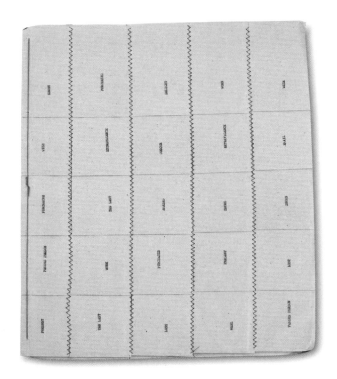

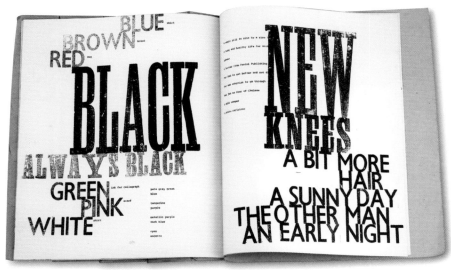

TITLE: *The Last*
DESIGN FIRM/AGENCY: The Caseroom Press
DESIGNER: Philippa Wood
YEAR: 2008

<u>**TITLE:**</u> *¿Me acompañas?*
<u>**DESIGN FIRM/AGENCY:**</u> Cyla Costa Studio
<u>**DESIGNERS:**</u> Cyla Costa, Esther Maré and
Maria Carvalho
<u>**YEAR:**</u> 2008

CYLA COSTA
¿Me acompañas?

¿Me acompañas? is a fanzine created in 2008 by Cyla Costa for Martin Lorenz's workshop 'Libros como churros' as part of the Master's programme in Editorial Design at ELISAVA, the Barcelona School of Design and Engineering. The inspiration was Costa's own life in Barcelona, and the impressions made on the artist by the city – both good and bad. It was made completely manually, without computers – just using collage, a Xerox machine, stickers and flyers about Barcelona cultural events.

The book is a loop that can read upside down: the end is the beginning and the middle closes the circle. The theme is Barcelona's huge cultural offering, and how it can often wear you out and paralyse you.

'I always try to use different forms of lettering,' says Costa, 'like collage in this case.' At the time of this project she was just beginning to work with type and lettering, so it was an important experiment for her. 'Lettering is my favourite way of communicating, and it shows in most of my work nowadays,' she adds.

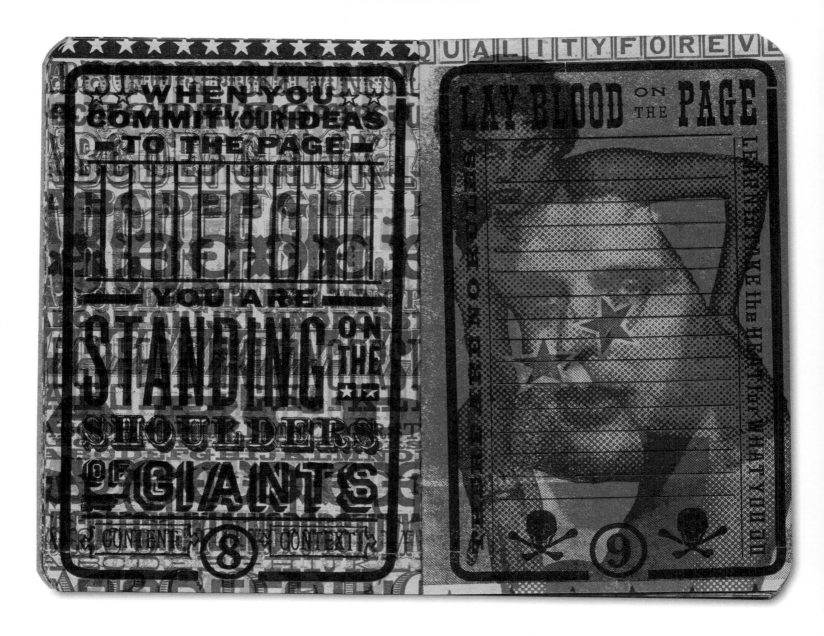

CHURCH OF TYPE
The Typography Codex

The Typography Codex came about because Kevin Bradley, of the Church of Type, saved scrap paper from a previous job and didn't want to throw it away. He also has over 1,700 examples of movable type in his collection, from 4pt to three feet tall: 'I've had my hands on all of them, over the years. Controlled chaos is my mantra.' In addition, a huge personal archive of small type and images are just collecting dust, so this project became a way to share them.

Bradley's entire creative practice has been explicitly tied to the use of original letterpress typography, except when he draws and carves the type into woodblocks: 'I keep the computer far away.'

'The *Codex*,' he explains, was a way to 'get off the grid of the letterpress format' and explore the use of typography as symbol; mark and metaphor 'provide a playground for me to explore relationships of the letter form in a completely different approach to the meaning of the letter form and the communication that ensues, either real or implied'.

The book itself is something of an insider joke. Or, as he says, 'an age-old story of love, lust, magic and betrayal combined with passion and elbow grease and a message of home to us poor suckers who live with deadlines and clients'.

For over twenty-five years Bradley has maintained a very prolific output. 'I produce everything by hand and offer the world something beautiful and authentic, in a time where very few things are real,' he says. 'I know how to letter-space, and I kern with a power saw! It pleases me no end that I work on the same playing field as my heroes. Creatively, I have had a very unique existence, but I've had to work very hard.'

TITLE: *The Typography Codex*
DESIGN FIRM/AGENCY: Church of Type
DESIGNER: Kevin Bradley
YEAR: 2015

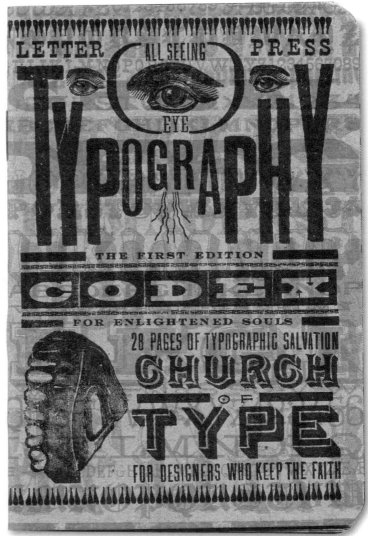

TITLE: *Justification Posters*
DESIGNER: Wael Morcos
YEAR: 2011

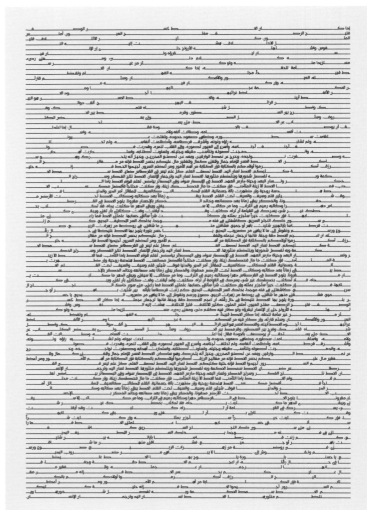

WAEL MORCOS
Justification Posters

These posters are explorations of expression through Arabic typography. The two posters use the typeface Kufam Arabic to push the concept of justification, and they question readability, texture and figure/ground relationships. Kashida, also called Tatweel, is a type of justification used in the cursive connected Arabic script. In contrast to the Latin white-space justification (which increases the length of a line of text by expanding spaces between words or individual letters), kashida justification is accomplished by horizontally elongating connections between characters at certain chosen points.

The content is a collection of statements and aphorisms relating to the aesthetic of the Arabic letterform. In this sense the narrative is reflexive.

Using the baseline elongations to create formal affectations within Arabic text is not new practice. Calligraphers have long used it to add emphasis to titles, modulate the speed of reading or the word emphasis, and to shape the line of text.

Perhaps what's unique here are two things: the conceptual purpose of the piece and the typeface choice of Kufam. In fact, Kufam is the result of the collaboration between Dutch type designer Artur Schmal, and Wael Morcos. The Arabic is inspired by early Kufi inscriptions (from the seventh century) while the Latin forms are inspired by Dutch urban lettering from the 1920s.

The scale of the posters plays a critical role in how they are viewed in contrast to how they are read. 'From afar one sees a letter forming in the centre of each poster,' Morcos says. 'In one poster the letter "waw", the twenty-seventh letter of the Arabic alphabet, is formed by the accumulation of letters in the middle. In the other poster the shape of the letter "kha", the seventh letter of the Arabic alphabet, is suggested by the absence of letters or by the horizontal lines stretching across the poster.' Meanwhile up close, the reading experience is meant to amplify the back and forth movement of the eye as it scans the poster looking for the next letter to form a word, and then a sentence.

إذا كان الخط كسر الوصف، فليح الرصف، مفتح العيون، أملس المتون، كثير الائتلاف، قليل الاختلاف، هشت إليه النفوس، واشتهته الأرواح حتى إن الإنسان ليقرؤه ولو كان فيه كلام دني، ومعنى ردي، ومستزيدا منه ولو كثر من غير سأمة تلحقه. إذا كان الخط قبيحاً، مجته الفهام ولفظته العيون والأفكار، وسلم قارئه، وإن كان فيه من الحكمة عجائبها ومن الألفاظ غرائبها. أجود الخط أبينه، وأحسن الحسن هو البير الرائق البهيج. ألق دواتك، واصل شباه قلمك، وفرق بين السطور، وقرمط بين الحروف. وسأل الصولي بعض الكتّاب عن الخط: متى يستحق أن يوصف بالجودة فقال: إذا اعتدلت أقسامه، وطالت ألفه ولامه، واستقامت سطوره، وصفى صعود حدوده، وتفتحت عيونه، ولم تشتبه راؤه ونونه، وأشرقت قرطاسه، وأظلمت أنفاسه، ولم تختلف أجناسه، وأسرع إلى العيون تصوره، وإلى القلب تنمره، وتناسب أصوله وتناسب فصوله، وتحمجت أصوله وجليلا، وتساوت أطنابه، واستدارت أهدابه، واستدارت أطنابه، وكخرج عن نمط الوارقين، وخيل أنه يتحرك وهو ساكن. الخط الحسن للإمام جمال وللفقير مال، عليكم بحسن الخط فإنه من مفاتيح الرزق. أكرموا أولادكم بالكتابة فإن الكتابة من أهم الأمور ومن أعظم السرور. أجيدوا الخط فإنه حلية كتبكم. الخط نصف العلم، كل علم ليس في القرطاس ضاع. الخط سمط الحكمة وبه تفصل شذورها وينتظم منثورها. الخط لسان اليد وسراج الذكر ولسان البعد وحياة حارس العهد. الخط في الإبصار سواد وفي البصائر بياض. تعلم قوام الخط إذا التأدب، فما الخط إلا زينة المتأدب، فإن كنت خا مال فخطك زينة، وإن كنت محتاجاً فأفضل مكسب. الخط هندسة روحية وإن ظهرت بآلة جسمانية. القلم للحكّاب كالسيف للمقاتل. أمر الحير والدنيا فوق شيئين قلم وسيف والسيف تحت القلم. الخط يبقى زماناً بعد كاتبه والذكر يبقى زمانا بعد صاحبه وخالد الذكر بالإحسان مقروناً. بلوج الخط في القرطاس دهرا وكاتبه رميم في التراب. وما من كاتب إلا سيفنى ويبقى الدهر ما كتبت، يداه، فلا تكتب بخطك غير شيء، يسرك في القيامة أر تراه. كتبت، وقد أيقنت بأن تفنى ويبقى كتابها، فإن كتبت، خيراً ساجزى بمثله وإن كتبت، شراً سألقى حسابها.

OPPOSITE, TOP LEFT AND BOTTOM RIGHT

TITLE: *Second Glance*
DESIGNER: Ebon Heath
PHOTOGRAPHER: Max Merz
YEAR: 2013

OPPOSITE, TOP RIGHT

TITLE: *Aku*
DESIGNER: Ebon Heath
PHOTOGRAPHER: Max Merz
YEAR: 2010

OPPOSITE, BOTTOM LEFT

TITLE: 'Push Me' chandelier
DESIGNER: Ebon Heath
PHOTOGRAPHER: Max Merz
CLIENT: Villeroy & Back
YEAR: 2012

EBON HEATH
Second Glance
Aku
'Push Me' chandelier

The typographic chandelier entitled 'Push Me' is inspired by the poetry found in the lyrics of 'The Message' by Grandmaster Flash and the Furious Five. It is an edition of twenty, hand crafted to order.

Each is made of laser-cut maple-wood veneer, individually assembled, numbered and signed. Three short films accompany the structure, with original sound design by Stimulus and Aybee (Deepblak).

Ebon Heath makes typographic sculpture because, he says, 'words are trapped by the page, or the screen, like butterflies with their wings pinned'. He has built a design philosophy based on how words are used every day, 'but rarely do we stop and look at the small details that make up their forms'.

If letters could jump off the page they would dance and scream the content that their author wanted them to have – just as a musician writes notes for a specific melody, a coder writes characters for a specific piece of software, or a graffiti writer signs their name with the uniqueness of a snowflake. 'When I was younger I could see the words dance when I closed my eyes and listened to hip-hop or jazz as almost experiencing synaesthesia [like tasting shapes or hearing colours]. Since my commercial clients were not asking these questions of me as a graphic designer, I decided to become my own client and write my own brief.'

Heath fused the forms of 'our typographic language with the physicality of our body language'. The process to solve this question began with countless drawings, research, and model making to find a method (without any expectations) of visualizing this concept. Along the path to this goal the typographic studies had their own finite qualities separated from the body. His type is visual music that forces the viewer to listen with their eyes.

'Creating visual rhythms found in the patterns of letters is a large component of what dictates the forms of my sculptural work,' he explains. 'I have a growing set of architectural grids [based on simple three-dimensional shapes like the cone, spiral or stripe] that I can use as a foundation for building type.' The letters dictate most of the aesthetic choices. 'It is the construction and assembly of all the specific characters combined that creates the collective form. The content of each piece informs many of my choices in its construction method, materials, scale, structure, colour, movement and light.'

Heath's fascination with letters came from admiring his parents' jazz record covers and the beautiful encoded intricacies of graffiti culture, to the massive glowing billboards of Times Square that lined the walls of his childhood in New York City. From his experience as an art director, 'I started to consider the page as a window looking into three-dimensional space,' he says. 'Once letters become liberated from the page (or screen) they can dance in space to have a more dynamic relationship to their content.'

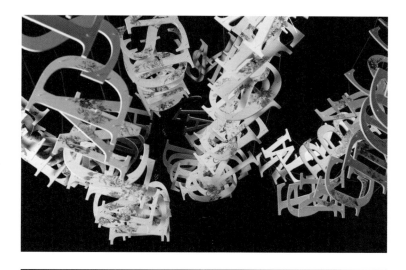

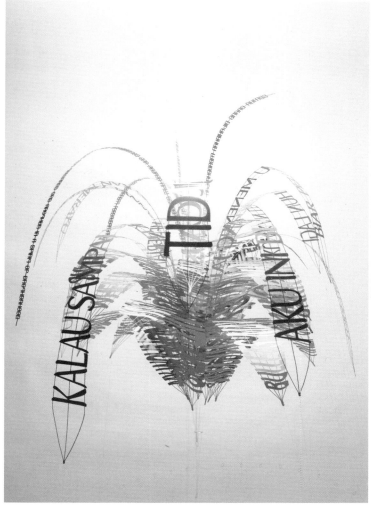

<u>**TITLE:**</u> *Open House*
<u>**DESIGN FIRM/AGENCY:**</u> The Caseroom Press/ABPress
<u>**DESIGNERS:**</u> Angie Butler and Philippa Wood
<u>**YEAR:**</u> 2012

 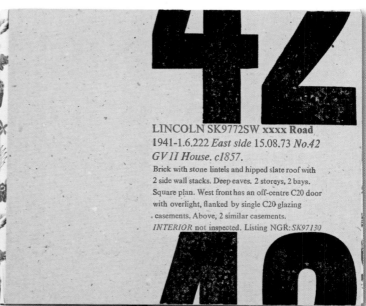

ANGIE BUTLER AND PHILIPPA WOOD
Open House

Open House is a collaborative artists' book project consisting of two volumes, 'No. 18' and 'No. 42', which are the designers' house numbers. The goal is to raise awareness of how people are connected to the places where they live, and to understand the psychology that underpins everyone's household furnishings and decor. In turning pages (opening doors), different thoughts and narratives are revealed. The twenty-four-page hardback cloth-bound book is divided into three sections, with decorative endpapers. It is letterpress, silk-screen and digitally printed, with additional manually typewritten text, and ornamented with both badges and buttons.

The designers joined together for this project because of a mutual passion for artists' books and letterpress printing. Angela Butler admired the work of Philippa Wood and Barrie Tullett, who form part of a collective called The Caseroom Press, an independent UK publisher whose work explores the function and format of the book, from traditional print to the artists' book.

'To work collaboratively with another practitioner is a reflexive process,' Butler said of her interest, 'and I wanted to have that kind of working relationship with someone else, but not just anyone. It was vital to be supportive of each other's work and share particular affinities within our practice to enable a successful outcome.'

Wood's practice of developing a rhythm through sequential narrative made Butler think more about the way that her images and text could interrelate to form different meanings, depending on how the reader turned the pages of the book. Also the placement of items in her own home reflected a particular narrative aesthetic. The duo engaged in domestic archaeology, giving each other an online tour of each other's houses, to unearth a variety of narratives.

Butler says she 'is one of few practitioners in the UK' who has aligned letterpress printing with her book arts practice. She prefers to have as much control over each aspect of the book-making process as possible, and to evidence human touch within it, saying 'so I tend to use more traditional processes ... As my background and training is in fine art practice, I am not bound by the rules of graphic design practice, so have a liberated approach to what is acceptable within book arts practice: the weight and shape of each character, the rhythm across the page, using letters and characters to create visual images, the tactility of using the letterpress process to physically create and print a text, and the relationship of the printed page to the object of the book.'

TITLE: *The Travelling Font Salesman*
DESIGN FIRM/AGENCY: Anne Ulku
FONT DESIGNER: Chank Diesel
DESIGNER: Anne Ulku
AUTHOR: Peter Hajinian
CLIENT: Chank Co.
YEAR: 2014

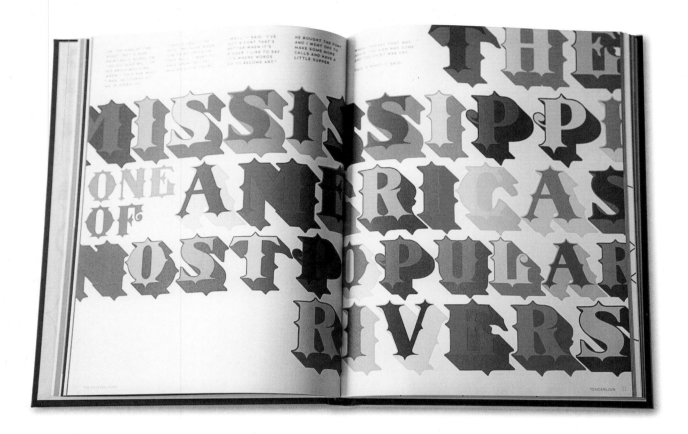

CHANK DIESEL AND ANNE ULKU
The Travelling Font Salesman

Anne Ulku wanted to create something that would show off some new type work from Chank Diesel (aka Peter Hajinian), but not a typical type-specimen promo piece. 'After coming up with a few concepts and directions,' she recalls, 'I realized the most prominent, quirky and endearing part of Chank was that he considered himself a door-to-door salesman of fonts.' The idea was to create a book containing a variety of his personal travel experiences, moments, observations and thoughts.

The story encompasses life on the road of a travelling salesman in his off-hours. The stories are like journal entries of simple moments, personal encounters, emotions, thoughts and visual observations. Though each story is different and unrelated, there is a sense of connection throughout the entire book, not just in the way the pages are designed, but in the way that Diesel is so descriptive that the reader feels involved.

The typographic scheme is rooted in how Diesel's fonts were made and the inspiration for their creation, which helped to guide some of the stories in the book. Some of the different layout ideas and font styles were better suited to smaller body copy, and others for larger headlines. 'I wanted each spread to be different – colours, expressive layout, text length, type sizes,' says Ulku. Each page or spread was individually composed to express both the typography and the story. 'I pictured each page or spread being its own frameable work of art,' she adds.

Diesel's fonts usually contain lots of personality and flavour: 'They are not perfect and grand, but they are charming and endearing in their own way,' he says. 'For their use in this book I wanted them showcased in an array of bright and uplifting colours. I am so tired of seeing the twentieth-centuryish "black and white and red" palette in typography, and I wanted my fonts to contrast with that, to be presented in a more diverse bunch of colours to show their place in the present and the future.'

The book was designed as a vibrant art book, displaying a collection of short stories while showing off the type styles in the best way for pleasure and commerce. The result is an enticing series of contrasts, or as Ulku says: 'I never thought I'd use eighteen different fonts in one single book!'

196

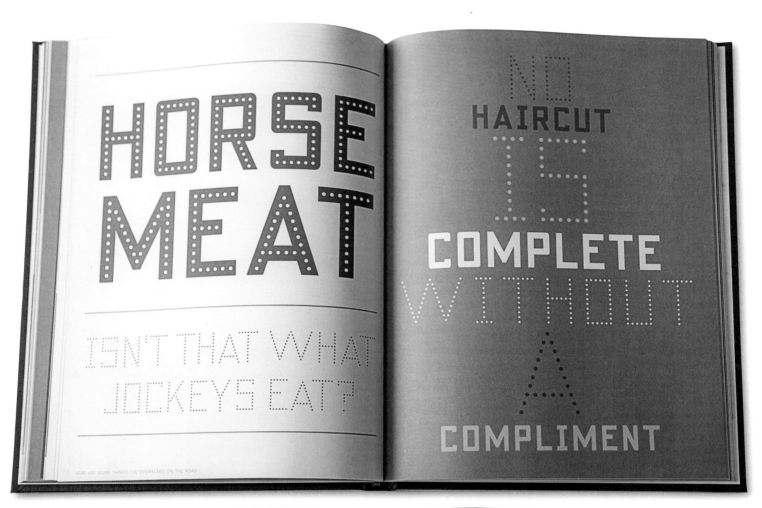

BRIAN SCOTT BAGDONAS
A Linotype Matrix-Slide-Being Distributes Gifts That Fulfill
A Linotype Matrix-Slide-Being Contemplates the Night Sky...
The Fir Tree

A Linotype Matrix-Slide-Being distributes gifts that fulfill

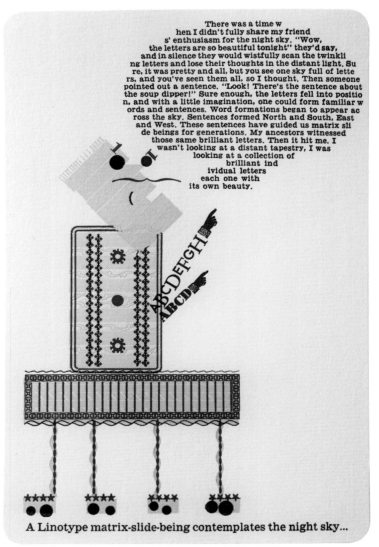

A Linotype matrix-slide-being contemplates the night sky...

Brian Scott Bagdonas made a series of typographic prints for the Grand (International) Letterpress holiday print exchange organized by a group of letterpress printers in the UK. They belong to the 'Linotype Matrix-Slide-Being' series; made-up Linotype composition cast for the print. Logically, Bagdonas was inspired to use pre-digital, pre-computer commercial print production and composition tools to make beautiful printing; he says he is particularly interested in Linotype machine composition, 'and wished to honour this technology'.

The 'typographical narrative' prints were initially born out of a desire to continue to learn the operation and maintenance of type-casting and hot-metal composition machinery. 'It has been a great exercise to cast type forms in this way,' Bagdonas says, noting that 'I'm inspired by mid-twentieth-century commercial printing. During this time, I believe that the designer, printer and machine influenced the print work equally.'

Bagdonas savoured the resourceful and creative approaches to print design of the hot-metal era. In spite of the increase in both production speed and volume, the hand of the craftsperson was not lost. 'Because of that,' he eulogizes, 'I think even the most utilitarian single-colour printing of that time was a beautiful thing.'

OPPOSITE, LEFT

TITLE: *A Linotype Matrix-Slide-Being Distributes Gifts That Fulfill*
DESIGN FIRM/AGENCY: Fiddleink
ART DIRECTOR/DESIGNER: Brian Scott Bagdonas
YEAR: 2014

OPPOSITE, LEFT

TITLE: *A Linotype Matrix-Slide-Being Contemplates the Night Sky...*
DESIGN FIRM/AGENCY: Fiddleink
ART DIRECTOR/DESIGNER: Brian Scott Bagdonas
YEAR: 2015

ABOVE

TITLE: *The Fir Tree*
DESIGN FIRM/AGENCY: Fiddleink
ART DIRECTOR/DESIGNER: Brian Scott Bagdonas
YEAR: 2014

JAMIE CLARKE
Brighton Letterpress Print

Initial capital letters constructed from diverse imagery and decoration, used to enhance the stories they illustrate, are among Jamie Clarke's favourite design elements. 'I love beautiful drop caps, both historical and modern,' he says. 'For me, they need to be in context, partnered with the relevant text, reinforcing its message.' His goal is to bring the surrounding words to life and make the reading experience more vivid and memorable: 'I like to use these illustrative capitals to compose interesting typographic layouts, experimenting with their positioning; using them to break up long paragraphs, sign off at the end of a section, or even to invite the words to flow into them.'

Clarke made this typographic treatise after several visits to the seaside city of Brighton, England, made over the course of a few years. 'I always felt rejuvenated on returning to London,' he says. 'Full of new ideas. And I wasn't alone in feeling this way; Brighton has attracted many famous people over the years and enticed them to make a home there. It's inspired Oscar Wilde, King George IV and many notable writers, filmmakers and artists. I wanted to design a piece that would capture this culture and spirit of Brighton, over time.'

So to achieve the balance of contemporary and historic he made use of modern illuminations to illustrate key points, together with little icons, which are playfully scattered within the typography.

This piece (a limited edition of 100 prints, 640mm × 425mm, typeset in Sentinel by Hoefler & Co.) briefly charts the town's rapid development from a fishing village, noted in the Domesday Book, to a cultural destination that attracts 8.5 million visitors a year. One drop cap lists the historical names and nicknames for Brighton over the centuries. However, with so much to say about the city, 'I focused the story on its contemporary arts and entertainment scene,' Clarke says, regarding how this work describes the vibrant music scene, its film culture, the entertainment piers, museums and galleries, the Royal Pavilion and the unparalleled regency architecture. It also lists the huge variety of annual festivals the city hosts each year.

The various illustrated cap references are:

B: From the famous Brighton Pier signage
R: Lettering based on the iconic Golden Gallopers carousel
I: A list of the historical names and nicknames for Brighton
G: Illustrating the city's vibrant music scene
H: Representing its Regency-style architecture
T: The seafront, pier and Vespa scooters (from the film *Quadrophenia*)
O: The Royal Pavilion architecture and dragons
N: Colophon, featuring Gill Sans (Eric Gill was born in Brighton)

BRIGHTON has long been a popular cultural and entertainment destination. Its seafront attractions, frequent festivals, landmark architecture and proximity to London make it unique. Capitalising on these assets, Brighton and Hove has earned its place among the most visited cities in Britain'. While many of its top attractions thrive on hasty day-trippers and hen & stag parties, the magnificent history and diverse culture that underpins the city are easily discovered just beyond the flashing lights and fish & chip shops. ¶ Once a fishing village, noted in the Domesday Book as *Bristelmestune*, its development as a leisure hub took off in the 1750s when Dr Richard Russell of Lewes began prescribing the medicinal use of drinking and bathing in its seawater. Advised that these waters would benefit his gout, the Prince Regent (later King George IV), spent considerable time here and built a grandiose palace as his seaside retreat. The Prince's patronage was fundamental to the village's swift transformation into a fashionable, high-class resort, which became known as Brighton. Rapid growth boosted demand for entertainment venues and the impressive Regency buildings that still characterise the seafront and surrounds. ¶ With the arrival of the London and Brighton Railway in 1841, visitors flocked to the town to enjoy the seaside and burgeoning leisure activities that developed into the city we know today. ¶

REGALLY GAZING OVER its pebble beach, which swarms with activity in the warmer months, the city is set just far enough from the seafront to make it easy to hop between the two. The beach is a focal point for a variety of events and festivals and each section of frontage has its own distinct personality. In the east you'll find the Volk's Electric Railway and the Madeira Colonnade, while in the arches between the two piers, more than 20 artists have taken up residence. The Hove end is home to rows of picturesque striped beach huts and the Hove lawns. Peppered between these points you'll find the beautifully lettered Golden Gallopers carousel, built in 1888, the recently refurbished Bandstand, said to be one of the finest Victorian examples in England, and iconic public art including Bruce Williams' *Kiss Wall*, *Afloat* by Hamish Black and *Passacaglia* by Charles Hadcock.

VARIOUS OFFICIAL & UNOFFICIAL NAMES AND MOTTOS OF BRIGHTON: BOPEEPSTRTA BRISELMESHE A DEEP ED BOG OLD OCEANS BAUBLE LONDON BY THE SEA TR QUEEN OF WATERING PLES SKID ROW SEA MERBY DR BRIGHON SILLENBEACH BETWEEN DWN & SEA WE FLOURISH 2000 AD NW THE CITY OF BRIGON & HOVE

IN FRONT OF THE WEST PIER, whose metal skeleton is slowly being consumed by the sea, work has begun on the i360 observation tower. Billed as a "vertical pier" the 162 metre-high lookout is due to open in 2015. Until then Brighton's Palace Pier remains the city's most famous attraction. Looking beyond its tacky adornments, the structure still offers a glimpse of why it was called *The Finest Pier in the World*. Its amusement arcade, the Palace of Fun, is housed in an original domed building with a fine ironwork interior and stained glass windows, while a number of original kiosks are dotted about, as small heirlooms of the Victorian era. The benches along its length still face inwards, recalling a time when promenading along the pier was an opportunity to see and be seen. Arguably the best time to see the pier is at night, when its length is illuminated with over 60,000 lights. ¶ ROWING CONTINUALLY, Brighton's live music scene offers a variety of gigs every night, from an estimated 500 resident bands. Venues are all over; beneath the railway station, under the colonnade, and in many of the city's pubs. Distinguished venues include Concorde 2, housed in a former Victorian teahouse and The Brighton Dome, once the Prince Regent's lavish riding school and stables. Large music events include The Great Escape, attracting over 400 up-and-coming bands to play over its three days, and the Shakedown Festival featuring more established acts. ¶ Brighton also has a rich cinematic history, playing its part both in the early development of filmmaking, and as a setting for films. Its most famous is surely *Quadrophenia* (1979), starring the mods and scooters that have become synonymous with Brighton. Other popular films shot here include *The End of the Affair* (1999), *The Young Victoria* (2009), *Brighton Rock* (1947 & 2010) and *The Boat that Rocked* (2009). ¶ You'll find the country's oldest purpose-built cinema here too: The Duke of York's Picture House has been in operation since 1910, and displays a pair of iconic, 20ft can-can dancer's legs atop of its striking Edwardian baroque-style façade. The Duke of York's is also part of the annual CINECITY Film Festival, that has recently been joined by the Big Screen On The Beach, whose 2014 screenings were watched by 100,000 people in just ONE MONTH.

There seems to be a major festival or event every weekend in the city, the greatest of which is the Brighton Festival. For three weeks each May the city hosts the biggest arts and entertainment festival in England. Approaching its 60th year, the event highlights the full spectrum of Brighton's cultural heritage with live music, theatre, dance, art, film and literature. ¶ Alongside the main festival is the fringe, which includes the Open Houses event where 1,000 artists display their work in 200 homes and studios all over the city ¶ Summer brings the acclaimed Pride event, the most colourful weekend of the year; a visual and audio extravaganza to celebrate diversity and promote equality of the lesbian, gay, bisexual and transgender community. Over 160,000 revellers enjoy a vibrant parade, dance events, cabaret, funfair and a main stage of activities. ¶ Other regular events include; the Brighton Science Festival, the Food and Drink Festival, the Brighton Comedy Festival and the Untouchables Weekender when Vespa and Lambretta scooters descend on the seafront. Several events have developed over the years covering the 54 miles from London to Brighton. The most notable are The Veteran Car Run which began in 1896, the record-holding Mini Run, featuring over 2000 cars and the Bike Ride, now in its 40th year. Towards the end of the year, many Brightonians observe winter solstice with the Burning the Clocks event, during which homemade paper lanterns are paraded through the city and then burnt on a large beach bonfire, launching a huge firework display.

HOSE VENTURING just beyond the seafront will unearth some of Brighton's other treasures. The Lanes form Brighton's historic quarter. Renowned for jewellers and antique stores (and 'twittens') formed the original fishing village. Just north of this is the young and fashionable North Laine, packed with independent shops, pubs and cafes nestled between well-kept seaside terraced houses. On either side of the city, Kemp Town and Brunswick Square both exemplify the finest Regency architecture in the country. In the city centre is the impressive Brighton Museum and Art Gallery, which is located in the opulent Royal Pavilion grounds ¶

OFTEN used as a symbol of the city, the Royal Pavilion represents the pinnacle of Brighton's arts and cultural heritage. This extravagant and exotic pleasure palace was built between 1787 and 1823 as a monument for the Prince Regent. Its Indian style exterior was conceived by architect John Nash and features a fantastic tangle of domes, towers and minarets. Its luxurious interior also fires the imagination. Filled with oriental dragons (there are 108 dragons in the music room alone), it boasts the finest examples of Chinoiserie style in Britain. ¶

CITES & acknowledgements: Thanks to Brighton & Hove Museum and Visit Brighton. ¶ John Pritchard for putting me up and giving me a local's view. Ben Mitchell for typographic support and local insight. Ryan Gillard for lettering and typographic feedback, my wife, Nicola Gibbons, for her support and proof-reading. ¶ Bibliography David Bramwell and Tim Bick, *Cheeky Guide to Brighton*, 2009 ¶ Tim Carter, *Encyclopaedia of Brighton*, 1990, *My Brighton and Hove* [Available Online, 2014]. ¶ Brighton is the most popular UK seaside destination for foreign tourists and 8th in the top 20 UK destinations reached (via London). Office for National Statistics, 2013 ¶ Letterpress printed by Richard Lawrence, in Oxford. Set & Screened by H&Fj and Gill Sans by Eric Gill born in Brighton ¶ Jamie Clarke MMXIV

TITLE: Brighton Letterpress Print
DESIGNER/PHOTOGRAPHER/ILLUSTRATOR:
Jamie Clarke
YEAR: 2013

JASON PERMENTER
Erosion & Typography

After years of being a volcanologist and professor of geology, 'I decided that I just wasn't happy,' says Jason Permenter, about hanging up his rock hammer and returning to school to study graphic design.

Understanding the relationship between the space, shapes, crags and contours of letterforms was a gruelling process: 'It was difficult to stop seeing an A as an A,' he says. As a result he struggled back in design school, certain that he was a scientist, and that no one 'would ever believe I was now a designer'. But over time it dawned on Permenter that the difference between design and science is a very thin line. 'It's problem solving, it's iteration, it's challenges, it's about success and failure and starting from scratch. And it's always about facts, somehow.'

He needed to face this feeling of scientist vs. designer head-on. 'So I put on my geologist hat once again, and I looked at a block of text set in Univers. The text is from an essay by Wolfgang Weingart (the "father of Swiss Punk typography"). Made sense to me. What would Wolfgang do? As hokey as it sounds, the design for *Erosion & Typography 2* came to me in a dream.'

Permenter stopped looking at the essay as words and started looking at it as a collection of little crystals, tiny rocks in a million different shapes. 'I let the water flow through the essay, slowly, just like groundwater does, a millimetre at a time, taking years to move a metre, and I watched how it eroded the forms from the inside, creating sinkholes, stalactites, stalagmites, cavities, cleavage planes. I watched how the space between words became weak points or strong points, and I let it erode away just as it should.'

Every letter was a specific form in the system. 'I forgot that they were letters – I had to, in fact. I spent time with each individual letter, adjusting and spinning and dropping and catching them on each other like grains of sand or bits of broken rock. The style here was deliberately meant to be from the inside out, starting in one single point of weakness, sometimes random, and letting the erosion happen as it would naturally. I let gravity and water take over and the letters just fell where they wanted.'

In the end, he says, 'I imagine that these designs are just waiting for geologic time to catch up with them, and have another part break off entirely.'

TITLE: *Erosion & Typography 1* (opposite);
Erosion & Typography 2 (page 204);
Erosion & Typography 3 (page 205)
ART DIRECTOR/DESIGNER: Jason Permenter
YEAR: 2007

Typographisches Bewußtsein ist engagiertes Experimentieren und kritische Distanz. Oder: Unter welchen Umständen diese Publikation zustande kam. Meine Unterrichts-Konzepte für die Typographie: 1. Versuch einer Definition. Beob-Feststellungen achtungen ForderungenZur Verfügung stand eine typographische Werkstatt. Meine dringlichste Aufgabe, Typographie zu zeigen und weiterzugeben, sehe ich darin, dem Interessier ten relativ alle Möglichkeiten zu zeigen, die in einer Werkstatt Stecken. Das sind Materialien und technische Möglichkeiten. Besonders diejenigen, welche sich aus der wechselseitigen Beeinflussung gestalterischer Ideen, typographischer Elemente und technischer Verfahren ergeben. In diesem sa en ng ist es von Notwendigkeit, auf die weite Variabilität des typographischen Materials und die Dehnbarkeit seiner Bedeutungsfunktionen hinzuweisen. Leider bleiben ch e Untersuchu gen meist auf das syntaktische, suf die Beziehung unterschiedlicher gestalterischer Elemente beschränkt. Es wäre daher von Notwendigkeit, die z sch nd prag ti hen Funktionen der Typographie, also die Bedeutung typographischer Zeichen und ihr Funktionieren in Kommunikationsprozessen stärker zu untersuchen u andein. Doch bereit etzt reicht die Zeit nicht, mit gründlicher Methodik Beizubringen, wie der Schüler mit den gegebenen Möglichkeiten fertig werden kann. ie ographen‹ waren Schüler mit ve chiedenartigen Interessen. Und mit unterschiedlichem Niveau und Ausbildungsstand. Die erst ufg eim vorliegenden Heft wurd au schließlich von Schülern gelöst, die am Anfang ihres Typographie-Unterrichtes standen. Dabei d ß größte Schwier kei beim logischen Gliedern eines Textes auftraten. Diese Erfahrung machte ich mit Klassen der z r ebenfalls. Das ze w he komplexe Materie im Fach ‹Typographie› vermittelt wird une wie langwierig dieser Prozeß l v rläuft. rän sich immer stärker die Frage auf: Wie kann man Typographie innerhalb von zwei Jahren so itteln, daß der Schüler selbständig entscheiden lernt, ein gegebenes Manuskript in einen D rap ischen Entwurf umzusetzen? Erste Voraussetzung dafür scheint mir das Gefühl absoluter Ent c eidungsfreiheit zu sein. Freilich eine Freiheit, unter der mehr die V füg rkeit der typographischen Möglichkeiten zu verstehen ist. Und E sc ungen, die aus der Aufgabe und deisen Möglichkeiten abgeleitet rde Da jede Entscheidung, die weitgehed durch Vorlieben, Unkenntnis d erständnis bestimmt wird, die also weitgehend schon zuvor t e ht, kann beim Umsetzen eines Textes in Typographie eine scheidung sein. Auch das muß der Schüler lernen zu u erk nnen, um daraus vielleicht einen neuen h Ansatzpunkt für seine Arbeit zu gewinnen. Das alb wird in meinem Unterricht nicht skizziert. Die ypographische Realität ist das abgesetzte W nUnd nur die zeigt seine Länge, sein o tnis zu anderen Wörtern, zum gesamten um ihn umgebenden Raum mit sein n F nzungen. Wenn der Schüler di s i hen Motive verstanden und e m ittelten Kriterien beg z wird er im Sinne der das muß die zei g scheiden können nn er die Funk

diesen idealen orientieren müssen. Zur Verfügung stand jedem Schüler ein maschinengeschriebenes Manuskript. Unsere Schule kennt keinen Unterricht im Texten. nd auch keine L ehrfächer, in denen Textprobleme behandelt werden. Die Schüler können aus diesem Grund keine selbst konzipierten Texte in die Typographie-Werkstatt mitbringen. Das wäre zum n eispiel deshalb sinnvoll, damit die solchem Texte zugrunde liegende Konzeption auch für die Konzeption der Typographie verwendet werden kann. Wie eine ausgezeichnete Hilfe für die logische Strukturierung des Textes und für die Bestimmung von Schrift und Satzart wäre. Ohne diese Kenntnis der textlichen Konzeption —also ohne Kenntnis der praktischen Aufgabe und geplanten Bedeutung eines Textes —bleibt die Typographie auf ihren syntaktischen Möglichkeiten beschränkt. Also: Wenn die semantische und pragmatische Funktion h eines Textes erkannt und verstanden sind, können die vielfältigen syntaktischen Möglichkeiten sinnvoll eingesetzt werden. Ich betone das deshalb, weil ich mir davon eine entscheidende Objektivierung des Lehrprozsses verspreche. Einfacher ausgedrückt: Ein bißchen weniger auf Lehrmeinungen und Gefühlen gegründeten und damit letztich für Schüler und Lehrer noch produktiveren Unterricht. Zur Verfügung standen den Schüler 4 Wochenstunden, um in der Typographie-Werkstatt zu arbeiten. Für das immer wichtiger werdende Kommunikationsmedium ‹Typographie› sind 4 Wochenstuden anachronistisch. Sie reichen kaum für die Vermittlung handwerkiicher Fertigkeiten. Der vorliegende Druck entst a zwischen November 1970 und März 1971. Daran ist abzulesen, daß ein Viertel der Schulzeit dieser Aufgabe geopfer werden mußte. Night aus Ignoranz gegenüber anderen Aufga b sondern aus Gründen zeitlicher und didaktischer Not. Daran ist weiterhin abzulesen, daß andere dringende Probleme überhaupt nicht behandelt werden konnten. Ich de n beispielsweise an die Aufarbeitung der verschiedenen typographischen Theorien. An nichtwerbliche, sogenannte ‹technische Typographie›. An komplexe Typographie-Projekte als Teil visueller Erscheinungsbilder oder Orientierungssysteme. Oder, zum Beispiel wenig er anspruchsvoll: Rasterprobleme und typographische Programme im Verlagswesen. Die Liste ließ

Typographisches Bewußtsein ist engagiertes Experimentieren und kritische Distanz. Oder: Unter welchen Umständen diese Publikation zustande kam. Meine Unterrichts-Konzepte für die Typographie: 1. Versuch einer Definition. Beob-Feststellungen achtungen ForderungenZur Verfügung stand eine typographische Werkstatt. Meine dringlichste Aufgabe, Typographie zu zeigen und weiterzugeben, sehe ich darin, dem Interessier ten relativ alle Möglichkeiten zu zeigen, die in einer Werkstatt Stecken. Des sind Materialien und technische Möglichkeiten. Besonders diejenigen, welche sich aus der wechselseitigen Beeinflussung gestalterischer Ideen, typographischer Elemente und technischer Verfahren ergeben. In diesem Zusammenhang ist es von Notwendigkeit, auf die weite Variabilität des typographischen Materials und die Dehnbarkeit seiner Bedeutungsfunktionen hinzuweisen. Leider bleiben entsprechende Untersuchungen meist auf das syntaktische, suf die Beziehung unterschiedlicher gestalterischer Elemente beschränkt. Es wäre daher von Notwendigkeit, die semantischen und pragmatischen Funktionen der Typographie, also die Bedeutung typographischer Zeichen und ihr Funktionieren in Kommunikationsprozessen stärker zu untersuchen und zu behandeln. Doch bereits jetzt reicht die Zeit nicht, mit gründlicher Methodik Beizubringen, wie der Schüler mit den gegebenen Möglichkeiten fertig werden kann. Die ‹Typographen› waren Schüler mit verschiedenartigen Interessen. Und mit unterschiedlichem Niveau und Ausbildungsstand. Die erste Aufgabe im vorliegenden Heft wurde ausschließlich von Schülern gelöst, die am Anfang ihres Typographie-Unterrichtes standen. Dabei zeigte sich, daß größte Schwierigkeiten beim logischen Gliedern eines Textes auftraten. Diese Erfahrung machte ich mit Klassen der letzten Jahre ebenfalls. Das zeigt, welche komplexe Materie im Fach ‹Typographie› vermittelt wird une wie langwierig ieser Prozeß verläuft. Daher drängt sich immer stärker die Frage auf: Wiekann man Typographie innerhalb von zwei Jahren so vermitteln, daß der Schüler selbständig entscheiden lernt, ein gegebenes Manuskript in einen typographischen Entwurf umzusetzen? Erste Voraussetzung dafür scheint mir das Gefühl absoluter Entscheidungsfreiheit zu sein. Freilich eine Freiheit, unter der mehr die Verfügbarkeit der typographischen Möglichkeiten zu stehen ist. Und Entscheidungen, die aus der Aufgabe und deisen Möglichkeiten abgeleitet werden. Da jede Entscheidung, die weitgehed durch Vorl... verständnis bestimmt wird, die also weitgehend schon zuvor feststeht, kann beim Umsetzen eines Textes in Typographie eine Fehlen... lernen zu erkennen, um daraus vielleicht einen neuen Ansatzpunkt für seine Arbeit zu gewinnen. Deshal wird in mehlen... ität ist das abgesetzte Wort. Und nur die zeigt seine Länge, sein Verhältnis zu anderen Wörtern, zum gesamten T... grenzungen. Wenn der Schüler diese didaktischen Motive verstanden und die vermittelten Kriterien begriffen hat... iden können. Und nur wenn er die Funktion dieser Entscheidungsfreiheit in der typographischen Gestaltung... onen der Typographie begreifen. (Im Idealfall, muß ich einschränken). Ich bin überzeugt, daß wir die Ausbildung anversta... die Grundfunktigung stand jedem Schüler ein maschinengeschriebenes Manuskript. Unsere Schule kennt keinen Unterricht im Texten... reu müssen. Zur Verfüeme behandelt werden. Die Schüler können aus diesem Grund keine selbst konzipierten Texte in die Typographie-Werksta... n denen Texteshalb sinnvoll, damit die solchem Texte zugrunde liegende Konzeption auch für die Konzeption der Typographie verwendet werden ka... n. Was... ichnete Hilfe für die logische Strukturierung des Textes und für die Bestimmung von Schrift und Satzart wäre. Ohne diese Kenntnis der textlichen Konzepti... also ohne Kenntnis der praktischen Aufgabe und geplanten Bedeutung eines Textes—bleibt die Typographie auf ihren syntaktischen Möglichkeiten beschränkt. Als Wenn die semantische und pragmatische Funktion eines Textes erkannt und verstanden sind, könnnen die vielfältigen syntaktischen Möglichkeiten sinnvoll eingesetz werden. Ich betone das deshalb, weil ich mir davon eine entscheidende Objektivierung des Lehrprozesses verspreche. Einfacher ausgedrückt: Ein bißchen weniger au Lehrmeinungen und Gefühlen gegründeten und damit letztlich für Schüler und Lehrer noch produktiveren Unterricht. Zur Verfügung standen den Schüler 4 Wochenstund n, um in der Typographie-Werkstatt zu arbeiten. Für das immer wichtiger werdende Kommunikationsmedium ‹Typographie› sind 4 Wochenstuden anachronistisch. Sie reichen kaum für die Vermittlung handwerklicher Fertigkeiten. Der vorliegende Druck entstand zwischen November 1970 und März 1971. Daran ist abzulesen aß ein Viertel der Schulzeit dieser Aufgabe geopfer werden mußte. Nicht aus Ignoranz gegenüber anderen Aufgaben, sondern aus Gründen zeitlicher und didaktisc er Not. Daran ist weiterhin abzulesen, daß andere dringende Probleme überhaupt nicht behandelt werden konnten. Ich denke beispielsweise an die Aufarbeitung d verschiedenen typographischen Theorien. An nichtwerbliche, sogenannte ‹technische Typographie›. An komplexe Typographie-Projekte als Teil visueller Erscheinungs ilder oder Orientierungssysteme. Oder, zum Beispiel wenig er ans pruchsvoll: Rasterprobleme und typographische Programme im Verlagswesen. Die Liste ließe sich beließ ig fortsetzen. Zur Verfügung stand ein Lehrer, der (bei 20 Schülern) pro Schüler und Woche 10 minuten investieren kann. Mit 10 Minuten pro Schüler und Wo ist es unmöglich, auf die natürlichen individuellen Probleme jedes Schülers einzugehen. Was im Hinblick auf die Probleme ‹kreativer› Gestaltung und die wirksam Vermittlung von Fertigkeiten mir unbedingt notwendig erscheinen. Zudem waren die Klassen überfüllt, wordurch das Niveau der Ausbildung nicht verbessert wurde. Ei e Beobachtung, die durch die Arbeiten in dieser Publikation teilweise bestätigt wird. Einheitsware entsteht, wenn die Möglichkeiten für Differenzierungen knapp sind. Das soll nicht heißen, daß das Niveasu dieser Arbeiten hier ausschileßlich von der Überfüllung der Klassen beeinflußt ist. Aber eine größere Variationsbreite von zeitlich und thematischer Ausbildung hätte sich sicher positiver auf die Schüler und den hier gezeigten Arbeiten ausgewurkt. Diese Publikation solite vor allem zur Diskus ion beitragen. Arbeiten einfach abzubilden, um sie kommentarios sich selbst zu überlassen—dazu ist der vorliegende Druck nicht gedacht. Er soll vielmehr Problem zeigen, die bei der Reflexion über einen bestimmten Ausbildungszeitraum und die darin enstandenen Arbeiten aufgetaucht sind. Deshalb erlaube ich mir diese Beobac... Feststellungen und Forderungen. Sie sollten im Einzelnen noch konkretisiert und diskutiert werden. Der Prozeß einer breiten Meinungsbildung erscheint mir er als die Vorstellung fertiger Meinungen. W. Weingart, Basel im März 1971.

Typographisches Bewußtsein ist engagiertes Experimentieren und kritische Distanz. O Unterrichts-Konzepte für die Typographie: 1. Versuch einer Definition. Beob-Feststellungen ach Meine dringlichste Aufgabe, Typographie zu zeigen und weiterzugeben, sehe ich darin, dem Interessier Stecken. Des sind Materialien und technische Möglichkeiten. Besonders diejenigen, welche sich aus typographischer Elemente und technischer Verfahren ergeben. In diesem Zusammenhang ist es von Not Materials und die Dehnbarkeit seiner Bedeutungsfunktionen hinzuweisen. Leider bleiben entsprechende Unters unterschiedlicher gestalterischer Elemente beschränkt. Es wäre daher von Notwendigkeit, die semantischen un Bedeutung typographischer Zeichen und ihr Funktionieren in Kommunikationsprozesse stärker zu untersuchen und zu beh mit gründlicher Methodik Beizubringen, wie der Schüler mit den gegebenen Möglichkeiten fertig werden kann. Die ‹Typo Interessen. Und mit unterschiedlichem Niveau und Ausbildungsstand. Die erste Aufgabe im vorliegenden Heft wurde a ihres Typographie-Unterrichtes standen. Dabei zeigte sich, daß größte Schwierigkeiten beim logischen Gliedern eines Textes Klassen der letzten Jahre ebenfalls. Das zeigt, welche komplexe Materie im Fach ‹Typographie› vermittelt wird une wie langwi sich immer stärker die Frage auf: Wie kann man Typographie innerhalb von zwei Jahren so vermitteln, daß der Schüler selbst Manuskript in einen typographischen Entwurf umzusetzen? Erste Voraussetzung dafür scheint mir das Gefühl absoluter Ent Freiheit, unter der mehr die Verfügbarkeit der typographischen Möglichkeiten zu verstehen ist. Und Entscheidungen, die aus der Auf abgeleitet werden. Da jede Entscheidung, die weitgehed durch Vorlieben, Unkenntnis und Unverständnis bestimmt wird, die also weitgehend kann beim Umsetzen eines Textes in Typographie eine Fehlenscheidung sein. Auch das muß der Schüler lernen zu erkennen, um daraus vielleicht ei nen neuen Ansatzpunkt für seine Arbeit zu gewinnen. Deshalb wird in meinem Unterricht nicht skizziert. Die typographische Realität ist das abgesetzte Wort. Und nur die zeigt seine Länge, sein Verhältnis zu anderen Wörtern, zum gesamten Text un zum ihn umgebenden Raum mit seinin Begrenzungen. Wenn der Schüler diese didaktischen Motive verstanden und die vermittelten Kriterien begriffen hat, wird er im Sinne der oben geforderten ‹Freiheit› entscheiden können. Und nur wenn er die Funktion dieser Entscheidungsfreiheit in der typographischen Gestaltung verstanden hat, wird er auch die Grundfunktionen der Typographie begreifen. (Im Idealfall, muß ich einschränken). Ich bin überzeugt, daß wir die Ausbildung an diesen idealen orientieren müssen. Zur Verfügung stand jedem Schüler ein maschinengeschriebenes Manuskript. Unsere Schule kennt keinen Unterricht im Texten. Und auch keine Lehrfächer, in denen Textprobleme behandelt werden. Die Schüler können aus diesem Grund keine selbst konzipierten Texte in die Typographie-Werkstatt mitbringen. Das wäre zum Beispiel deshalb sinnvoll, damit die solchem Texte zugrunde liegende Konzeption auch für die Konzeption der Typographie verwendet werden kann. Was aber ausgezeichnete Hilfe für die logische Strukturierung des Textes und für die Bestimmung von Schrift und Satzart wäre. Ohne diese Kenntnis der textlichen Konzeption – also ohne Kenntnis der praktischen Aufgabe und der plantan Bedeutung eines Textes –bleibt die Typographie auf ihren syntakischen Möglichkeiten beschränkt. Also: Wenn die semantische und pragmatische Funktion eines Textes erkannt und verstanden sind, können die vielfältigen syntaktischen Möglichkeiten sinnvoll eingesetzt werden. Ich betone das deshalb, weil ich mir davon eine entscheidende Objektivierung des Lehrprozesses verspreche. Einfacher ausgedrückt: Ein bißchen weniger auf Lehrmeinungen und Gefühlen gegründeten und damit letztich für Schüler und Lehrer noch produktiveren Unterricht. Zur Verfügung standen den Schüler 4 Wochenstunden, um in der Typographie-Werkstatt zu arbeiten. Für das immer wichtiger werdende Kommunikationsmedium ‹Typographie› sind 4 Wochenstuden anachronisch. Sie reichen kaum für die Vermittlung handwerklicher Fertigkeiten. Der vorliegende Druck entstand zwischen November 1970 und März 1971. Daran ist abzulesen, daß ein Viertel der Schulzeit diieser Aufgabe geopfer werden mußte. Night ingende Probleme aus Ignoranz gegenüber anderen Aufgaben, sondern aus Gründen zeitlicher und didaktischer Not. Daran ist weiterhin abzulesen, daß andere d bliche, sogenannte überhaupt nicht behandelt werden konnten. Ich denke beispielsweise an die Aufarbeitung der verschiedenen typographischen Theorien. An nichtweriig er anspruchsvoll: ‹technische Typographie›. An komplexe Typographie-Projekte als Teil visueller Erscheinungsbilder oder Orientierungssysteme. Oder, zum Beispiel weil (bei 20 Schülern) pro Rasterprobleme und typographische Programme im Verlagswesen. Die Liste ließe sich belieb ig fortsetzen. Zur Verfügung stand ein Lehrer, der me jedes Schülers Schüler und Woche 10 minuten investieren kann. Mit 10 Minuten pro Schüler und Woche ist es unmöglich, auf die natürlichen individuellen Probleme eint. Zudem waren einzugehen. Was im Hinblick auf die Probleme ‹kreativer› Gestaltung und die wirksame Vermittlung von Fertigkeiten mir unbedingt notwendig erschn teilweise bestätigt die Klassen überfüllt, wodurch das Niveau der Ausbildung nicht verbessert wurde. Eine Beobachtung, die durch die Arbeiten in dieser Publikation schließlich von der wird. Einheitsware entsteht, wenn die Möglichkeiten für Differenzierungen knapp sind. Das soll nicht heißen, daß das Niveau dieser Arbeiten hier aus die Schüler und den Überfüllung der Klassen beeinflußt ist. Aber eine größere Variationsbreite von zeitlicher und thematischer Ausbildung hätte sich sicher positiver auf gszeitraum und die hier gezeigten Arbeiten ausgewurkt. Diese Publikation solite vor allem zur Diskussion beitragen. Arbeiten einfach abzubilden, um sie kommerta rios sich selbst zu überlassen—dazu ist der vorliegende Druck nicht gedacht. Er soll vielmehr Probleme zeigen, die bei der Reflexion über einen bestimmten Ausbildun noch konkretisiert darin enstandenen Arbeiten aufgetaucht sind. Deshalb erlaube ich mir diese Beobachtungen, Feststellungen und Forderungen. Sie sollten im Einzelnen und diskutiert werden. Der Prozeß einer breiten Meinungsbildung erscheint mir hier wichtiger als die Vorstellung fertiger Meinungen. W. Weingart, Basel im März 1971.

der: Unter welchen Umständen die tungen Forderungen Zur Verfügungs se Publikation ten relativ alle Möglichkeiten zustande kam. Meine der wechselseitigen Beein zu zeigen, graphische Werkstatt. wendigkeit, auf die weite Varia flussung gestal in einer Werkstatt uchungen meist auf das syntakti bilität des typographischen d pragmatischen Funktionen der Typographie, als o die andein. Doch bereits jetzt re icht die Zeit nicht. graphen› waren Schüler mit vers chiedenartigen usschließlich von Schülern auftraten. Diese Erfahrung machte ich m it erig dieser Prozeß verläuft. Daher drängt ändig entscheiden lernt, ein gegebenes scheidungsfreiheit zu sein. Freilich eine gabe und deisen Möglichkeiten schon zuvor feststeht, nen neuen

SEVEN

ALPHA
BETICS

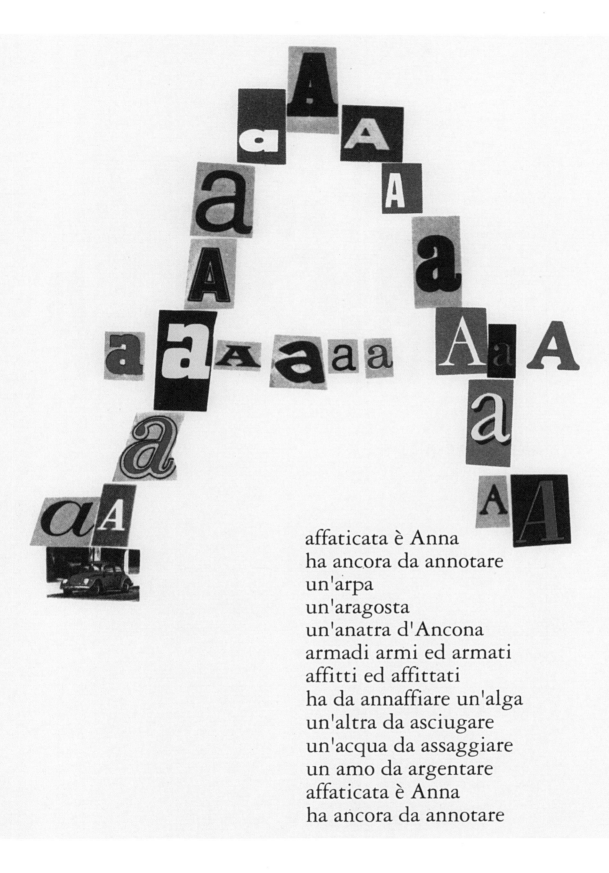

affaticata è Anna
ha ancora da annotare
un'arpa
un'aragosta
un'anatra d'Ancona
armadi armi ed armati
affitti ed affittati
ha da annaffiare un'alga
un'altra da asciugare
un'acqua da assaggiare
un amo da argentare
affaticata è Anna
ha ancora da annotare

BRUNO MUNARI
Alfabetiere

come un caso
ch'accadesse
come un cucciolo di cucco
come un calcio
come un sacco
Carlo cade
accoccolato
tra una capra con la coda
ed un can color cannella
caro amico
cosa accade
a Como

ci circonda un cinerama
di cilindri cinerini
di cipressi e cipolline
di ciliegie
di cicale
e cinque ciotole
con cinquanta cirri in cima

Bruno Munari (1907–1998) was the quintessential Futurist. His work looked beyond the status quo, becoming the model for progressive Italian designers and illustrators up to the current age. In the 1930s he produced the requisite Mussolini-inspired illustrations of aeroplanes and motorcars, representations of speed and mechanics that defined the Fascist era and its avant-garde aesthetic. He designed the iconic 1934 Futurist book/object, *L'anguria lirica*, with poetic text by Tullio d'Albisola, known for its metallic, mechanistic cover and interior pages featuring uncompromisingly progressive typography. For subsequent books he never settled for a formulaic approach. His collages and typographical concoctions might today be considered markers of a wider experimental period, but he remained forever experimental in heart and soul.

There are many other works by Munari that could exemplify the theme of type that thinks, notably his interpretation of F.T. Marinetti's 1937 *Il poema del vestito di latte* – an example of *parole in libertà* – about how milk is produced. Munari was a proponent of active book design, and produced works for adults and children, many of which have been widely reprinted. Among the most distinctive is a pre-school alphabetic – an interactive book in which cut-out letters (what today is called 'ransom note lettering') invited children to find, cut and paste their own discoveries.

Alfabetiere, a slender and alphabetically robust volume, initially published in 1960 by Einaudi and then reprinted in 1972 and 1998 (the latter by Corraini Edizioni, which has reissued much of Munari's work, and *Alfabetiere* for the eighth time in 2014), has no equal. The compositions of letters form letters, and the wacky rhymes, composed of words that begin with the letter that is featured, cannot but encourage young readers to discover the variety and versatility of our twenty-six-letter alphabet. It is also a joy for the adult reader to find the mysterious letters.

One of many Munari-illustrated alphabet books, this is not about learning words but rather experiencing the shapes and forms; what makes words come to life. The characters were cut and torn from newspapers and magazines precisely to demonstrate that the same letter can be typeset or hand-lettered in different forms, tenors and timbres. The reader learns, too, to find other options, as if on an expedition, by pasting those similar letters they've found on their own. Or, as one critic noted, *Alfabetiere* could be considered a game in which Munari allows his reader to hunt for alphabetic prey.

zitti zitti
dice Zazà
suoniamo lo zufolo qua e là
con la zazzera di zinco
lo zimbello e la zimarra
la zizzania nella zucca
nello zoo tutto s'inzuppa
siate pronti ad ammazzare
con la zampa della zebra
le zanzare

chi del chianti
chiede a Chiasso
chiaramente china il capo
ma chi chiede chianti a Chiasso?
chitarristi
smacchiatori
archivisti
macchinisti
tutti chiacchierano
e chi spera
chiede chianti fino a sera

nell'alba lilla
una lama luccica
un'anguilla s'allunga
allora
la laguna allagata
pullula di lumache
lontano Luca livido
in livrea
lucida lingue di lupo
lesto lega legumi
con lacci di lana
Luca
è una leggenda
su lastre di latta

sussurrar sente Susanna
un sospetto nella scranna
solitario un sorcio secco
succhia solo il suo sorbetto
sibillini sassolini
son tra sugheri e sterpini

TITLE: *Alfabetiere*
DESIGNER/AUTHOR: Bruno Munari
PUBLISHER: Einaudi and Corraini Edizioni
YEAR: 1960

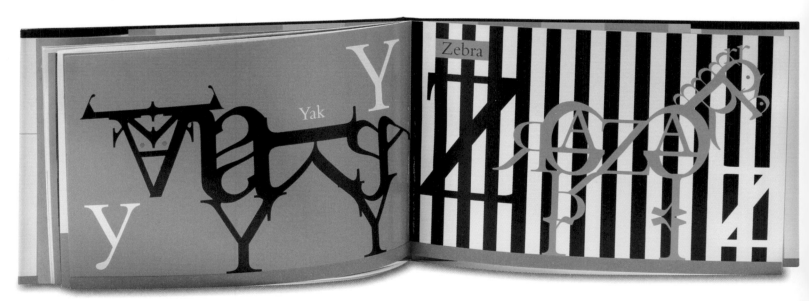

TITLE: *Bembo's Zoo*
DESIGN FIRM/AGENCY: de Vic
ART DIRECTOR/DESIGNER/PHOTOGRAPHER/
ILLUSTRATOR: Roberto de Vicq de Cumptich
CLIENT: Henry Holt
YEAR: 2000

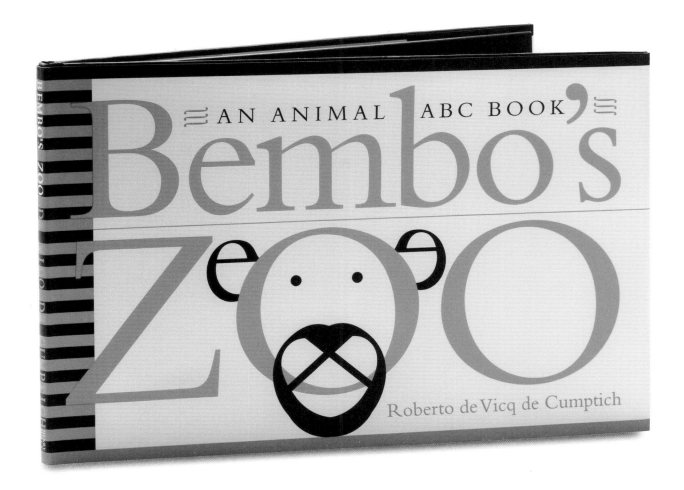

ROBERTO DE VICQ DE CUMPTICH
Bembo's Zoo

Roberto de Vicq de Cumptich was trying to teach his two-year-old daughter to learn Portuguese, his native tongue. He was unable to find an alphabet book that would work in both languages, he says. For instance, 'A is fine for "Alligator", but in Portuguese it is "*Jacaré*".' He resolved to fulfil the need himself but, being a graphic designer rather than an illustrator, de Vicq decided to make his own typographic menagerie, using only typefaces to form the animals. 'I gave myself limits by using only the letters of the animal's name and a reduced palette (cream, orange, green and black),' he explained.

The Bembo typeface was chosen for its elegant proportions and the way it works in both small and large sizes. The book also has a unique resonance because of the way de Vicq refers to the characteristics of each face. 'I can never recall the proper names for the different parts of the typeface; it is always embarrassing calling the "hole" for the "counter", or "the thing sticking up or down" instead of "ascenders" or "descenders". Looking at type charts, I realized most of the names are related to the human body, such as the "ear", the "arm" or the "spine". The idea was to create a little inspirational/reference guide by playing with silhouettes and type, and to play with humour.'

As well as being an alphabet book, *Bembo's Zoo* is a love poem to expressive typography. 'I love to experiment with type, to make it more expressive and playful,' de Vicq adds. 'Almost like playing with playdough – you stretch, pinch and punch, and try not eat it.'

211

ROSS MACDONALD
Achoo! Bang! Crash! The Noisy Alphabet

Ross MacDonald wanted to make a piece that showcased all of the wood type he had amassed for his private Brightwork Press. Rather than just do a straight type specimen book, he wisely decided to make an old-fashioned primer, or ABC book, using 'sound words', or onomatopoeia. He planned to illustrate it with simple linocut illustrations, print it letterpress, and send it out as a promo piece to art directors and designers. 'I pictured it as being very beautiful and tasteful,' he recalls, 'but every time I tried to think up illustrations to go with the sound words, I kept coming up with goofy slapstick images.'

Every page tells a different story – each has anywhere between one and eight sound words, printed from wood type, and incorporated into a single illustration. The type is always very much a part of the illustration, and the scenes are as silly and weird as possible.

MacDonald loves using nineteenth-century wood type, but, he says, 'in a way that looks modern, hopefully'. The type was hand-inked and printed using split fountain, overprinting and multiple passes. The words are often set on curves, or bouncing around the page, or overlapping, so the overall effect does not look anything like a nineteenth-century poster. In a way, it still functions well as a type specimen book. 'You can really see the type and appreciate the beauty of the letterforms,' MacDonald says, 'but you are seeing them in a setting that's stripped of period references, so the type stands on its own.'

<u>**TITLE:**</u> *Achoo! Bang! Crash! The Noisy Alphabet*
<u>**DESIGN FIRM/AGENCY:**</u> Brightwork Press
<u>**ART DIRECTOR/DESIGNER/PHOTOGRAPHER/**</u>
<u>**ILLUSTRATOR:**</u> Ross MacDonald
<u>**CLIENT:**</u> Roaring Brook Press
<u>**YEAR:**</u> 2002

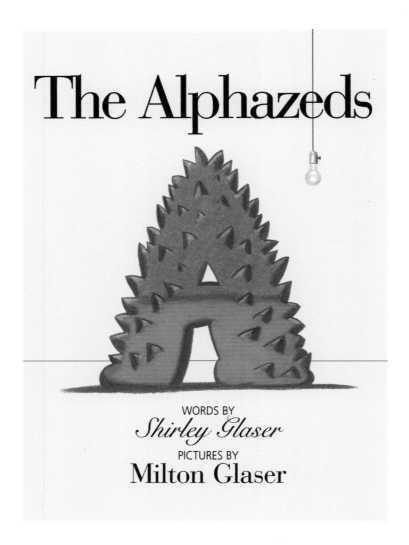

MILTON AND SHIRLEY GLASER
The Alphazeds

Letters and type are the heart and soul of a graphic designer. Invariably, illustrators who are also graphic designers and typographers who like illustration will eventually produce an alphabet book.

Milton Glaser agrees. His *Alphazeds* is, however, not just any alphabetorium or letterform primer but an analysis of division, distinction and an evolving community. As Glaser notes, 'It is a story that is based on the pay-off.' (You might be able to guess what that is.) He had a vague idea of the outcome, but it came together when he and his wife Shirley agreed on the concept of an origin story of sorts that proceeds from twenty-six different letters, each with their own personality types (or typefaces), in an unfurnished room. They argue among themselves and learn to find commonality.

First to enter is the Angry A, with ugly spikes on its cactus-like body, then the Bashful B, a slender and shy blue Bodoni character.

The letters immediately find themselves in conflict: 'What are you doing here?' demands A. 'Excuse me ...'

materializes above B in a quiet thought bubble.

As the pages turn, more typefaces make their presence known. The Confused C and Dynamic D, a dark-red extrovert who yells 'Ta-da!' regardless of what the others say. Elegant E is an upscale black script letter ('I dare say, it's getting a bit crowded'), and Flamboyant F, a voluptuous form, exclaims: 'I seem to be the only one here who knows how to dress.'

There are party letters including a Kicking K, which shoves the other guests with its lower extension, and an R that speaks in silly rhymes. One small overcrowded room is filled with anarchic and senselessly scrawled letter doodles where nothing pertains to anything else. Then at they end they somehow make the sense that letters are meant to do. They become words.

'It was a complicated process,' Glaser says. 'Not sketching the idea, but achieving the goal' – referring to the days before the computer, when photostating, cutting and pasting were time-consuming and frustrating. This often caused the production artists, in this case George Levitt, to angrily shout out a few choice words that did not always start with A.

TITLE: *The Alphazeds*
DESIGNER/ILLUSTRATOR: Milton Glaser
AUTHOR: Shirley Glaser
PUBLISHER: Hyperion/Miramax
YEAR: 2003

Lovely L, Mighty M, and Negative N came in, followed by Ornate O.

WERNER DESIGN WERKS
Alphabeasties and Other Amazing Types,
Alphasaurs and Other Prehistoric Types

RIGHT AND OPPOSITE, TOP

TITLE: *Alphabeasties and Other Amazing Types*
DESIGN FIRM/AGENCY: Werner Design Werks, Inc.
ART DIRECTOR: Sharon Werner
DESIGNERS/ILLUSTRATORS: Sharon Werner
and Sarah Forss
PUBLISHER: Blue Apple Books
YEAR: 2009

OPPOSITE, BOTTOM

TITLE: *Alphasaurs and Other Prehistoric Types*
DESIGN FIRM/AGENCY: Werner Design Werks, Inc.
ART DIRECTOR: Sharon Werner
DESIGNERS: Sharon Werner and Sarah Forss
ILLUSTRATORS: Sharon Werner, Sarah Forss
and Carly Wright
PUBLISHER: Blue Apple Books
YEAR: 2012

'We are accidental authors,' says Sharon Werner, referring to her colleagues Sarah Forss, Meghan O'Hare, Lori Benoy and Carly Wright. 'We didn't set out to create a children's book, or any other book for that matter.' The first book, *Alphabeasties and Other Amazing Types*, started life as the result of a Type Directors Club call for entries. From there, two publishers suggested it would make a great children's book. 'Great! We can design it, but we don't fancy ourselves writers, and certainly not writing for kids.'

Type, however, was their expertise, so the group set out to create a book that would stimulate children to become excited about type and the personality of different typefaces and letterforms. Animals, bugs and dinosaurs were, they say, 'fun vehicles or tools for our lessons'. And as kids have access to so many different fonts, Werner and company wanted to show them as having a personality and character traits, like people.

An 'A' is always an 'A', but it can be tall and thin or short and stout; rounded, jagged or even shaggy.

After the first book they created an activity book, *Alphabeasties Amazing Activities*, and then it 'seemed natural to do a second book about numbers … but what is the vehicle?' The solution was *Bugs by the Numbers*. 'Knowing nothing more than the average person about bugs, we set out to learn everything we could; anything that had to do with numbers. We wanted to put the often gigantic numerical facts into perspective for a kid. For instance, did you know that a termite can lay one egg every fifteen seconds?' After *Bugs* they dived into *Alphasaurs and Other Prehistoric Types*. Each one was created with typography.

Letters are part of the picture storytelling. The large animals and bugs were created one letter at a time – like digital needlepoint – literally moving pixels. Using a singular font family for each creature, they created shadow and shape with bold letters and highlights with the light typeface. 'We needed to select type families that would allow us to get the details we needed, such as thin spindly legs or massive spikes. Each page was carefully laid out – we didn't want to rotate any of the type or of course flop any letters, so we had to know fairly exactly where it was going to go and how large. We didn't want the type to be out of scale with the creatures' details.'

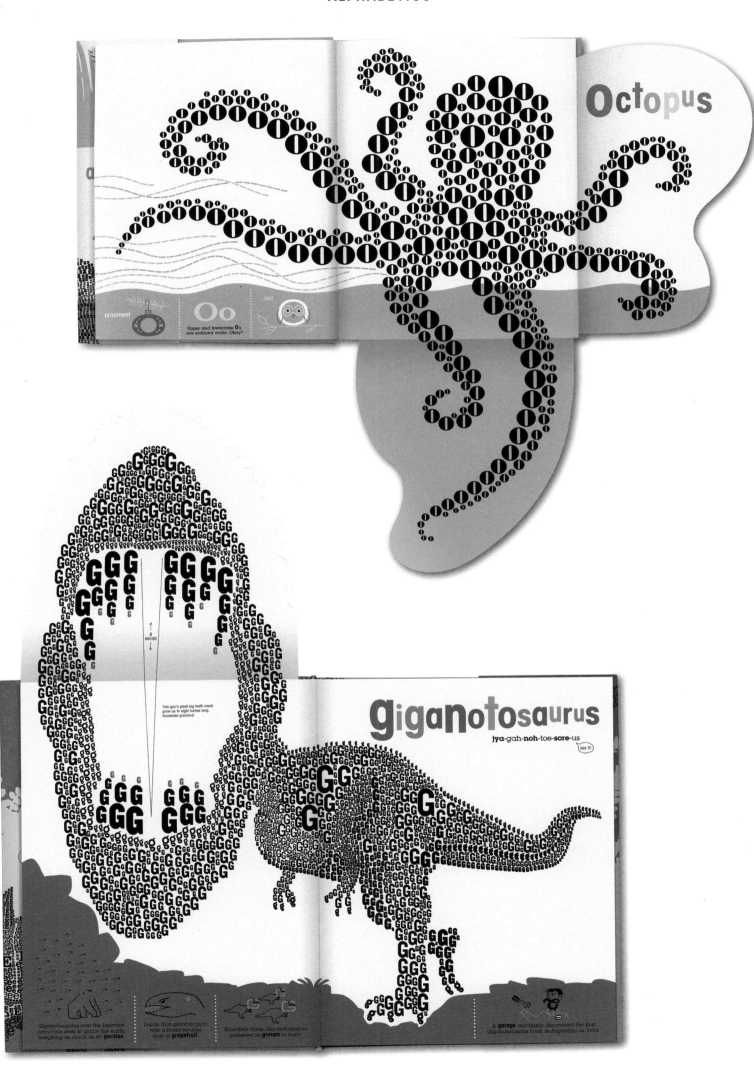

Octopus

ornament · Oo · owl

Upper and lowercase O's are ordinary ovals. Okay?

giganotosaurus

jya-gah-noh-toe-sore-us (say it!)

This guy's great big teeth could grow up to eight inches long. Goodness gracious!

8 INCHES

Giganotosaurus was the heaviest carnivore ever to grace the earth, weighing as much as 40 gorillas.

Inside that giant noggin was a brain smaller than a grapefruit.

Scientists think Giganotosaurus gathered in groups to hunt.

A garage mechanic discovered the first Giganotosaurus fossil in Argentina in 1993.

List of Designers

AGRAFKA STUDIO
agrafkastudio.com

BRIAN SCOTT BAGDONAS
www.portlandmade.com/stumptown-printers-brian-bagdonas

MARIAN BANTJES
bantjes.com

ALEXANDRA BEGUEZ
www.alexandrabeguez.com

PILAR GONZALEZ BERGEZ
www.behance.net/pilargbergez

NOTA BENE VISUAL
www.notabenevisual.com

**PETER BLEVGARD
AND ANDREW SWAINSON**
www.leviathan.co.uk/menu.html
www.burningshed.com/store/ape/
product/351/4146/
www.andrewswainson.com

ANTONIUS BUI
www.antoniusbui.com/work-avenue/

BIANCA BUNSAS
www.behance.net/biancabunsas

**ANGIE BUTLER AND PHILIPPA WOOD,
BARRIE TULLETT**
www.the-case.co.uk

CHURCH OF TYPE
churchoftype.com

JAMIE CLARKE
www.jamieclarketype.com

CYLA COSTA
www.cylacosta.com

ALLEN CRAWFORD
www.allencrawford.net

ROBERTO DE VICQ DE CUMPTICH
devicq.com

CHANK DIESEL AND ANNE ULKIU
chank.com

JOHANNA DRUCKER
www.johannadrucker.net

LORA FOSBERG
www.lorafosberg.com

MILTON AND SHIRLEY GLASER
www.miltonglaser.com

TIMOTHY GOODMAN
tgoodman.com

DIRK HAGNER
www.dirkhagnerstudio.com

JONNY HANNAH
www.stjudesprints.co.uk/collections/
jonny-hannah

EBON HEATH
www.listeningwithmyeyes.com

DANIEL PATRICK HELMSTETTER
danielpatrick.org/#poetry

JOHN HENDRIX
johnhendrix.com/portfolio

TOM HINGSTON
www.hingston.net

HERMAN INCLUSUS
www.hermaninclusus.co.uk

MAIRA KALMAN
www.mairakalman.com

CORITA KENT
corita.org

PATRICK KING
typographyshop.tumblr.com

MOLLY LEACH
www.lanesmithbooks.com/
lanesmithbooks/bio.html

WARREN LEHRER
www.earsay.org

LUST
lust.nl

ROSS MACDONALD
www.ross-macdonald.com

HERMES MAZALI
www.hmazali.com

DYLAN MCDONOUGH
dylanmcdonough.com

WAEL MORCOS
www.waelmorcos.com

OLIVER MUNDAY
omunday.tumblr.com

JOHN PASSAFIUME
johnpassafiume.com

JASON PERMENTER
jasonpermenter.com

BRIAN REA
www.brianrea.com

NICK REEVE
www.creativereview.co.uk/with-this-suit

ROGERS ECKERSLEY DESIGN
red-partners.com

LAURIE ROSENWALD
www.rosenworld.com

SAWDUST
www.madebysawdust.co.uk

ALIDA SAYER
www.alidasayer.com

PAULA SCHER
www.pentagram.com/#/home

CAROLYN SEWELL
www.carolynsewell.com

STUART SHARPE
www.ssharpe.com

ISABEL SEIFFERT
www.isabelseiffert.net

SIGLIO PRESS (JOHN CAGE BOOK)
sigliopress.com

ARIANE SPANIER DESIGN
arianespanier.com

JACK SUMMERFORD
www.designpastime.com/design-pastime-
graphic-designers/jack-summerford

ANNIE VOUGHT
annievought.com

WERNER DESIGN WERKS
wdw.com

SAM WINSTON
www.samwinston.com

KIRIL ZLATKOV
www.behance.net/rand0mabstract

Index

Acknowledgments

First and foremost, a huge thank you to our editor, Lucas Dietrich, who has supported the work of designers and the design process consistently for well over a decade. Our deep gratitude goes to assistant editor Bethany Wright, who has shepherded this project with intelligence, respect and patience.

We are indebted to Abigail Steinem, our loyal researcher, for her keen ability to find the unfindable and her dogged pursuit of delinquent materials. And thanks, as well, to our interns who pitched in along the way: Gina Roi, Maria Sofie Rose, and Luisa Ulhoa.

We obviously celebrate the designers, typographers and artists who allowed their work to be used and thank them for providing the insights into how and why they transformed the printed word and page into unconventional graphic communication.

To Louise Fili, Nicolas Heller, and an array of Andersons and Arangos, our respective families, we are forever grateful for inspiring us. To colleagues and friends like Joe Newton and Mirko Ilic, who provided suggestions, original material, an ear, and on occasion a Coke Zero with ice, we tip our hats and bow.

And to the School of Visual Arts (SVANYC), president David Rhodes and executive vice president Tony Rhodes, thank you for the opportunities to work in an environment where we see designs make art and design grow and prosper.

-SH and GA

Dedication:
Louise Fili and Nicolas Heller —SH
Lloyd Artist Anderson —GA

Published in the U.S. and Canada in 2017 by
Yale University Press
P.O. Box 209040
302 Temple Street
New Haven, CT 06520-9040
yalebooks.com/art

Published by arrangement with
Thames & Hudson Ltd, London

Designed by Therese Vandling
Manufactured in China by Imago

Library of Congress Control Number: 2016959712
ISBN 978-0-300-22679-9

10 9 8 7 6 5 4 3 2 1